CONTEMPORARY MUSICAL FILM

Music and the Moving Image

Series Editor
K. J. Donnelly, University of Wales Aberystwyth

Titles in the series include:

Film's Musical Moments
by Ian Conrich and Estella Tincknell (eds)

Music and the Moving Image: A Reader
by Kevin Donnelly (ed.)

Music, Sound and Multimedia
by Jamie Sexton (ed.)

Music Video and the Politics of Representation
by Diane Railton and Paul Watson

Contemporary Musical Film
by K. J. Donnelly and Beth Carroll (eds)

www.edinburghuniversitypress.com/series/mami

CONTEMPORARY MUSICAL FILM

Edited by
K. J. Donnelly and Beth Carroll

EDINBURGH
University Press

Edinburgh University Press is one of the leading university presses in the UK.
We publish academic books and journals in our selected subject areas across the
humanities and social sciences, combining cutting-edge scholarship with high editorial
and production values to produce academic works of lasting importance. For more
information visit our website: edinburghuniversitypress.com

Edinburgh University Press Ltd
The Tun – Holyrood Road
12 (2f) Jackson's Entry
Edinburgh EH8 8PJ

First published in hardback by Edinburgh University Press 2017

Typeset in 10/12.5 Adobe Sabon by
Servis Filmsetting Ltd, Stockport, Cheshire,
and printed and bound by
CPI Group (UK) Ltd, Croydon CR0 4YY

A CIP record for this book is available from the British Library

ISBN 978 1 4744 1312 1 (hardback)
ISBN 978 1 4744 3168 2 (paperback)
ISBN 978 1 4744 1313 8 (webready PDF)
ISBN 978 1 4744 1314 5 (epub)

CONTENTS

ILLUSTRATIONS

CONTRIBUTORS

Stefano Baschiera is Lecturer in Film Studies at Queen's University Belfast. His main research areas include European cinema, film industries, film distribution and transnational productions. His work has been published in a variety of edited collections and journals including *Film International*, *Bianco e Nero* and *The New Review of Film and Television Studies*. He is the co-editor with Russ Hunter of *Italian Horror Cinema* (2016) for Edinburgh University Press.

Geena Brown is a doctoral student of Film Studies at the University of Southampton researching the cross-media aesthetics of Studio Ghibli. Her key area of study is the films of Hayao Miyazaki, but she also has interests in Asian cinema, Hollywood musicals, global animation and video game adaptation.

Ryan Bunch is a musicologist with research and teaching interests in American music, stage and film musicals, and cultures of childhood and youth. He has taught at Temple University, the Community College of Philadelphia, Holy Family University, and Rutgers University-Camden, where he is currently a graduate assistant and PhD student in the Department of Childhood Studies.

Beth Carroll is a lecturer in Film and Literature in the English and Film departments at the University of Southampton. Her research interests include space, musicals, music, gestalt theory, haptics, disgust and video games. She has recently published a chapter on the Pet Shop Boys in *Today's Sounds for Yesterday's Films: Making Music for Silent Cinema* (2016). Her monograph

Feeling Film: A Spatial Approach (2016) explores a spatial methodology for the reading of films.

Jack Curtis Dubowsky is a prolific composer, author and filmmaker. He is author of *Intersecting Film, Music, and Queerness* (2016), which bridges musicology, cinema studies and queer theory. He writes about film, music, sexuality, popular culture, production practices and animation. He has scored six feature films, from dramas such as *Redwoods* to documentaries such as *I Always Said Yes*, and television, for example, AMC's *Lookalike*. He is a member of the Motion Picture Editors Guild and has worked extensively as a music editor, with screen credit on Pixar features including *Monsters Inc.* and *Toy Story 2*. Dubowsky's own films have screened at the British Film Institute and festivals worldwide. His documentary feature examining architecture and gentrification, *Submerged Queer Spaces*, premiered at Frameline36. His major concert music works include *Harvey Milk: A Cantata* and an oratory with orchestra, *Eisenhower Farewell Address*.

Todd Decker is Professor of Music and Chair of the Music Department at Washington University in St Louis. His books include *Hymns For the Fallen: Combat Movie Music and Sound after Vietnam* (2017) and *Who Should Sing Ol' Man River? The Lives of an American Song* (2015). He has lectured at the Library of Congress, London's Victoria and Albert Museum, and LabEx Arts-H2H in Paris.

K. J. Donnelly is a Reader in Film Studies at the University of Southampton. He is the author of *Magical Musical Tour: Rock and Pop in Film Soundtracks* (2015), *Occult Aesthetics: Sound and Image Synchronization* (2012), *British Film Music and Film Musicals* (2007), *The Spectre of Sound* (2005) and *Pop Music in British Cinema* (2001), as well as editing five books concerning music and different forms of media.

Stephanie Fremaux is a lecturer in Media Theory at Birmingham City University. She completed her PhD thesis about the Beatles on film in 2009 at Exeter University, and a manuscript titled 'The Beatles on Screen' is forthcoming with Bloomsbury Academic. She has strong research interests in music tourism, heritage and fandom, as well as popular music trends in general. Stephanie's work has appeared in *Celebrity Studies* and the *Journal of Heritage Tourism*, and she has published on music performance and identity in relation to David Bowie's use of personae.

Craig Hatch is a researcher and freelance writer specialising in film sound and Asian cinema, and is currently based in Japan. He has a chapter on music in Dario Argento's films in the collection *Italian Horror Cinema*, edited by Stefano Baschiera and Russ Hunter (Edinburgh University Press, 2016). He currently runs www.horrorjapan.com, a project that looks to review and document media from all aspects of Japanese horror culture.

Catherine Haworth is Senior Lecturer in Music at the University of Huddersfield. Her research focuses upon musical practices of representation and identity construction across various media, with a particular focus on film music. Recent projects include publications on identity and the soundtrack in female detective films, the female gothic genre, and the James Bond series, as well as guest editorship of the gender and sexuality special issue of *Music, Sound and the Moving Image* (2012), and the co-edited collection *Gender, Age and Musical Creativity* (2015).

Ian Sapiro is a Lecturer in Music at the University of Leeds. His research interests include film-score production, musical theatre, orchestration and the crossovers between them. He is author of *Scoring the Score: The Role of the Orchestrator in the Contemporary Film Industry* (2016), *Ilan Eshkeri's Stardust: A Film Score Guide* (2013), and book chapters on screen orchestration as a creative process, rock operas and film composer Trevor Jones.

INTRODUCTION: REIMAGINING THE CONTEMPORARY MUSICAL IN THE TWENTY-FIRST CENTURY

K. J. Donnelly and Beth Carroll

Film musicals are one of the key places where music and film join most clearly. They are the antecedent of modern digital audio-visual culture, where sound and image combine, and film aesthetics and music aesthetics merge into something different and more than the sum of their parts. Sonic excess becomes visual spectacle, both vying for ascendency. The film musical is a site of tension: between innovation and tradition, between sound and image, musical number and narrative, and between professionalism and amateurism. It is the continuous discord and synthesis that these tensions raise that forces the musical to never be in stasis, but rather always in a constant state of transition. It is the extent and form of these transitions that this collection focuses upon.

Although one of the staples of classical Hollywood, the film musical became more intermittent in the post-studio era. Indeed, in the last decades of the twentieth century it had become almost a rarity, the tent-pole musical productions of the 1960s, such as *Star!* (Robert Wise, 1968) and *Hello Dolly!* (Gene Kelly, 1969), heralding an era of lower budget caution and 'independent' production. However, in recent years there has been a remarkable resurgence in the success of film musicals. This edited collection explores the breadth and diversity of recent film musicals, celebrating their energy and diversity, and addressing the genre traditions and innovations, looking to the essential relationship between film and live entertainment, innovation and conservatism.

While at times the film musical genre might have seemed over, merely a historical curio, in the last couple of decades it has re-emerged with a renewed vigour. Although the 'classical musical' of Hollywood's heyday – the big white sets, full orchestral scores, dancing stars and elaborate production numbers – might seem long gone, its modes are still very much alive, and its sibling on the stage (embodied by Broadway and London's West End) remains tremendously successful. The old mantra that the musical is dead has long taken on muted tones and the form's past popularity discussed with diminishing reverence excepting by those who have remained stalwart to the genre. Yet, it has never been proven true. The musical has simultaneously morphed, reimagined itself, gone back to basics, and managed to be all but a permanent fixture of cinema going and culture more widely over the last several decades. It has ably danced a path that spans both high and popular culture: from theatre to television, to the Internet and blogs; it has moved beyond the silver screen. The musical has continued to carve a relationship with its audiences, of ranging demographics, which challenges conventionally held understandings of interaction and perception, not least of which is through its primary focus on the audio-visual relationship. The importance of music and sound more widely to the musical has allowed the genre a privileged position as a spectrum, encompassing characteristics that eschew absolute generic delineation in favour of transferable traits. An overriding characteristic of the genre is the dynamic interaction between sound and image, discernibly demonstrated in musical numbers that culminate with a distinct interaction with the audience, (through both a physical reaction and a direct address). The genre has proven its longevity, with recent films such as *Mamma Mia!* (Phyllida Lloyd, 2008) and *Les Misérables* (Tom Hooper, 2012) providing Hollywood with successful box office receipts, and yet academic discourse has been slow at both re-evaluating the genre's position and understanding its unique audio-visual experience.

The arrival of the twenty-first century saw the resurgence of the musical genre: there were closer cross-ties with the stage, for instance *Hedwig and the Angry Inch* (John Cameron Mitchell, 2001), *The Phantom of the Opera* (Joel Schumacher, 2004) and *Chicago* (Rob Marshall, 2002); with *Shrek* (Andrew Adamson, Vicky Jenson, 2001), *Legally Blonde* (Robert Luketic, 2001) and *Silence of the Lambs* (Jonathan Demme, 1991) making the alternative journey from film to stage. There was also a revival of TV singing shows, from *The X Factor* (2004–) to *American Idol* (2002–), to dance-orientated programmes such as *Strictly Come Dancing* (2004–). Although not musicals in the traditional sense, they exist as a larger peripheral market of music focused on audio-visual entertainment and audience engagement. Culturally the musical has re-established itself as a permanent fixture in need of a new and updated theoretical exploration into its status and modes. The growing importance of synergy, and in particular soundtrack and theatrical sales, have made musicals a booming financial industry, crossing the divide and attracting tourists and diehard fans alike. As such, the musical has come to represent a multiplicity of things for the various audiences, exploiting several wide-ranging modes as a consequence.

Barry Keith Grant notes that writings about musicals have tended to see them as reflective of their historical context of production (new deal politics, cold war anxiety, more recent concern with identity politics).[1] In this current age of instability and irony no single spirit of the age is reflected. Fragmented demographics have led to an abundance of voices, at times flirting with union, at others independent and disconnected. However, this manifests as an eclecticism; a simultaneous return to traditionalism and a matching concern with refurbishing and redeveloping the genre hold sway. Since 2000, a kaleidoscopic range of musicals has been made. The date, in part, marks a larger dependence on the theatre/cinema relationship for musicals, but also the infiltration of the genre into wider media, such as the aforementioned radio, blogs, Internet miniseries and podcasts. An effect of this is a broadening of the musical forms. Thus, since 2000, there has been a simultaneous return to known musical models, demonstrably illustrated through a reliance on the West End and Broadway theatres, and an exploration into unconventional modes. It is a period that moves wildly between tradition and experimentation and, therefore, is worthy of academic investigation into the nuances of the genre. The financial success of the genre has also had a hand in its conservatism. The desire to replicate past successes, to stick to the known, the tried and tested both formally and musically, has created a dominant form in the wider public imagination. Distorting discussions of the innovative and the 'different', the stage's current omnipresence has cast the film musical in its own likeness. The integrated dramatic musical, with a strong connection to musical theatre's proclivity for show tunes, has relegated the broader film musical styles to exceptions that prove the rule rather than key and rich examples of the genre. In short, the 'tourist' musical's success on the stage has eclipsed the abundance of riches that the film musical (and indeed off-Broadway and the West End) have to offer. The rise and history of the musical has been well documented with regards to classical Hollywood cinema, and so too has the position of the genre in New American cinema with the fall of the Studio System and the passage to tent-pole productions by major conglomerations, such as *The Sound of Music* (Robert Wise, 1965). What has as yet been omitted by academic discourse is the place of the musical more recently, in an era of changing technologies, cultures and modes of spectatorship. The musical should be reconsidered with this in mind, but also with an ear to the position and use of music as a dominant mode of reading films more generally.

Scholars must consider the balance between tradition and experimentation, the capacity for new media to both rejuvenate conventional forms and conceive innovative modes. Podcasts such as *The Set List* (Victor Legrá, 2014–) allow an audio exploration into live performances on New York's cabaret scene, engaging enthusiasts and encouraging them to 'complete' the audio-visual performance with knowledge, expectation and personal expertise. Blogs such as *Dr. Horrible's Sing-Along Blog* (Joss Whedon, 2008) use direct address to an aware and knowing contemporary audience to blend the personal blog form with the more traditional Hollywood musical number revealing character's hidden desires and feelings. Both new and stalwart audiences alike are reached by the synthesis of tradition and experimentation. This coalescence is evident on the big screen as well as the small. A film such as *Dancer in the Dark* (Lars von Trier, 2000) belies the classical musical's archetypal high spirits that isolate many from the genre, whilst simultaneously referencing its conventional musical form. The battle between the old and the new cannot disguise audiences' continued desire for musical expression. The musical style may change, the show tune in constant battle with popular musical forms contemporary to the era: rock and roll, pop, rap, but the emphasis on musical performativity remains the same. Films such as *Kill Bill: Volume 1* (Quentin Tarantino, 2003), featuring The 5.6.7.8's singing 'I Walk Like Jayne Mansfield', and Pedro Almódovar's *Volver* (2006), in which Penelope Cruz (dubbed by Estrella Morente) sings the titular song 'Volver', demonstrate the importance of music to both the narrative and the creation of set sequences. These 'musicals by any other name' should not be overlooked in our examination of the musical, for both their growing number and their similarities to the traditional musical give them value. Indeed, the critical and financial success of *Black Swan* (Darren Aronofsky, 2010) and *Quartet* (Dustin Hoffman, 2012) demonstrate the popularity of such films with broad audiences. We might ask ourselves to review such films as *Casablanca* (Michael Curtiz, 1942) and *Blue Velvet* (David Lynch, 1986) through the lens of the musical and question whether these are film musicals or musical films. Is the differentiation one of form or quantity of musical performance? In the modern era's featuring of a varied musical palette, what place is there for theoretical discussions on 'ideal' forms? Beneath the ever-changing nuances of the musical, is there an underlying 'constant' and essence to the genre?

The existence of a strong tradition of format and aesthetics allows for the persistent possibility of experimentation, of 'kicking against' the conservative and perennially popular norm. One of the pillars of the format is the demarcation between number and narrative. Rick Altman notes that this is the single most defining aspect of the classical Hollywood musical genre. He defines the musical corpus as utilising the classical narrative hierarchy, where the soundtrack of music is subordinate to the image track but significantly at climactic moments a reversal of their relationship occurs in song sequences.[2] Alan Williams points out a formal reason for this: 'The musical film's alternation between music and diegesis seems both permitted and required by the strong boundaries that popular songs set for themselves.'[3] So the form of the music dictates film form, an uneasy joining of two aesthetic and temporal schemes. Musical sequences are based on the logic of music, where: 'If the music's rhythmic consistency lends order to diegetic time, the irregularities of diegetic space are made to conform to a pattern in the same way [. . .] freed from the realistic and causal constraints of the diegesis, the image can now reflect the music.'[4] Though musicals initially were often backstage musicals, with the songs as part of the show within a show and the drama derived from backstage antics, the so-called 'integrated musical' aimed instead to cohere all the film musical's aspects.[5] The stage version of Rodgers and Hammerstein's *Oklahoma!* in 1943 was hailed as the first integrated stage musical, being based around songs that all had relevance to narrative development. The stage musical was developing alongside the film musical, and the move toward 'integrated' musicals also involved smoothing over the divide between dance or song sequence and dialogue scenes with songs effortlessly emerging during action rather than the film effectively stopping and restarting. The increasingly integrated musicals had a sense of being more 'sophisticated' than their backstage or operetta counterparts.[6] Developing from Fred Astaire and Ginger Rogers films in the 1930s, by the 1950s MGM was producing aesthetically outstanding integrated musicals such as *An American in Paris* (Vincente Minnelli, 1951), *Singin' in the Rain* (Gene Kelly, Stanley Donen, 1952) and *It's Always Fair Weather* (Gene Kelly, Stanley Donen, 1955), and in particular those films made by the Freed Unit. The increasing development of film musicals as 'integrated musicals' in the 1950s involved a desire to stop the solid division between narrative development and the song sequence, which was most clear in the backstage musical. In its place, songs had narrative valence and also appeared seamlessly out of action in any location, with characters simply bursting into song with a musical backing from outside the diegesis. Perhaps the increased integration of songs with films sustained and led to 'non-musical' films increasingly including songs but as an integrated element rather than stopping for a song sequence. The 'musical in all but name' is thus a continuation of this process, whereby music increasingly becomes integrated with action, diegesis and narrative – therefore colonising the mainstream dramatic film. A number of films occupy an 'interzone' between the mainstream dramatic film and the musical, including *A Clockwork Orange* (Stanley Kubrik, 1971), *Natural Born Killers* (Oliver Stone, 1994), *Trainspotting* (Danny Boyle, 1996) and most of Quentin Tarantino's films, where musical sequences are foregrounded. Indeed, Tincknell and Conrich note that songs appearing in a film do not necessarily mean it is a musical, but where should the delineation start and stop?[7]

Currently there are many film musicals that are not billed as such (for example, *South Park: Bigger, Longer and Uncut* [Trey Parker, 1999]), while in other cases films may not seem to be a musical at all until they are given closer scrutiny (for example, *Sucker Punch* [Zack Snyder, 2011] and *O Brother,*

Where Art Thou? [Ethan Coen, Joel Coen, 2000]). These constitute the afore-mentioned 'musicals in all but name', and mix both form and aesthetics. Their omission from the musical genre is in no small part due to the current influence of musical theatre on the stage; the historical development of trends in the genre, from the backstage to the integrated, is forgotten in the face of theatre's dominance. Frequent criticisms of the genre's 'bursting into song', paradoxi-cally dismissing the backstage musical's importance in classical Hollywood cinema, illustrate an erosion of understanding. The genre's history, its desire to frame musical numbers within the diegesis, is cast away. The stage musical, and its accompanying filmic adaptations, has become so primary in the pub-lic's imagination that it has distorted our understanding of what a musical is. Consequently, the genre's spectrum becomes unnecessarily narrow. Films such as *Sucker Punch*, with clearly delineated musical sequences containing visual expressions of the music, are seen as innovative only when we permit the stage musical to be the de facto musical standard, representing 'tradition'. By not exploring these films within the musical context, we are permitting market-ing and promotional departments to set their own terms without academic scrutiny.

Arguably, there has been a convergence between incidental music in films (non-diegetic music) and the modes of the film musical. The musical may remain as a genre but its impetus, aesthetics and attractions now also exist in many mainstream films. Indeed, one could argue that such characteristics have always been there, most clearly in mainstream films that included a featured song or two. With the recession of the musical as a perennial film genre, its role of selling music has migrated to mainstream films, taking with it something of the aesthetics that film musicals derived from their dominance by music dynamics and requirements. The musical's selling of songs, whether in the form of sheet music, dance crib sheets or album sales, has in many respects come full circle. The rise of MTV and its accompanying aesthetics, developed through a desire to visually represent and sell the attached record or song, has found its way back into the musical. Not only have we witnessed the rise of the jukebox musical, but so too the rise of increased editing rates and musi-cally driven visual style so evocative of MTV and seen in films such as *Moulin Rouge!* (Baz Luhrmann, 2001).[8] New media becomes old as the aesthetics developed on blogs, online and on TV come full circle with their appearance on the silver screen. The sonic driving force remains a constant, however.

Although academic theorising on the musical is experiencing an increase in popularity, the dominance of ocularcentric readings still predominates. Such discourses, though providing fecund material for analysis, omit any nuanced understanding of the musical's sonic nature, audio primacy, and the trans-formative audio-visual relationship. A central tenet of this edited collection will be a focus on sound and music and how it can and should be seen as a principal approach to Film Studies. Recent theoretical books, such as Steven Cohan's edited collection *The Sound of Musicals,* have aided the rise of the musical in academe, discussing the genre in terms of alternative readings; looking at established texts in light of newer theoretical models such as queer theory.[9] Studies such as these are important reassessments of the genre, but do not take as their focus contemporary musicals. The same is true of texts such as *Musicals: Hollywood and Beyond* by Bill Marshall and Robynn Stilwell, unfortunately published before the musical resurgence of the 2000s and largely focusing on older musical texts.[10] Corey K. Creekmur and Linda Y. Mokdad's *The International Film Musical* does invaluable work in assessing the range of musicals in non-Hollywood and international contexts, but due to its geographical diversity, does not suitably explore the reasons behind the current diversity of the musical.[11]

This edited collection takes a range of different contemporary musicals as case studies in order to highlight a range of views. It discusses the position of the musical in today's cultural milieu, not just within Hollywood but also within a wider geographical and cultural context. These range from an historic understanding of the genre's relationship with live entertainment and the stage, to television and music videos, and the evolving relationship with the Internet. The collection contains three sections: 'Original Musicals', 'Stage to Screen' and 'Musicals by Another Name'. Within each section the chapters are arranged in chronological order, as determined by their primary case study, highlighting how historical contexts have altered our understanding of the tension between experimentation and tradition.

Part One, 'Original Musicals', begins with a chapter by Craig Hatch that explores the Japanese film *The Happiness of the Katakuris* (Takashi Miike, 2001), with a view to understanding how its director Takashi Miike uses musically guided aesthetics. This is followed by K. J. Donnelly's chapter, which analyses the status of rock in film. Jack Curtis Dubowsky then examines how *Team America: World Police* (Trey Parker and Matt Stone, 2004) is indicative of Parker and Stone's use of the musical form in their wider oeuvre. Beth Carroll's chapter follows and uses *Romance & Cigarettes* (John Turturro, 2005) to assess how auteurist discourses have obscured our understanding of the musical genre and whether perceived innovation in the genre is but a facade. Stephanie Fremaux's focus on the Beatles' music in *Across the Universe* (Julie Taymor, 2007) examines how the music's meaning is deliberately and visually evoked. Here the music becomes the primary driving force behind the film's aesthetics. Finally, Ryan Bunch's chapter investigates the extent to which *Frozen* (Chris Buck and Jennifer Lee, 2013) varies from the canonical Disney structure.

Part Two, 'Stage to Screen', sees Catherine Haworth explore the musical genre's changing form through an examination of the jukebox musical

Mamma Mia!, whose success is indicative of the dominance of the stage. Pop music has played a long and varied role in the musical, for instance as a form of youth expression (*Summer Holiday* [Peter Yates, 1963]); here Catherine Haworth looks at how our understanding of 'quality' is shaped by the music of ABBA and the jukebox musical more generally. The tension between amateurism and professionalism is evoked in the performances of *Mamma Mia!*. Personal identity and performativity become key aspects of both the newness and familiarity of the film's music. Continuing to explore the important relationship between stage and screen in the recent resurgence of the film musical, Ian Sapiro uses interviews with key personnel from *Les Misérables* to explain how the director and his support staff recorded the music for the film. The success of the stage is in part due to the 'liveness' of performance, but as Ian Sapiro makes clear, replicating this feeling in a large budget film is fraught with difficulties and practical considerations.

Part Three, 'Musicals by Another Name', explores how the rise of the musical film has been important to audiences as well as film studios. Stefano Baschiera's chapter examines the story telling functions of the music track in *O Brother, Where Art Thou?*. Todd Decker explores the *Fast and the Furious* (2001–15) film franchise and the importance it places on music. He argues that the strong visual aesthetic of underground car racing becomes musical numbers, sonically driven. Finally, Geena Brown explores how Quentin Tarantino makes use of the musical genre's form and focus on spectacle to choreograph violence in *Kill Bill: Volume 1*.

NOTES

1. Barry Keith Grant, *The Hollywood Film Musical* (Oxford: Wiley-Blackwell, 2012), p. 38.
2. Rick Altman, *The American Film Musical* (Bloomington: Indiana University Press, 1989), p. 108.
3. Alan Williams, 'The musical film and recorded popular music', in Rick Altman (ed.), *Genre: The Musical* (London: Routledge and Kegan Paul in association with the British Film Institute, 1981), p. 156.
4. Altman, *The American Film Musical*, p. 81.
5. Martin Sutton, 'Patterns of meaning in the musical', in Rick Altman (ed.), *Genre: The Musical* (London: Routledge and Kegan Paul in association with the British Film Institute, 1981), p. 191.
6. John Mueller, 'Fred Astaire and the integrated musical', *Cinema Journal*, 1984, 24(1): 28–40; Cari McDonnell, 'Genre theory and the film musical', in David Neumeyer (ed.), *The Oxford Handbook of Film Music Studies* (New York: Oxford University Press, 2014), p. 252.
7. Ian Conrich and Estella Tincknell, *Film's Musical Moments* (Edinburgh: Edinburgh University Press, 2006), pp. 4–5.
8. Carol Vernallis, *Experiencing Music Video: Aesthetics and Cultural Context* (New York: Colombia University Press, 2004).
9. Steven Cohan, *The Sound of Musicals* (London: British Film Institute, 2010).

10. Bill Marshall and Robynn Stilwell, *Musicals: Hollywood and Beyond* (Exeter: Intellect Books, 2000).
11. Corey K. Creekmur and Linda Y. Mokdad (eds), *The International Film Musical* (Edinburgh: Edinburgh University Press, 2012).

PART ONE

ORIGINAL MUSICALS

1 AESTHETIC ABSURDITIES IN TAKASHI MIIKE'S *THE HAPPINESS OF THE KATAKURIS*

Craig Hatch

The late 1990s were an exciting time for Japanese cinema. After significant competition from television in the early 1970s saw studios such as Nikkatsu turn to erotic films (*pinku*) and Daiei face bankruptcy, the nation was experiencing something of an international resurgence by the late 1990s. Aided by the worldwide proliferation of DVDs, the charge was led predominantly by a number of filmmakers who had cut their teeth on V-cinema. Originally a branding specifically for Toei's line of straight-to-video productions, V-cinema became a catch-all for OV (Original Video) films; an arena which granted the freedom for newcomers to try their hand at directing and assistant directors such as Hideo Nakata and Takashi Shimizu the freedom to break away and develop unique voices of their own.[1]

Arguably the most successful of the V-cinema graduates is Takashi Miike, who remains one of the biggest names in Japanese cinema, both domestically and internationally. Due to his breakthrough film *Audition* (Takashi Miike, 1999), distributors were quick to paint Miike as the new 'king of extreme', despite only having produced two real horror films by the time of *The Happiness of the Katakuris* (Takashi Miike, 2001). As a self-proclaimed 'director for hire', it is not the choice of projects or genres that define him as a director, but rather his approach to genre. As a director, Miike's career is more akin to filmmakers such as Teruo Ishii and Norifumi Suzuki than someone like John Carpenter, producing up to seven films a year in the early 2000s, almost always as assignments rather than personal projects. Whilst as an assistant director for television Takashi Miike worked with directors such as Yukio

Noda, perhaps best known in the west for *Zero Woman: Red Handcuffs* (Yukio Noda, 1974) and the second Golgo 13 film, *Golgo 13: Assignment Kowloon* (Yukio Noda, 1977). More importantly, however, he moved on to working as assistant director for film, most notably under Shohei Imamura (on *Zegen* [Shohei Imamura, 1987] and *Black Rain* [Shohei Imamura, 1989]), a director well known for blurring styles and the lines between feature films and documentary performance.[2]

The Happiness of the Katakuris is a musical remake of the Korean comedy horror film *The Quiet Family* (Kim Jee-woon, 1998). The debut film of Kim Jee-woon, who would go on to find international success with *A Tale of Two Sisters* (Kim Jee-woon, 2003), *The Quiet Family* has much the same set-up as Miike's film until half way through, at which point the film takes a darker turn through the involvement of a hitman, which Miike's film substitutes with the subplot of an incompetent conman. *The Happiness of the Katakuris* follows the titular Katakuris, and patriarch of the family Masao Katakuri's attempt at bringing the family closer together by opening an inn as a family venture along a soon-to-open road in the vicinity of Mount Fuji. Things quickly take a turn for the worse, however, when guests begin to die through no fault of the Katakuris – heart attacks, suffocation and suicide; the family nevertheless choose to hide the corpses to ensure that their business is a success, and the family unit stays united. Despite the grim premise, however, *The Happiness of the Katakuris* is a more light-hearted film than its inspiration, with Miike's farcical approach to the musical genre bringing levity in place of the thriller nature of the original.

Typical of the director's initial exposure to the West, *The Happiness of the Katakuris* was marketed with the tag line of 'The hills are alive with the sound of screaming', and the American poster containing pull quotes such as 'graphic violence, kinky sex and parodies of Rodgers and Hammerstein'.[3] Dave Kehr's review from which the quote is pulled is in fact a slating of the film, going as far to remark how 'each new death [is] celebrated by the Katakuris in song, or at least as close to song as Japanese pop music, surely among the world's worst, can come'.[4] It seems not to matter that there is in fact no 'kinky sex' in the film or that the violence is light and cartoonish, as it is extremity that Miike's films were initially sold on, not his creative approach to genre. Miike, however, staunchly rejects the idea that he makes films of a particular genre, stating 'I don't think about genre at all. My films are categorized as being in a certain type of genre. But myself, I don't make the movie thinking about which category the film belongs in.'[5] Despite this, however, Miike retains a reputation in the West as a director of particularly violent films, although this is largely the result of the selective international distribution of his films, that causes even his lighter films to be viewed through an 'extreme' slant. 'It's very interesting to me that the movies selected by European and American film festivals and critics always seem to be my most violent ones', he observes. 'But if people think I just make one violent movie after another that's OK, because I really enjoy making movies.'[6]

The tag line and pull quotes selected unfortunately follow the tone of Tartan's 'Asia Extreme' style of marketing (the film's UK distributor), which has been criticised for marketing Asian cinema indiscriminately as 'sexually explicit and transgressively violent'.[7] However, they do at least inadvertently hint at the unusual tone of the film and its flirting with genre for comedic effect. As noted by Steve Rawle's essay on the marketing of the film and its place as a cult hybrid:

> the marketing was reductive and more or less pre-empted the critical response that saw this as a 'zombie musical'. The attempt to position the film within the boundaries of a single genre ignores its cult sensibilities, its transgression of genre boundaries and the sheer lunacy of its camp appeal.[8]

The Happiness of the Katakuris therefore, at least in reviews, has often been viewed through the lens of horror comedy rather than as a stylistic, musical farce.

Whilst the main focus of the chapter will be on *The Happiness of the Katakuris*, it will be supported with references to musical moments in other Takashi Miike films, specifically *For Love's Sake* (Takashi Miike, 2012), Miike's only other musical so far. This will be supplemented by a look at musically guided aesthetics, and how the introduction of music grants a greater allowance for a shift in directional and performance style, as evidenced in the wider filmography of Takashi Miike.

DIRECTION

Despite the production of *The Happiness of the Katakuris* marking Miike's first attempt at the musical as a genre, his films by this point had already garnered attention for the way in which they use music to frame the editing; condense story, play an active role in the story, or in some cases comment on the medium of delivery itself. The most discussed moment of one of Takashi Miike's international 'breakthrough' films, *Dead or Alive* (Takashi Miike, 1999), is the film's explosive montage opening. Reviews upon the film's release and those written in retrospect often dedicate a substantial portion of their evaluation of the film to the one scene and its music video aesthetics. A retrospective appraisal of the particular scene in *The Guardian* notes how

> It's essentially five minutes of continuous sleaze, resembling more an 18-rated trailer than it does the establishing moments of a film [. . .]. It

starts with a count-in – 'One, two; one two three four' – before a rock riff kicks in, there's a scream, and a (not entirely convincing) body is seen falling from a building.[9]

The scene is constructed of brief flashes of separate narratives, seemingly unrelated to each other apart from their unifying theme of excess, the location of Kabukicho and the connecting tissue of the rock soundtrack. With no context for the images on screen, the opening five minutes of *Dead or Alive*, as Boult states, play out as a trailer for the film rather than its establishing moments. The clarification for this scene, however, does not so much reside within the scene itself, but in the twelve second shot that immediately prefigures the chaos. The scene opens with an optical effect of film being loaded into a projector, as the frame flickers for half a second before one of the film's leads, Sho Aikawa, kneeling on a grimy jetty, turns his head to notice the camera and begins to count down the opening moments to his film with co-star Riki Takeuchi. The film's leads count into the film as if to launch into a rock song, which is in essence what happens as the electric guitar kicks in and, detached from continuity and realism, the film barrels through its opening moments as if it were a musical number. The moment is also notable for pairing two V-cinema favourites together for the first time, in a theatrical film no less. The opening twelve seconds of the film is metatextual, announcing the music video compilation (of what in the script were entire scenes) that is about to ensue and making an attraction out of the film's stars.[10]

Previous to his theatrical endeavours, however, Miike's most audacious manipulation of the way in which his films interact with music and genre can be found in one of his V-cinema movies *Osaka Tough Guys* (Takashi Miike, 1995). *Osaka Tough Guys*, Miike's V-Cinema Yakuza parody film, contains a karaoke musical number that plays not only with musical performance but as Mes states, 'directly plays with and pays tribute to the film's V cinema origins.'[11] The scene takes place in a club that the protagonists are visiting, when one character takes to the stage to perform a karaoke number so inept that it not only destroys the venue itself, but also the medium upon which the film has been recorded. The character's musical performance is deemed to be so excruciating that video cassette tracking lines appear on screen and the visuals shift off centre frame, as if the film is looking to escape the medium of its own existence. The scene then ends with a blank blue screen, and as if prefiguring *The Ring* (Hideo Nakata, 1998) somewhat, the dreadfulness of the moment has infected not just the tape, but the video player itself, expanding beyond the reality of the cassette tape. Much of V-Cinema, was in fact shot on 16 mm film rather than video, but Miike's intent in targeting the associated characteristics of the genre and medium of delivery was clear.[12] With *Osaka Tough Guys* there is a clear understanding of what the audience and their expectations bring to a viewing experience that is being played with. As with *The Happiness of the Katakuris*, however, the intertextuality extends beyond directorial stylistics as characters audition for V-Cinema films as part of the plot, poking at the V-Cinema scene and in particular the Yakuza films that made up most of the releases, prefiguring the reflective genre study of *The Happiness of the Katakuris*, again through music.[13]

Incorporating music video aesthetics, karaoke culture, claymation and rock performance through the inclusion of musicians Kenji Sawada and Kiyoshiro Imawano, *The Happiness of the Katakuris*, and Miike's later musical *For Love's Sake*, invites the audience to find comedy in the absurdity of musical aesthetics, performance and rules of continuity editing. The genre of the musical allows for a conscious manipulation of aesthetics and performance that, as already noted, is also evident in the wider narrative of Takashi Miike's manipulation of genre codes through music within his filmography.

The most notable way in which the cinematic style is framed within the narrative is how the film is portrayed as being through the eyes of the young granddaughter of the family, Yurie Katakuri. Although this framing device is not particularly consistent, with the character absent for many scenes, it provides an early 'excuse' for the farcical way in which the film plays out as it switches from claymation to horror to musical number. It grants the film the lens of a child viewing adults 'being silly', singing, dancing and struggling to deal with realities of life without much luck, nor seriousness. Both the adult characters and actors help the young girl through the dance routines, and her childlike approach even to dancing alongside the dead highlights the nature of the musical performances at play within the film. It is through this lens that the film gains much of its comedy, but being a musical, it could be said that the genre codes at play already give the film a reason to break not only from reality, but also from its own style.

The key to the absurd aesthetics of *The Happiness of the Katakuris*, however, is the way in which despite being largely surreal, launching from claymation, to karaoke music video, to musical numbers with reanimated corpses, in an inverse of traditional musicals, the characters never break from their own capabilities as performers musically, even as the spatial and sequential parameters of the film deform the reality around them. The joy of the film comes from a partial sense of irony about the musical, but also from the endearing nature of a 'real' family attempting to force themselves through spontaneous musical numbers, as hard as they try. The characters break from the moment to strike poses that are equal parts *Ultraman* as they are musical stances, yet when the time comes to actually dance together, they struggle to keep strict synchronicity with each other, gleefully moving forward with a 'close enough' approach to the choreography.

This is nothing new of course, for, as Feuer states regarding various MGM musicals of the 1950s, 'Clowning may compensate for the lack of choreography'.[14] Yet with *The Happiness of the Katakuris* clowning is purposefully under-rehearsed rather than a purposeful goof in order to achieve such an effect. It is not the staging that gives the impression of non-choreography, as in *For Love's Sake*, but instead the performance style itself. It is obvious that Miike had his actors rehearse to at least some degree, but with musicals having the reputation of typically being rehearsed to such an extreme, even the slightest movement out of time breaks the illusion of unity of a musical in to a farce.

The film plays upon cynical viewings of musicals and raises questions regarding how each character knows the lines to the songs and the moves to the dances. *The Happiness of the Katakuris* makes a point of going halfway with these ideas and then takes a 'this will do' approach. All of the family members know the words to their songs, most of them know their dance moves, but it is all so wildly unrehearsed that the farcical nature of the musical still comes across.

This is also repeated in Miike's second musical, *For Love's Sake* (although not to the same degree), in which the love interest of the film, Ai, reacts in embarrassment when her elderly parents embark on a musical number about their love for one another. Sporadically she attempts to join in with a choreographed arm movement, but with a grimace on her face, having been forced into a musical number when all she wanted to do was ask to borrow money from her parents. This happens almost immediately after Ai has her own musical number, in which she struggles and fails to convince her crush to join in on the moment. At an earlier point in the film her secret admirer decides to confess his love through song; here she looks increasingly uncomfortable throughout the entire number, almost looking for an exit from the film. By the end of the scene the character is on his knees, perspiring from the amount of effort that has gone into such a production.

Although *For Love's Sake* and *The Happiness of the Katakuris* share a similar ethos on the musical and the absurdity of musical aesthetics, there is a key difference in that whilst *For Love's Sake* contains performances that are more professionally choreographed, the film is purposefully shot with long and often wide shots to expose the awkwardness of such a moment were it to occur in reality. *The Happiness of the Katakuris*, however, attempts a more musical style, yet features characters that have no place in being in such an environment. Another is that in *The Happiness of the Katakuri* the characters that want to be in on musical numbers possibly should not be, whilst in *For Love's Sake*, being a love story, characters are purposefully attempting to stay out of them, as suits their characters' motivations.

It is because of this approach to musical numbers that it has been presumed that Miike's musicals are cynical. In a write-up on the Fantasia International Film Festival, Dru Jeffries deridingly terms *For Love's Sake* 'a musical for people who hate musicals, a love story seemingly for people incapable of the feeling'.[15] However, Miike and his cast argue that the reason for this approach is quite the opposite. In reference to the choreography of *Happiness of the Katakuris*, the actor Kenji Sawada reasoned:

> I mean, the Japanese musical which is not sophisticated at all . . . I can't dance gracefully, but the audience would see us try very hard. Not only with the dancing, but with the singing, we could make the film more unique than ever, I thought. All the cast are doing their utmost to make the best film.[16]

Although this quote is taken from a 'making of' feature produced for the film's release and therefore should be understood as marketing, his reasoning does line up clearly with the themes of family that run through the film. Similarly, Katakuri's choreographer, Ryohei Kondo, comments how he likes to

> intuitively choreograph dance on the spot. Normally, it's very tough but I like it and the director also encourages me . . . there are a lot of people dancing but they are not professional dancers. So, a unique charm has been added.[17]

PERFORMANCE

Indeed, the performances within the film play a large part of the film's farcical nature. Before continuing, however, it is important to give a little background on two of the main stars of the film, Kenji Sawada, who plays the father of the family, and Kiyoshiro Imawano's enigmatic Richard Sagawa.

Kenji 'Julie' Sawada is a pop idol who emerged from the 'group sounds' movement as the singer of a band called The Tigers. Group sounds was a movement that took off in earnest in the mid to late 1960s, with the second and most notable wave of group sounds coming after the Beatles' perfor-mances in Tokyo in the summer of 1966.[18] It was in the wake of these concerts that The Tigers emerged. Amongst similarly mop-haired Japanese rock and roll bands capitalising on the moment, The Tigers appealed directly to teen culture of the time with a mix of covers of Western songs and those written for them by professional songwriters. The Tigers in particular had a song written for them by Barry and Maurice Gibb of the Bee Gees, entitled 'Smile For Me', in an attempt to crack the United Kingdom. Although the moment was rela-tively short lived as the youth came to crave a more 'authentic' style of rock, numerous stars from the movement such as Kenji Sawada went on to embark on solo careers once the movement was over, with others moving into film.

Sawada managed to carve out a considerable film career for himself, starring in films for directors including Kinji Fukasaku, Paul Schrader, in *Mishima: A Life in Four Chapters* (Paul Schrader, 1985), and two films for Seijun Suzuki, *Yumeji* (Seijun Suzuki, 1991) and *Pistol Opera* (Seijun Suzuki, 2001), a semi follow-up to *Branded to Kill* (Seijun Suzuki, 1967), which was released in the same year as *The Happiness of the Katakiris*.

Most important to this chapter, however, is Sawada's participation in The Tigers films. The Tigers in particular have a history of 'rock films', such as *Hanayahanaru shôtai* (Kunihiko Yamamoto, 1968), which attempted to mimic the success the Beatles found with similar pictures. As with films such as *A Hard Day's Night* (Richard Lester, 1964), one of the primary functions of *Hanayahanaru shôtai* was to display the personalities of the band members and deliver a fictionalised idea of their interactions to form a collective identity for the fan base. What results, as with *A Hard Day's Night*, is an 'ambiguity between the group action and as non-actors "being themselves".'[19] What is often overlooked in the West with regards to the performance style found in *The Happiness of the Katakuris*, however, is just how much this element is also in play in Miike's film, in which we see characters (and deceptively actors) who 'can't dance, nor barely sing'; except in Japan viewers are aware that they can, an element that is reflected within the narrative itself with the Richard Sagawa character.

Sawada is a musician who knows how to perform and it would be a mistake to overlook the layers of performance at play in *The Happiness of the Katakuris*; not only from his time as an actor, but musically too, in the group films from his time as a pop idol. Kenji Sawada was what is known as a *bishōnen*, an androgynous male commonly found in romance manga and the type most commonly associated with Japanese pop stars. Sawada found himself voted one of the 'sexiest' men, even in the 1980s, as he retained his *bishōnen* characteristics through the 1970s and into the 1980s through the adoption of heavy make-up.[20] With Sawada's role as family patriarch in *The Happiness of the Katakuris*, however, you have a character that cannot perform, can barely sing, but also, as an ex *bishōnen*, cannot keep his family together.

As a result, you have musicians effectively portraying the everyman, out of place in a musical number. This premise reaches its conclusion at the climax of the film in *The Happiness of the Katakuris*' most overtly parodic moment, the last number of the film, 'That's Happiness', in which the family take to the mountains for a scene that clearly evokes *The Sound of Music* (Robert Wise, 1965). Though the majority of the film lampoons the farcical idea of musicals and their performances rather than specific films, this final number allows the newly united family to enact a real stage musical number that stands outside of the karaoke performances and rock musical moments that preceded it.

Much of the promotion around the film in the West revolved entirely around the idea of *The Happiness of the Katakuris* being a horror take on the *The*

Sound of Music, which of course it is not, yet arguably the most enduring image from the film (and the one that frequently appeared on posters) is of the Katakuris running through the hills holding hands, mimicking the image of the Von Trapps doing the same thing. In Japan, however, this scene would play very differently to how it would in the West, leaning not so much on the side of parody but rather again playing with the idea of metatextual duality and musical performance. While a member of The Tigers and subsequently the rock supergroup Pyg, Kenji Sawada often went by the moniker of Julie Sawada, taken from one of his idols Julie Andrews.[21] After over thirty years of being known as 'Julie', Kenji Sawada finally gets to give his performance of 'Julie', but not Julie the musician, Julie the actress.

The duplicitous nature of the performances, however, are commented upon more strongly in arguably the film's most enduring character, Kiyoshiro Imawano's Richard Sagawa, who acts as a narrative meta commentary on the casting and performances in the film. Kiyoshiro Imawano is something of a contemporary of Sawada's, although he found greater success in the glam rock era of the 1970s, rather than the pop star position of Sawada. With only two films to his credit at the time of *The Happiness of the Katakuris* (neither of which were the kind of mainstream pictures that Sawada had starred in since the 1960s), Imawano's performance is not as subtle, and his role more anarchistic.

Imawano's camp conman Sagawa enters the film and promptly snatches up the affection of the daughter of the Katakuri family, Shizue. As with the partial cast of musicians pretending to be amateurs, Imawano's character, a Japanese native, adopts the identity of a half Japanese US navy man who, to be more precise and in the words of the character, is in 'Britain's Royal Navy' and also a 'British secret agent by order of Queen Elizabeth'. The character himself is a performer struggling to hide his real identity from the other characters in the movie.

Furthermore, Sagawa's inability to keep his story straight could in itself be a reflection of the film's own reluctance to adhere to any particular style, particularly with regards to the performances. Imawano as an actor, looking every bit natively Japanese and without any make-up to hide the fact, nonetheless stuns Shizue when it is revealed that he is in fact Japanese and not a foreign serviceman. Shizue's willingness to accept Sagawa as non-Japanese (or at least through the eyes of her daughter) is reflected in the performance of Imawano himself. An audience watching the film would be well aware that the musician can perform, yet due to their willingness to see actors in their role, the audience accepts that he cannot and is on the same level as the non-musicians in the film. This is furthered by Sagawa's broken Japanese speech in the film. Not only has the performance robbed the character of his ability as a world class performer, but also of his speech.

Finally, towards the end of the film, Sagawa is revealed to be a fraud parading as a foreigner in a service uniform stolen from Shochiku, the production company behind *The Happiness of the Katakuris*. At this point the metatextual parody of the character is complete as we are introduced to a Japanese man, pretending to be a character that cannot perform and cannot speak Japanese whilst dressed up in a rental costume from a film company. Both Sagawa and Imawano have been found out, and the performance as style nature of the film becomes clear.

Blurring the lines between professional and amateur to create a stylistic effect was part of the ethos behind *The Happiness of the Katakuris*.

> Miike believes that if you cast a non actor, you sort of force the professional actors to let go of their normal routines and their normal ways of approaching their craft as they have to deal with someone who doesn't use those methods, who doesn't know the craft in a sense, and who works in a more instinctive fashion.[22]

Although Kenji Sawada, Kiyoshiro Imawano and also Shinji Takeda (the son of the family) all come from a musical background, the grandfather, daughter, mother and granddaughter do not. As Tom Mes hints, the purpose of this method of casting was to have just enough musical talent within the film for it to function effectively as a musical, yet to even it out with amateurs unfamiliar with music resulting in the endearing earnestness and familial tone that runs throughout the film, despite its absurd story and aesthetics. The mix forces the professionals to let go of their training, but also adds pressure to the actors who are not musicians to try their hardest to live up to the accomplishments of the more established cast members.

In conclusion, whilst *The Happiness of the Katakuris* certainly succeeds in its musical ambitions, it is understandable how the film, along with *For Love's Sake*, has come to be known as a musical for people that 'don't like musicals'.[23] Rather than embarking upon numbers in earnest, each musical moment in the film instead works to make wry comment on the stylistics of various forms of musical cinema; from music videos, to musicals, to karaoke videos. The film functions successfully as more of a musical farce than the horror musical that the film was sold as. Through this farcical nature, however, the film attains an earnestness that would not exist had it been produced as a 'straight faced' film.

The Happiness of the Katakuris achieves its absurdist tone not just through Takashi Miike's directorial style, but also the way in which the characters within the film attempt to match up to the traditional sequential breaking tropes of the musical whilst never successfully breaking free from the capabilities of their characters. Although partially lost in the West, this is exacerbated by the audience's awareness that whilst the characters cannot indeed match the musical-based non-realism of the film that surrounds them, some of the actors themselves, being pop stars, could, adding metatextual quality to the genre play within *The Happiness of the Katakuris*.

Notes

1. Jasper Sharp, *Historical Dictionary of Japanese Cinema* (Lanham, MD: Scarecrow Press, 2011), p. 271.
2. Tom Mes, *Agitator: The Cinema of Takashi Miike* (Guildford: FAB, 2003), p. 18.
3. Dave Kehr, 'Film Review. Well, the hills are alive but the tourists aren't', *New York Times*, 15 August 2002, available at <http://www.nytimes.com/movie/review?res= 9F03E3DA1F3AF936A2575BC0A9649C8B63> (last accessed 9 August 2016).
4. Ibid.
5. Tom Mes and Kuriko Sato, 'Takashi Miike', Midnight Eye Interview: Takashi Miike, 1 May 2001, available at <http://www.midnighteye.com/interviews/takashi-miike/> (last accessed 9 August 2016).
6. Steve Rose, 'Controversial Japanese director Takashi Miike talks to Steve Rose', *The Guardian*, 2 June 2003, available at <https://www.theguardian.com/film/2003/jun/02/artsfeatures.dvdreviews2> (last accessed 9 August 2016).
7. Daniel Martin, 'Between the local and the global: "Asian Horror" in Ahn Byung-ki's *Phone* and *Bunshinsaba*', in Daniel Martin and Alison Peirse (eds), *Korean Horror Cinema* (Edinburgh: Edinburgh University Press, 2013), pp. 145–57, esp. p. 152.
8. Steven Rawle, 'The ultimate super-happy-zombie-romance-murder-mystery-family-comedy-karaoke-disaster-movie-part-animated-remake-all-singing-all-dancing-musical-spectacular-extravaganza: Miike Takashi's *The Happiness of the Katakuris* as "cult" hybrid', in Leon Hunt, Sharon Lockyer and Milly Williamson (eds), *Screening the Undead: Vampires and Zombies in Film and Television* (London: IB Tauris, 2013), pp. 208–32, esp. p. 219.
9. Adam Boult, 'Why I love . . . the first five minutes of Dead or Alive', *The Guardian*, 28 August 2013, available at <https://www.theguardian.com/film/2013/aug/28/why-i-love-dead-alive-takashi-miike> (last accessed 12 August 2016).
10. Mes, *Agitator*, p. 172.
11. Ibid. p. 61.
12. Jasper Sharp, *Historical Dictionary of Japanese Cinema*, p. 271.
13. Mes, *Agitator*, p. 60.
14. Jane Feuer, *The Hollywood Musical* (Bloomington: Indiana University Press, 1982), p. 9.
15. Dru Jeffries, 'Fantasia International Film Festival', *SYNOPTIQUE: An Online Journal of Film and Moving Image Studies*, 2013, 2(1): 61–6, esp. 62.
16. Naoto Kumazawa, *Making of the Happiness of the Katakuris*, 2001.
17. Ibid.
18. Michael K. Bourdaghs, *Sayonara Amerika, Sayonara Nippon: A Geopolitical Prehistory of J-pop* (New York: Columbia University Press, 2012), p. 125.
19. K. J. Donnelly, *Magical Musical Tour: Rock and Pop in Film Soundtracks* (New York: Bloomsbury Academic, 2015), p. 21.
20. Kenneth G. Henshall, *Dimensions of Japanese Society: Gender, Margins and Mainstream* (New York: St Martin's Press, 1999), p. 46.
21. Julian Cope, *Japrocksampler: How the Post-war Japanese Blew Their Minds on Rock 'n' Roll* (London: Bloomsbury, 2007), p. 91.
22. Tom Mes, *The Happiness of the Katakuris Commentary* (Arrow Video, 2015).

23. Kyle Warner, 'Happiness of the Katakuris, The (2001) Review', *City on Fire*, 23 June 2015, available at <http://cityonfire.com/the-happiness-of-the-katakuris-2001-review-takashi-miike/> (last accessed 29 August 2016).

BIBLIOGRAPHY

Boult, Adam, 'Why I love . . . the first five minutes of Dead or Alive', *The Guardian*, 28 August 2013, <https://www.theguardian.com/film/2013/aug/28/why-i-love-dead-alive-takashi-miike> (last accessed 12 August 2016).

Bourdaghs, Michael K., *Sayonara Amerika, Sayonara Nippon: A Geopolitical Prehistory of J-pop* (New York: Columbia University Press, 2012).

Cope, Julian, *Japrocksampler: How the Post-war Japanese Blew Their Minds on Rock 'n' Roll* (London: Bloomsbury, 2007).

Donnelly, K. J., *Magical Musical Tour: Rock and Pop in Film Soundtracks* (New York: Bloomsbury Academic, 2015).

Feuer, Jane, *The Hollywood Musical* (Bloomington: Indiana University Press, 1982).

Henshall, Kenneth G., *Dimensions of Japanese Society: Gender, Margins and Mainstream* (New York: St Martin's Press, 1999).

Jeffries, Dru, 'Fantasia International Film Festival', *SYNOPTIQUE: An Online Journal of Film and Moving Image Studies*, 2013, 2(1): 61–6.

Kehr, Dave, 'Film Review. Well, the hills are alive but the tourists aren't', *New York Times*, 15 August 2002, <http://www.nytimes.com/movie/review?res=9F03E3DA1F3AF936A2575BC0A9649C8B63> (last accessed 9 August 2016).

Martin, Daniel, 'Between the local and the global: "Asian Horror", in Ahn Byung-ki's *Phone* and *Bunshinsaba*', in Daniel Martin and Alison Peirse (eds), *Korean Horror Cinema* (Edinburgh, Edinburgh University Press, 2013), pp. 145–57.

Mes, Tom, *Agitator: The Cinema of Takashi Miike* (Guildford: FAB, 2003).

Mes, Tom, *The Happiness of the Katakuris Commentary* (Arrow Video, 2015).

Mes, Tom and Kuriko Sato, 'Takashi Miike', Midnight Eye Interview: Takashi Miike, 1 May 2001, <http://www.midnighteye.com/interviews/takashi-miike/> (last accessed 9 August 2016).

Rawle, Steven, 'The ultimate super-happy-zombie-romance-murder-mystery-family-comedy-karaoke-disaster-movie-part-animated-remake-all-singing-all-dancing-musical-spectacular-extravaganza: Miike Takashi's *The Happiness of the Katakuris* as "cult" hybrid', in Leon Hunt, Sharon Lockyer and Milly Williamson (eds), *Screening the Undead: Vampires and Zombies in Film and Television* (London: IB Tauris, 2013), pp. 208–32.

Rose, Steve, 'Controversial Japanese director Takashi Miike talks to Steve Rose', *The Guardian*, 2 June 2003, <https://www.theguardian.com/film/2003/jun/02/artsfeatures.dvdreviews2> (last accessed 9 August 2016).

Sharp, Jasper, *Historical Dictionary of Japanese Cinema* (Lanham, MD: Scarecrow Press, 2011).

Warner, Kyle 'Happiness of the Katakuris, The (2001) Review', *City on Fire*, 23 June 2015, <http://cityonfire.com/the-happiness-of-the-katakuris-2001-review-takashi-miike/> (last accessed 29 August 2016).

2 FILM AND THE TWILIGHT OF ROCK (ROCK IS DEAD AND FILM KILLED IT): POST-MILLENNIAL ROCK MUSICALS

K. J. Donnelly

For a number of years, I have been wrestling with the notion of rock music being dead and have eventually reluctantly admitted that it has suffered an ignominious but unspectacular slow fade out. I do not wish to lament, merely to register a significant change that is evident in film and across culture generally. Perhaps the grotesque corpse of rock can be summed up by rock group AC/DC's last tour. Founder member Malcolm Young retired to a nursing home with Alzheimer's disease in 2014 and later in the year drummer Phil Rudd was arrested and found guilty of drug possession and threatening behaviour. They were replaced. In early 2016 singer Brian Johnson withdrew from the band for medical reasons (due to hearing issues), to be replaced on the 2016 world tour by Guns N' Roses singer Axl Rose. For much of the tour, Rose had his leg in plaster and was confined to a 'throne' on casters in the middle of the stage throughout the performances. Little was left of the 'real' group and the spectacle was bizarre and confounding in the extreme, but perhaps emblematic of rock music.

This chapter is an attempt to write about films in which I can find few redeeming features. Since the millennium, a number of film musicals have presented a particularly tame and standardised image of rock music. This appears to correspond very directly with the increasingly prominent notion of rock being 'dead'. Films such as *School of Rock* (Richard Linklater, 2003), *Camp Rock* (Mathew Diamond, 2008), and *Rock of Ages* (Adam Shankman, 2012) depict a world where rock's socially and culturally problematic aspects have been dissipated or assimilated. This chapter investigates how this cycle of films makes a cultural statement on the death and transfiguration of rock music, as well as embodying rock's destiny.

This recent cycle of films appears to mark nails in the coffin of rock. While over the years many journalists have declared rock moribund, scholars have been slow to have an opinion on something that is not easily substantiated. Although rock-style music continues to be produced, it seems to me that the crucial point is the loss of its socio-cultural milieu. Two decades ago, one of the defining popular music scholars, Lawrence Grossberg, noted that, 'rock's conditions of possibility have been transformed so radically as to suggest that rock's operating logic might no longer be either effective or possible' – that is, in vernacular terms, 'rock & roll is dead'.[1] I concur. The context of the music has changed alongside rock's potential value in a specific cultural system where it developed through its, often negative, relationship with other cultural elements. So, if rock has 'died', what happened to it? Most clearly dominant culture assimilated it. It became 'daddy's music', with rich businessmen and businesswomen as stars, with advertisers manipulating a few iconic images and sounds into something approximating what rock once had been. Of course, there are still new records that sound like rock – and some of them are very good – but they are in fact something else. The context has changed so radically that what was once (perhaps just slightly) unacceptable and unstable as culture now has become a conservative cultural dominant.[2] The cycle of films that I listed above not only sets a solid headstone to mark rock's death as a living, organic music, but also illustrates the empty remainder of rock at the cultural continuum of the present and foreseeable future.

Perhaps rock should be seen as an *historical* object, as a *context* rather than text or style of music. This is similar to debates about film noir, as to whether it was an historically bound cycle or simply a perennial style of film (and thus a genre). Did it emanate from a particular sociocultural moment and worldview; or is it merely a selection of stylistic elements? There had been assumptions of rock music's permanence. Perhaps it merely emanated from a particular social condition (the post war baby boom in the West)? This would make current rock music like 'trad jazz', which is a vibrant live music form but no longer a living organic culture, having developed almost negligibly over decades.

This chapter is not interested in establishing that rock is dead as a going concern. This can be discussed by others elsewhere. I am assuming as a starting point that rock music is not what it once was and, as a working hypothesis, that it is 'dead'. I mentioned above that scholars are not particularly concerned to note this and that it seems like the sort of 'grand gesture' that besets journalism rather than academic scrutiny. Perhaps this is why I have little desire to argue the case but will merely use the notion as an heuristic tool to attempt a greater understanding of the startlingly stereotypical and unaffronting countenance of rock music in recent mainstream films.

Nor do I want to spend much space defining rock music, and merely wish to note that after the advent of rock 'n' roll in the mid-1950s, 'rock' became used for a less compromising form of music in the late 1960s. Tied directly to the counterculture of that era, rock music had retained something of the unruly and controversial aspects of rock 'n' roll culture of over a decade earlier. In an authoritative general guide to popular music, Roy Shuker noted that rock music came from 'grafting together of the emotive and rhythmic elements' of a number of musical formats and was derived from rock 'n' roll, while 'pop is seen to have merged as a somewhat watered-down, blander version of this [. . .]'.[3] Indeed, there has been a tension between rock music being something of an organic folk culture and a mass entertainment industry production line, and this is articulated in the films under scrutiny here, sometimes explicitly but more often implicitly.

CAMP ROCK

America has a well-established tradition of sending children to summer camps. These can be themed, and while sport has been the most popular camp theme, music has also been a preferred focus, although until relatively recently this would have been classical music or jazz rather than rock music. As well as drawing upon this tradition, *Camp Rock* owes much to the tradition of the American high school film, including such elements as the 'mean girl' and her gang, the 'outsider girl', and a group of young people of the same age concentrated together. Mitchie (Demi Lovato), an aspiring singer, goes to a teenage summer camp that is founded upon the principle that all its activities relate to popular music. While developing her popular music skills, Mitchie meets and falls in love with a visiting pop singer (Joe Jonas as Shane). This is a rather coy Disney television film, aimed at 'tweenies' or young teens. It is tempting to see this Disney product as an embodiment of American conservative culture. Indeed, the Jonas brothers made much in their publicity of their Christian beliefs and wearing of purity rings, indicative of their chastity, signifying that they would not indulge in carnal activities until their marriage day. It is therefore unsurprising that *Camp Rock* is a sexless teen movie, also not wishing to enflame its young teen audience too much. The central couple does not even manage a kiss. However, the exuberant song sequences might, of course, easily be interpreted as a sublimation of sex drive for the film's characters, much as in most classical film musicals.[4] In fact, *Camp Rock* is in most aspects a rather traditional teen pop musical. But it is hardly a 'rock' musical, which begs the question why the term appears so prominently in the title. After all, 'Camp Pop' would not have been a bad title. Perhaps the answer resides in a desire to engage the residual rebellious image of rock, with Shane Gray (Joe Jonas) being an over-indulged and slightly gruff figure, while the early song

'We Want to Rock' appears as a statement of intent, but one that is not clearly fulfilled. Indeed, it is hard not to think of 'rock' as a metaphor for sex, as has been common in rock music history. Def Leppard's clear message of 'Let's Get Rocked', for instance, does not seem a million miles from 'We Want to Rock'.

As a seemingly traditional pop musical, *Camp Rock* has well-defined song sequences. In fact, it even bears a strong resemblance to classical integrated musicals, with many functional songs that add something to narrative development rather than serving simply as momentary attractions in themselves. Certainly, in many ways *Camp Rock* follows the traditional classical film musical blueprint. For example, it has something of the 'dual focus narrative' as discussed by Rick Altman, where a male and female character who will come together in the film remain apart and have their own songs until the climactic 'consummation'.[5] Here, this takes place in the duet where Mitchie and Shane join together to sing 'This is Me'. Similarly, *Camp Rock* contains songs that have specific narrative functions, which move narrative on and tell us about character. Clear examples are 'Gotta Find You' and 'Who Will I Be'. These both resemble the so-called 'I Want' or 'I Wish' song (sometimes called the 'Wishes and Aspirations song'), which often comes early in a musical and sets out a principal narrative goal for the protagonist. The film's musical structure involves not only intermittent but regular song sequences, but also a large-scale big happy ending finale (the 'Final Jam'). The narrative is a fairly straightforward Cinderella story, alongside a stereotypical 'becoming honest to self and the world' narrative trajectory.[6] Shane hears but does not clearly see Mitchie singing at the piano after he runs away from some screaming fans. Her rather breathy performance states: 'No more hiding who I am. This is me.' Enchanted with the song/her, Shane declares, 'I've got to find that girl with the voice' ('Gotta to Find You'). There is a clear association of the singing voice with the 'real self', yet later in the film, when Shane sings to Mitchie ('who I am'), his diegetic performance is clearly enhanced by the song's chorus being bolstered by more non-diegetic voices rather than simply his own.

It is a curious point that almost all the music in *Camp Rock* is not rock music. In the film's only significant montage sequence, the non-diegetic music, which one might expect to be rock music, is instead the hip hop song 'Start the Party'. The film also includes girl band pop (when Tess, Ella and Margaret practice singing in harmonies), R & B (Lola singing 'What it Takes'), breakdancing and some electropop at the 'Final Jam' with choreographed dancing troupe and no instruments evident. Indeed, the use of iconic musical instruments is at the heart of popular ideas about rock music. The film shows off some electric guitars (including a cheap 1970s Japanese Teisco played by Mitchie early in the title sequence and a Les Paul Goldtop – though a cheaper copy rather than a Gibson – played by Peggy at the 'Final Jam'), but emphasises singing rather than playing music.

One notable aspect of *Camp Rock* is its use of hip hop at times in the film, making a strange bedfellow indeed with the film's 'rock' aspirations. Black characters appear rapping and breakdancing, and remain compartmentalised (often being together in a group and not as boyfriends of the main characters, etc.) and on the way towards a present but segregated tokenism. Early in the film, Dee LaDuke gives an introduction to the camp. She asks the campers to sing 'hello' to her, which is succeeded by a reverse shot of Mitchie in medium close-up. Two black rappers suddenly join her on stage, which is succeeded by a reverse shot (a medium close-up 2 shot) of two black characters. This structure is repeated later. When black girl Lola gets up to an R & B-type song ('What it Takes'), there is a cut from her to a reverse shot of very excited looking rappers from earlier. Dancers in the film's song and dance sequences are both black and white, but the form of dancing is associated more with pop music, and some of the other songs are clear girl band material. The 'Final Jam' is the film's climax and what all the characters have been anticipating. Could it be less 'rock'? It begins with the Hasta La Vista Crew's rap and dance performance (featuring Ella) and then has an R & B dance song performed by the IT Girls, Tess and ranks of choreographed dancers. Arguably, none of this is traditionally associated with rock music.

Overall, *Camp Rock* suggests very strongly that rock culture at present is a shadow of its former self. Although the film's 'old rocker' figure, Brown Cessario (played by British actor Daniel Fathers), is the boss of the camp, he is reduced to talking about great days in the past – solidifying the notion of rock music being a past endeavour that now simply constitutes some great memories of times long gone. His status as a middle-aged representative of rock seems to emphasise the 'pop' of the film's youth. He spouts clichés such as 'when the music calls you've got to answer' and 'if the class is a-rocking, I'm glad I came knocking'. There are some residual aspects of rock on show, perhaps most notably the appeal to a sense of the authentic. Shane's recent career development is not satisfactory for him. He calls it 'stupid cookie pop star stuff'. Brown says to Shane: 'what happened to the kid who just loved music?' and then forces him to teach 'Hip Hop Dance' classes.

The song sequence for the declaration song 'We Rock' involves a large ensemble. The music is light rock alongside choreographed dancing of the sort evident in lighter pop music such as boy or girl bands. *Camp Rock* consistently emphasises singing and dancing over ensemble instrument playing, with nothing remotely like a rock band ever materialising. The Jonas brothers (as 'Connect 3') do not include other musicians (bass guitar, drums, keyboards) on the stage with them, and Caitlyn's short solo performance behind the keyboard is truncated, while other sequences with elaborate gyrating dancers are far more extensive. In addition to all this, the singing style in evidence is fairly homogeneous and not really rock at all. Indeed, it owes far more to the television talent shows of recent years, such as *Pop Idol* and *X-Factor*, which have lauded a fairly circumscribed style of singing that is firmly based in chart pop rather than rougher vocal styles traditional to rock music. Rock aspects remain firmly in the margins or lack evidence in *Camp Rock*, which resembles a children's version or kindergarten understanding of rock music, and is much more comfortable with its deployment of the brand of boy and girl band culture that became prominent in the mid-1990s and after.

SCHOOL OF ROCK

School of Rock appears to be a film mostly about children but aimed at an adult audience. Is the film about school, or about rock? While it is clearly making pronouncements about the former, it is equally making assumptions and declarations about the latter. Like musical camps for teenagers, rock schools have increasingly become prominent, where children can go to weekend or evening classes to learn rock instruments and ensemble playing. The film's narrative concerns Dewey Finn (Jack Black), who illicitly gains a job in a school teaching fourth graders and lacking training decides to teach them rock music.[7] They form an ensemble called School of Rock and play at a 'Battle of the Bands' contest. Dewey takes rock music to the heart of education, verifying that it is important for the development of children. This proves that rock is not in any way threatening or destabilising but is in fact a life-affirming and positive thing for society. The film is a parable of society (the school) being 'converted' in a Christianity-like manner to a culture that was previously considered to have something of an 'outsider' character. The concluding stage show, however, exposes the truth: that the rock music is not really rebellious or problematic and is in fact acceptable to, if not the very culture of, the parents. In a populist twist, the school and a few conservative parents are the only ones who need convincing that rock is good for everyone. Jeff Smith's appraisal of the film is that, 'While it is tempting to claim that the kids truly learn the value of oppositional politics (i.e. stickin' it to the man) [. . . the film is ultimately] merely a performance of social opposition'.[8] Unlike *Camp Rock*, the music in the film is most decidedly rock. Rock instrumentation is constantly in evidence and almost all the music that appears is classic rock music from the 1970s and 1980s. *School of Rock* includes much 'album' (rather than hit chart) music, from bands such as AC/DC and Led Zeppelin. Indeed, some of these songs might be classified as part of an accepted 'repertoire' of classic rock, particularly hard rock and heavy metal. While this is a 'jukebox musical' in that it uses a roster of pre-existing songs, they are songs of a certain character and status. There is a good chance that the audience might know these songs already. For instance, when Finn sets the children in a line and he assigns musician roles to them, this is accompanied non-diegetically by AC/DC's 'Back in Black' (the opening section without singing). This rhythmic riff is well-known and the volume of the music simply ducks for his dialogue. When Dewey sees his class playing music with little enthusiasm, he opens a van and gets out rock instruments that he brings into the school. This is accompanied by Cream's 'Sunshine of Your Love' (again the opening of the song), which suddenly fades out as the children have finished their 'classical' music lesson and enter his classroom. One of Dewey's pupils, Zach, plays classical guitar but his father will not let him play electric guitar. Finn then gives him perhaps the most iconically 'rock' electric guitar: a Flying V. Dewey then demonstrates a succession of guitar riffs: Black Sabbath's 'Iron Man', Deep Purple's 'Smoke on the Water' and AC/DC's 'Highway to Hell'. He does not name them and in a 'name that tune' manner the film appears to assume they will be familiar to many members of the audience. This sequence deftly illustrates the film's central reference points in 1970s heavy rock, although the film also uses The Velvet Underground, David Bowie, The Who, The Stooges, T. Rex, and Kiss (with a cover of a song by punk band The Ramones), as well as more recent music by The Darkness, Metallica and The Black Keys in fragments as non-diegetic music.

Traditional film musicals (and stage musicals) often concluded with a big number. While the Beatles' *A Hard Day's Night* (Richard Lester, 1964) had a short live concert and *Camp Rock* had its 'Final Jam', *School of Rock* similarly contains its own live-on-stage culmination at the Battle of the Bands contest. As well as Dewey's old band No Vacancy, his new ensemble with the school children, School of Rock, performs three songs: 'School of Rock' and 'In the Ancient Times' (both original songs) and a cover of AC/DC's 'It's a Long Way to the Top (If You Want to Rock 'n' Roll)'. The on-stage performance owes much to rock traditions. Dewey is dressed up as iconic AC/DC lead guitarist Angus Young, in schoolboy attire, which is not doubled by the children on stage and is slightly perturbing in this context.[9] Lead guitarist Zach performs a virtuoso guitar solo on his knees in classic heavy rock style. This leads to a reverse of Zach's father and the keyboard player's father formally complimenting each other on their sons' skills.

In the spirit of racial and cultural diversity, *School of Rock* wishes to emphasise that rock is perhaps not as 'white' as it sometimes might seem. As well as an Asian American keyboard player, black girl Tomika gets her own soul-style singing cameo in the middle of a song. This inspires an immediate reverse shot of her proud and smiling parents. On the one hand, this acknowledges that rock music is not a wholly white form of music but also 'compartmentalises' black characters in a strikingly similar shot structure to *Camp Rock* (one of black performer-black audience). In the cause of social unity, all the school children are happy at the end, although School of Rock loses out to No Vacancy as winners (which echoes Mitchie not winning the 'Final Jam' in *Camp Rock*).

In summary, *School of Rock* certainly espouses rock music, particularly of the 1970s heavy rock variety. Dewey asks the children for their musical influences and balks at their mention of Christina Aguilera, Puff Daddy and Liza Minnelli. He then tells them it should be Led Zeppelin, Black Sabbath, AC/DC and Motörhead. Australian band AC/DC seem a dominant force in the film, with Dewey copying their guitar player's attire and his ensemble's extensive and memorable cover of one of their songs as the film's culmination, as well as Dewey quoting their lyrics and playing one of their famous guitar riffs, while their 'Back in Black' appears as non-diegetic music. Indeed, *School of Rock* was released a year after AC/DC had signed a lucrative deal with Sony Records not only for new albums but, significantly, to allow the re-release of their old material.[10]

Finn tells his class that rock 'n' roll music was opposed to the Establishment: 'There used to be a way to stick it to The Man. It was called rock 'n' roll. But guess what? Oh, no. The Man ruined that too, with a little thing called MTV.' Tellingly, he talks about it in the past tense. It is certainly possible to read the film as being self-conscious about what has happened to rock music and the processes of recuperation, which indeed it enacts. However, *School of Rock* suggests that rock is universal but that it also might be a means of infantilisation. Indeed, the film has a distinct ambivalence to its evangelism. Does it suggest that rock is worthwhile knowledge or that it is as useful as any knowledge, and that therefore education is useless?

ROCK OF AGES

Rock of Ages is likely named after a Def Leppard song from the early 1980s, which is, of course, a parody of the Christian hymn of that same title. In the early 1980s, there was still something slightly dangerous about this mild blasphemy which is now wholly lost. The film's story is as follows: in 1987, Sherrie arrives in Los Angeles hoping for a career as a singer.[11] She meets and falls in love with Drew, who gets her a job at the music venue the Bourbon Room, which is owned by Dennis (Alec Baldwin) and Lonny (Russell Brand). They need rock star Stacee Jaxx (Tom Cruise) to perform and make money that will save the club from bankruptcy while simultaneously being persecuted by the mayor and his wife who want to shut them down. As well as using a succession of well-known rock songs rearticulated in the film, *Rock of Ages* wields some distinctive and stereotypical rock imagery. Tom Cruise plays Stacee Jaxx as an archetypal dissipated rock singer who lives through following his immediate urges. Jaxx seems partly based on Axl Rose of Guns N' Roses and Bret Michaels of Poison, bands that are both well represented in the film's choice of songs. Although Cruise was clearly committed to the role, the character will always appear essentially as Tom Cruise, and his performance has something of the drag act about it. Certainly, his name is derived from the Blur song 'Tracy Jacks' (on *Park Life*, 1994), which is about a middle-aged transvestite.[12] Similarly, Alec Baldwin always looks like he is wearing a long-hair wig, while Lonny is played by British comedian Russell Brand, whose seems to have based his career on the adoption of something of a stereotypical 'rock' persona while not being a rock musician – and had already appeared as a rock star in comedy feature films *Forgetting Sarah Marshall* (Nicholas Stoller, 2008) and *Get Him to the Greek* (Nicholas Stoller, 2010).

Perhaps it is something of a surprise that a fairly traditional film musical such as this was derived from a stage original. The stage version first appeared in 2005 but the film makes a number of instructive amendments to the stage original. In the film, the misunderstanding between the romantic leads pulls them apart and motors the narrative: Drew thinks Sherrie has slept with Stacee Jaxx. She has not – but in the stage version she had. If the film seems coy, its joyous conclusion is less so on stage, with club owner Dennis dying. Furthermore, the stage version's darker ending also sees Stacee Jaxx charged with statutory rape and fleeing American justice, all of which Tom Cruise was spared. The film also removes the German developers forcing the 'clean up' of the strip and the closure of the Bourbon Room, replacing the motivation simply with hypocritical 'morality-selling' politicians, the mayor and his wife (who as it turns out once was involved with Jaxx).

Rock of Ages is very much premised upon the notion of a 'repertoire', being built around a group of known 'classic' rock songs from the 1980s, broadly speaking the period setting of the film. This is a very particular version of rock history evident in the film's roster of songs. It is dominated by radio friendly chart hits, mostly by American acts although including a few British groups who achieved chart success in the United States. Indeed, one can almost imagine that the film and the preceding stage show were conceived by initially setting out what would be the constituents of a best-selling compilation album of rock hits from the 1980s and a little beyond. This is remarkable in that rock music in the 1960s and 1970s tended to be album-oriented, and in some cases rock musicians disparaged the singles chart as crass pop commerce and distasteful. However, in the 1980s, a new 'chart friendly' rock music was particularly prominent in the US, and the film draws upon this rather than album-oriented music from the era. This repertoire runs from 'soft rock' such as Foreigner to pop-rock such as Pat Benatar, to so-called 'hair metal' such as Twisted Sister and David Lee Roth. What is striking about the rock music in the film is its credentials as pop music. While a sign in the street advertises rock group Motörhead, their music perhaps would have not been accessible or 'soft' enough for the film's musical consistency. So, the music upon which *Rock of Ages* is based is a highly particular brand of rock music. Furthermore, almost all the songs were big hits and have retained a certain profile for the public as classics, meaning that the film's audience would in many cases have recognised the songs, even if they did not like the music as such. For instance, *Rock of Ages* opens and closes with Jaxx singing Guns N' Roses' 'Paradise City', while he also sings Bon Jovi's 'Wanted Dead or Alive' and Drew sings Twisted Sister's 'I Wanna Rock', all of which were prominent MTV music videos in the early 1980s (as Dewey might remind us).

A film musical being based on a roster of known songs from diverse sources was not an uncommon procedure during the Hollywood studio era, and in many ways *Rock of Ages* appears like a traditional film musical.[13] It evinces a dual-focus narrative with respect to Sherrie and Drew, both of whom have separate songs and come together through music. Furthermore, *Rock of Ages* uses songs in a functional manner, with most of the songs being integrated with the narrative rather than a handful of 'backstage musical' isolated set-pieces. However, it seems slightly disquieting that the narrative situation is so clearly fabricated to fit the songs, which seems the wrong way round (see Stephanie Fremaux's discussion of this elsewhere in the volume). For instance, the extremely well-known 1980s Foreigner songs 'Waiting for a Girl Like You' (sung by Drew and Sherrie) and 'I Want to Know What Love Is' (sung by Stacee and journalist Constance Sack) are articulated into fairly stereotypical romantic narrative trajectories. The sense of cultural status of the film's songs, as known classics, guarantees the film's (soft) rock credentials and also forms the essential skeleton of the film, where enjoyment can come from recognising the next classic song rather than following the rather prosaic narrative development.

Along with *We Will Rock You* (which started in 2002 and is planned to be filmed in the future), *Rock of Ages* was a successful stage show based on a roster of classic hit rock songs. However, these are by and large slow 'power ballads' rather than straightforward rock songs. So, in terms of music, *Rock of Ages* tends towards the softer side of rock, and while it may use rock's iconography it tends to be a little toothless. For instance, Stacee Jaxx and the unconvincingly shy *Rolling Stone* journalist Constance have a lengthy sex scene on an air hockey table as they sing the Foreigner song 'I Want to Know What Love Is'. This is melodramatic but very demure, as is the film's attitude to 'sex, drugs and rock 'n' roll' more generally. While alcohol is flaunted, hard drugs are absolutely not in evidence.[14] Indeed, *Rock of Ages* presents a highly sanitised version of rock. The political opposition to rock (and the Bourbon Room) is also highly stereotypical and nothing like the sort of actual attacks made on rock in the 1980s. Tipper Gore's PMRC (the Parents Music Resource Center) hounded rock music, but significantly the sort of rock music targeted (political, Satanic, or 'violence-glorifying' music) is nowhere in evidence in this film.[15]

Indeed, there are some less than controversial singers making cameo appearances in *Rock of Ages*. Mary J. Blige, often known as the 'Queen of Hip Hop Soul', sings Quarterflash's 'Harden My Heart' and is something of a surprise in a rock-based film, replacing an ageing seemingly white hippie character in the stage version, while grown-up teen pop singer Debbie Gibson sings along-side Sebastian Bach (from rock group Skid Row) on Jefferson Starship's 'We Built This City (on Rock'n'Roll)'. The ridiculing of the boy band in concert is succeeded by the film's tumultuous and celebratory conclusion: a version of Journey's 'Don't Stop Believin'', which is less known these days for the original soft rock record of 1981 than it is for its more pop-inspired manifestation in TV high school choir drama *Glee* (2009–15, Fox) in 2009.

CONCLUSION

I certainly would not deny that rock music is being made at present, and in some cases by musicians who have been doing exactly the same thing for half a century. The crucial point is that the context has changed and the reason for rock music and the wider sociocultural implications of the music no longer have the same effect.[16] Rock music is no longer 'outsider' music, if indeed it ever was. As Glenn Frey's 1986 song 'Boys of Summer' noted with incredulity: 'Walking down the street today I saw a Dead Head sticker on a Cadillac'. The symbol for the Grateful Dead, the spearhead of the rock counterculture, had become acceptable to, and part of, the Establishment. This is the key cultural change and the image of rebelliousness has changed its cultural value. This has been a gradual process, arguably starting at the time of rock 'n' roll's appearance in the 1950s, but certainly accelerating in the 1980s and beyond.

Films have certainly played their part in helping to tame rock music. For example, Spoof mock rockumentary *This is Spinal Tap* (Rob Reiner, 1984) established a whole model of representing rock musicians, to the point where actual rock documentary *Anvil: The Story of Anvil* (Sacha Gervasi, 2008) appears so similar to the spoof that it resembles a sequel. Although the latter is a straightforward documentary, it is almost impossible to take seriously. Indeed, modern rock films might well mark a continuity with the pop film of the early 1960s, which aimed to make the music and culture acceptable to adult culture and was a road to assimilation. Early rock 'n' roll films aimed to retain the unruly excitement of rock 'n' roll culture while also trying to reassure parents that their children would not be made into degenerates. This impetus almost became a genre in itself, with a fine example of the 'misunderstood teenager' film being Cliff Richard's *The Young Ones* (Sidney J. Furie, 1961). Here, the wronged teenagers turn out to have the moral fibre lacking in the suspicious adults, a trope evident even earlier with films such as *Don't Knock the Rock* (Fred F. Sears, 1956). As Barry Keith Grant noted three decades ago,

'The strategy of validating rock, of making it acceptable, by asserting in some way its unifying power has been perhaps the major motif of rock movies'.[17] In more recent times, there has been no need to endeavour to make rock acceptable, as it has become part of the Establishment itself.

In the late 1950s and early 1960s, rock 'n' roll films tried to allay parental fears about their children indulging in illicit sex. By the late 1960s, films were admitting that they had actually been taking drugs as well. This period is the cradle of the term 'rock music', with an implied progression from rock 'n' roll and a differentiation from pop (and popular) music. This form was partially hybridised from a folk music stem, from which it derives its interest in authenticity and conception of itself as more of an organic folk art than a top-down entertainment industry. Rock's connection with the counterculture is imperative for understanding how its social unacceptability became arguably its principal cultural importance, as a values and taste-questioning, and unstable element in modern culture. Of course, much rock music never thought of itself as having a cultural-political efficacy in this manner and this perhaps was its most crucial characteristic. This process of cultural conflict was sometimes crudely caricatured in films. A good example is the over-reaction of dominant social elements to the potential difference offered by rather anodyne pop-rock in *Footloose* (Herbert Ross, 1984).

A sense of rock as historically bounded means that as a going concern it might well have become moribund. It may remain as a stable form but no longer constitute a living organic culture.[18] (Although some shards of rock may have remained underground.) Each decade has different dominant ideas of what constitutes 'rock': in the 1950s, rock 'n' roll; in the 1960s, pop crossover (embodied by the Beatles and the Rolling Stones) and the counterculture; in the 1970s, so-called 'dinosaur' hard rock bands like Led Zeppelin and Deep Purple; in the 1980s, chart-busting soft rock like Def Leppard and Bon Jovi; and in the 1990s, the 'grunge' rebirth. Each decade of rock has been different and demographics could well be the key. *Camp Rock*, *School of Rock* and *Rock of Ages* are the logical conclusion of this process.

Who are the intended audiences for each film? Respectively, they are minors, parents, and 'nostalgers' of middle age and beyond, perhaps. Strikingly, in comparison with traditional pop musicals, the crucial notion of the 'generation gap' in these films is firmly outdated, as explicitly illustrated in *School of Rock*. Instead, perhaps the defining aspect of the films is a sense of repertoire. They are both founded upon a grouping of accepted 'classic' songs, which give the film authenticity as well as providing an essential structure. This is reminiscent of the notion of 'repertoire' in classical music, where a number of pieces of music are the accepted roster that is representative of the form.[19] These constitute a consensus, a sense of the musical establishment, perhaps. Similarly, two of the three films under discussion here are premised upon the notion of 'classic rock' and 'rock classics', which have become a vaguely accepted grouping of songs. In the 1970s, such a process of packaging old 'classic' songs (such as in the film *American Graffiti* [George Lucas, 1973]) was considered a form of nostalgia, but as the songs in these films are in a sense dealt with as timeless, this is not nostalgia but an acceptance of the pastness of rock music.

Notes

1. Lawrence Grossberg, 'Is anybody listening? Does anybody care? On "the state of rock"', in Andrew Ross and Tricia Rose (eds), *Microphone Fiends: Youth Music and Youth Culture* (London: Routledge, 1994), p. 52.
2. Perhaps emblematised by the use of rock songs as well as pop songs as themes when political parties are campaigning. Some notable instances are Mitt Romney's use of Kid Rock's 'Born Free' in 2012 and Donald Trump's use of the Rolling Stones' 'You Can't Always Get What You Want' in 2016.
3. Roy Shuker, *Key Concepts in Popular Music* (London: Routledge, 1998), p. 226.
4. Barry Keith Grant, *The Hollywood Film Musical* (Oxford: Blackwell, 2012), p. 47.
5. Rick Altman, *The American Film Musical* (London: British Film Institute, 1989), p. 19.
6. The film's message is of personal honesty and music as a vehicle for the true self. Shane tells his class: 'Your Music has to be who you really are, it has to show how you feel or it doesn't mean anything.' Mitchie has lied about her mother (telling them she's a record executive rather than the cook). This is revealed, and she falls out with the mean 'popular girl', Tess; Mitchie has to sit with Caitlyn and the three black people.
7. Michael Webb suggests that the name Dewey Finn references pragmatist philosopher John Dewey, who had strong views on school's ability to reform society more generally. 'Rock goes to school on screen: a model for teaching non-"learned" musics derived from the films *School of Rock* (2003) and *Rock School* (2005)', Michael Webb, *Action, Criticism, and Theory for Music Education*, 2007, 6(3): 55.
8. Jeff Smith, 'The edge of seventeen: class, age, and popular music in Richard Linklater's *School of Rock*', *Screening the Past*, 2005, no. 18, available at <http://www.screeningthepast.com/2014/12/the-edge-of-seventeen-class-age-and-popular-music-in-richard-linklaters-school-of-rock/> (last accessed 5 July 2016).
9. Jack Black had performed in the parodic rock duo Tenacious D from 1994. They had their own film vehicle, *Tenacious D: The Pick of Destiny* (Liam Lynch, 2006).
10. Jennifer Ordonez, 'Sony is betting on long future with aging rock band AC/DC', *Wall Street Journal*, 5 December 2002, available at <http://www.wsj.com/articles/SB1039039340966799593> (last accessed 10 August 2016).
11. According to a convincing source (Steve Pond, '"Rock of ages": here's what's wrong with this picture', *The Wrap*, 15 June 2012), the film gets its history and representation wrong; available at <http://www.thewrap.com/rock-ages-heres-whats-wrong-picture-44121/> (last accessed 8 July 2016).
12. As well as possibly referencing the British electronic dance music artists Basement Jaxx and their club of the same name that began in the mid-1990s. In the film, Jaxx was the singer in the group Arsenal, which appears to have been named in ignorance of the 1980s group who were an offshoot of Big Black.
13. For instance, *Singin' in the Rain* (Stanley Donen and Gene Kelly, 1952) had songs mostly written by Nacio Herb Brown and Arthur Freed, but which had appeared over the years elsewhere rather than being written for the film.

14. Indeed, the film and stage show leave out one of the key elements of Sunset Strip in the 1980s: drugs. A good description of the place and lifestyle is available in Mötley Crüe and Neil Strauss, *The Dirt: Confessions of the World's Most Notorious Rock Band* (London: Regan Books, 2001).
15. See Eric D. Nuzum, *Parental Advisory: Music Censorship in America* (London: HarperCollins, 2001).
16. Indeed, earliest and foundational scholars writing about rock and pop music approached it as an essential part of youth culture. For example, Simon Frith's *The Sociology of Rock* (London: Constable, 1978) and *Sound Effects: Youth, Leisure, and the Politics of Rock* (London: Constable, 1983). Now it is dominated by middle-aged people.
17. Barry K. Grant, The classic Hollywood musical and the "problem" of rock 'n' roll', *Journal of Popular Film and Television*, 1986, 13(4): 201.
18. Like Habermas noting that modernism was 'dominant but dead'. Hal Foster, 'Introduction', in Hal Foster (ed.), *Postmodern Culture* (London: Pluto, 1985), p. vii.
19. Classical repertoire is closely related to the notion of canon, those pieces which are deemed to be the most worthy. Marcia Citron, *Gender and the Musical Canon* (Chicago: University of Illinois Press, 1993), p. 1. It is arguably more closely related to the notion of the 'Great American Songbook', a roster of popular song 'standards', mostly from the first half of the twentieth century.

BIBLIOGRAPHY

Altman, Rick, *The American Film Musical* (London: British Film Institute, 1989).
Citron, Marcia, *Gender and the Musical Canon* (Chicago: University of Illinois Press, 1993).
Foster, Hal (ed.), *Postmodern Culture* (London: Pluto, 1985).
Frith, Simon, *The Sociology of Rock* (London: Constable, 1978).
Frith, Simon, *Sound Effects: Youth, Leisure, and the Politics of Rock* (London: Constable, 1983).
Grossberg, Lawrence, 'Is anybody listening? Does anybody care? On "the state of rock"', in Andrew Ross and Tricia Rose (eds), *Microphone Fiends: Youth Music and Youth Culture* (London: Routledge, 1994).
Grant, Barry Keith, 'The classic Hollywood musical and the "problem" of rock 'n' roll', *Journal of Popular Film and Television*, 1986, 13(4): 195–205.
Grant, Barry Keith, *The Hollywood Film Musical* (Oxford: Blackwell, 2012).
Ordonez, Jennifer, 'Sony is betting on long future with aging rock band AC/DC', *Wall Street Journal*, 5 December 2002, <http://www.wsj.com/articles/SB1039039340966799593> (last accessed 10 August 2016).
Pond, Steve, '"Rock of ages": here's what's wrong with this picture', *The Wrap*, 15 June 2012, <http://www.thewrap.com/rock-ages-heres-whats-wrong-picture-44121/> (last accessed 8 July 2016).
Nuzum, Eric D., *Parental Advisory: Music Censorship in America* (London: Harper Collins, 2001).
Shuker, Roy, *Key Concepts in Popular Music* (London: Routledge, 1998).
Smith, Jeff, 'The edge of seventeen: class, age, and popular music in Richard Linklater's *School of Rock*', *Screening the Past*, 2005, no. 18, <http://www.screeningthepast.com/2014/12/the-edge-of-seventeen-class-age-and-popular-music-in-richard-linklaters-school-of-rock/> (last accessed 5 July 2016).
Strauss, Neil and Mötley Crüe, *The Dirt: Confessions of the World's Most Notorious Rock Band* (London: Regan Books, 2001).

Webb, Michael, 'Rock goes to school on screen: a model for teaching non-"learned" musics derived from the films *School of Rock* (2003) and *Rock School* (2005)', *Action, Criticism, and Theory for Music Education*, 2007, 6(3).

3 *TEAM AMERICA: WORLD POLICE:* DUPLICITOUS VOICES OF THE SOCIO-POLITICAL SPY MUSICAL

Jack Curtis Dubowsky

Team America: World Police (Trey Parker and Matt Stone, 2004) expertly subverts and redacts conventions of Hollywood and Broadway musicals, mixing parody and politics in a fertile intertextual landscape. The film employs an ambiguous voice, a complicated parody of both conservative and progressive politics, and uses musical voices to indicate or reference various racisms and ironies, as well as to provoke and bait audience sensibilities. The film became hugely influential, paving the way for other comedies such as *OSS 117 Le Caire: nid d'espions* (Michel Hazanavicius, 2006) and *The Interview* (Seth Roger and Evan Goldberg, 2014). While *Team America*'s absurdist politics grabbed most of the critical attention lavished on the film, its implementation of musical numbers was groundbreaking, traditional, effective, reverent and irreverent all at once.

The story centres loosely around Broadway actor Gary, who is recruited by Team America because of the acting ability he demonstrates in *Lease*, a show-within-a-show parody of *Rent*. So begins *Team America* as something of a backstage musical, a tired subgenre rejuvenated by the incisiveness of the spot-on showstopper 'Everyone Has AIDS'. But *Team America* progresses into a spy thriller cum action movie, parodied by the use of marionettes, in which situational musical numbers' moderate pace, communicate emotional subtext and provide witty commentary, much as in a traditional musical.

Kim Jong-il's 'I'm So Ronery' subversively gives the 'hopes and aspirations' number to the villain, rather than the hero; filmmakers Trey Parker, Matt Stone and Pam Brady pioneered this gimmick in their earlier film, *South Park:*

Bigger Longer & Uncut (1999), with Saddam Hussein's plaintive 'Up There'. *Team America* encapsulates every possible use of music, from underscore to diegetic music, to its self-referential 'Montage', wreaking havoc with a *Rocky* parody, breaking the fourth wall, and throwing everything into a fantastical gap, a liminal space confounding diegesis, genre and political posture.

BUT IS IT A MUSICAL?

Filmmakers Matt Stone and Trey Parker share a background in music, and musical theatre permeates virtually all their work. A cursory look at their creative partnership, from adolescence through past projects to the current day, shows consistent alignment, homage, deployment and subversion of musical genre conventions, show tunes and formal structures.

Trey Parker became interested in musical theatre as a teenager. He met Matt Stone in film school at the University of Colorado Boulder. In 1992, the two made an animated short called *The Spirit of Christmas*, also known as *Jesus vs. Frosty*, inspired by taking acid.[1] At ages nineteen and twenty, Stone and Parker raised $100,000 to make *Cannibal! The Musical* (1993). Thereafter, they moved to Los Angeles to try to break into show business. In 1995, Brian Graden, an executive at Fox television, paid Parker and Stone $2,000 to remake *The Spirit of Christmas* as an 'animated video Christmas card' he could send to his friends, which he did.[2] The video circulated wildly around Hollywood; this led to a contract for six episodes with a new cable channel, Comedy Central, and so the animated series *South Park* (1997–) was born. *South Park* would boldly incorporate music, and its offshoot feature film *South Park: Bigger, Longer & Uncut* (1999) is largely a musical. Parker was nominated for best song for 'Blame Canada'; he and Stone attended the 2000 Academy Awards resplendent in gowns, tripping on LSD, to the irritation of other indignant nominees. Parker and Stone (with Robert Lopez, co-creator, composer and lyricist of *Avenue Q*) would create *The Book of Mormon*, which opened on Broadway in 2011, winning nine Tony Awards, including Best Musical.

Within this context, it is easy to retrospectively frame *Team America* as a musical; but the most convincing argument to place it within the musical genre is that the film would be eviscerated without its music, which encompasses every utilisation, including show tunes, underscore, source music, visual vocal performances, visual instrumental performances, even song and dance numbers, however brief or frivolous they may seem.

Team America as a musical contrasts delightfully to the other genre it most directly derives from: the action adventure film. Says Matt Stone:

A big part of the movie is basically doing a huge Hollywood spectacle event movie, but with puppets. Like a Michael Bay film, or a Jerry

Bruckheimer film, like *Armageddon* or like *The Day After Tomorrow*. But all with puppets.[3]

The puppets are a subversion of the action adventure genre – awkward in motion, small in scale – as are the show tunes and reliance upon musical genre conventions. So while *Team America* is a musical, this genrefication fits into a larger system of subversion and alteration.

In reading *Team America* as a musical, one should note similarities to 'punk musicals' described by film scholar David Laderman, such as *Jubilee* (Derek Jarman, 1978), *Times Square* (Allan Moyle, 1980), and *Liquid Sky* (Slava Tsukerman, 1983). These earlier punk musicals, like *Team America*, simultaneously pushed against the musical form and followed its rigid, commercial constraints in order to make a broad argument that could be digested by a wide audience – wider than punk itself may have reached. *Team America*, like these films, is both traditional and irreverent. As Laderman notes:

> On the surface, most of these punk films convey a conspicuous subversion of conformity; they are loudly anti. In various ways, they deconstruct the musical genre, translating much of punk's anarchic, anticommercial energy into film narrative. Yet they also illustrate how punk music's 'revolution' against dominant music-industry trends depended largely upon a certain ironic embrace of popular culture.[4]

Likewise, *Team America*'s approach is wholly dependent upon an embrace of a jingoistic nationalism that it simultaneously mocks. *Team America* deliberately straddles multiple genres (musical, action adventure, comedy, puppet movie), enabling it to have an ambiguous or shifting cinematic sensibility. Similarly, the punk musicals confounded and expanded the musical genre.

> Indeed, one primary way these films engage in a radical revision of the musical is by fusing the genre with an independent- and cult-film sensibility. In distinct ways, these punk films force the musical and the indie film to join hands, undoing genre conventions while simultaneously expanding the formal terrain of the genre.[5]

In the case of *Team America*, it is the musical and the action adventure film that join hands, certainly a radical revision if there ever was one, leading to many pleasurable and memorable cinematic moments.

While the above analysis places emphasis upon where musicals are headed, we might also consider an assessment of *Team America* from the more traditional standpoint of where musicals have been. Author, film programmer, musical historian and theorist Martin Rubin offers these observations:

> [M]usicals are based on a central contradiction between the discourse of the narrative and the discourse of at least a significant portion of the musical numbers. [. . .] A possible working definition of the musical (at least in its traditional form) is: a musical is a film containing a significant portion of musical numbers that are impossible – i.e., persistently contradictory in relation to the realistic discourse of the narrative. [. . .] In most traditional musicals, this requisite impossibility is concentrated along the transitional points between narrative and performance – that is, at those points where the character 'feels a song (or dance) coming on' and bursts into spontaneous, purportedly unrehearsed, but perfectly executed performance.[6]

In *Team America*, what we must excuse under Rubin's definition is that every major character does not have their own song, and much of the music is applied in a non-diegetic manner, as source music, rather than onscreen performance. Nevertheless, it is accurate to say that the music contradicts the 'realistic discourse of the narrative', in as much as that realism is set up in the film world itself, and the impossible points exist: Kim Jong-il overcome by emotion, Team America's violence to the tune of a recurring anthem, and a montage – the cinematic editing technique – itself bursting with metacommunicative song. These moments create musical tension with a jingoistic, straight-faced narrative. As Richard Barrios notes,

> Musical film has always picked its way through an existential minefield. These movies try to be new at the same time as they regress and reconstruct. They are uncannily self-referential, yet they sneer at their past while celebrating it.[7]

Team America features many songs and musical numbers worthy of unpacking. The aforementioned 'Montage', written and performed by Trey Parker, describes the cinematic technique and its application within the narrative, name-checking *Rocky* (John G. Avildsen, 1976), which has a similar training montage. 'Freedom Isn't Free', written and performed by Trey Parker, is a patriotic, nationalist, militarist, country western song in the vein of Merle Haggard's 'Okie from Muskogee' (1969), 'The Fightin' Side of Me' (1970), Lee Greenwood's 'God Bless the USA' (1984), or Toby Keith's 'Courtesy of the Red, White and Blue (The Angry American)' (2002). Gary's visit to the Cairo tavern, a nest of terrorists, is accompanied by 'Derka Derk (Terrorist Theme)', written by Trey Parker and Marc Shaiman, a clear homage to and parody of John Williams's Tatooine cantina band music from *Star Wars* (George Lucas, 1977). Trey Parker's 'The End of an Act' parodies Berlin's drippy 'Take My Breath Away', written by Giorgio Moroder and Tom Whitlock, from *Top Gun*

(Tony Scott, 1986), a film name checked several times in *Team America*. There is other interesting licensed source music ('Magic Carpet Ride', 'Battle Without Honor or Humanity'), Harry Gregson-Williams's straight-faced action score, and of course Trey Parker's anthemic 'America, F**k Yeah'.

Given this wealth of material, it is for lack of space that I focus my attention on two particular numbers: Kim Jong-il's 'I'm So Ronery' and Gary Johnston's 'Everyone Has AIDS'.

'EVERYONE HAS AIDS'

Following a preliminary setup in Paris – the World Police's backfiring attempts at fighting terrorism ('Damn, I missed him!') as Le Tour Eiffel crashes on the Arc de Triomphe – *Team America* begins as a backstage musical. Just as Paris was reduced to an agglomeration of American clichés and stereotypes of France – fountains, mimes, Citroën DS19s – packed into the same frame, New York City is distilled to tourist essentials. An establishing shot of Times Square begins with the Theatre Development Fund's TKTS discount ticket booth; we see the iconic, round Guggenheim Museum right beside a Broadway theatre showing *Lease: The Musical*. The venue clearly resembles the Schubert Theatre – not the Nederlander where *Rent* ran for 12 years. These mash-ups inform us that the stereotyping, while idiotic, is intentional and carefully planned.

Inside, Gary Johnston, the reluctant hero of the film, performs a leading role in *Lease*, while Spottswoode, the mastermind of the World Police, holding a dossier on the actor, observes from a seat in the audience. The musical's stage set is humorously derived from *Rent*: a multi-level framework of industrial aluminium tubing, lit in dark blues, within a theatre stripped to black box.

The song, the musical

'Everyone Has AIDS', written by Trey Parker and Marc Shaiman, is the first real musical number of *Team America*. Marc Shaiman worked with Parker and Stone on *South Park: Bigger, Longer & Uncut*, and is himself a Broadway composer for shows including *Hairspray, Charlie and the Chocolate Factory*, and *Catch Me If You Can*. Given the sensitive nature of the humour, it is worthwhile to note that Marc Shaiman is gay, and married his partner Louis Mirabal in 2016.[8]

'Everyone Has AIDS', performed onstage by Gary (Trey Parker) and the company of *Lease*, establishes the backstage musical setting of *Team America*, as well as the film's overall parodic perspective (Figure 3.1). Musically, the song is a trite but catchy piano rock band show tune, the exact instrumentation and style employed by *Rent*, a conjunction similarly employed by *Hair* and *Urinetown*. This style, which eschewed the orchestra, helped lead to the

Figure 3.1 *Team America*, 'Everyone Has AIDS'.

2003 Broadway musicians strike, led by the AFM Local 802. (One might note the irony of a show about unemployed artists helping to push musicians out of work.)

The song, the closing number from the musical *Lease* within the musical *Team America*, tells us 'everyone is dead from AIDS'. The puppet audience cries. Spottswoode looks at his Gary Johnston folder. Gary, onstage, plays the part of a newly minted activist: 'Well I'm gonna march on Washington, lead the fight, and charge the brigades.' The song universalises the epidemic: 'The pope has got AIDS and so do you', and exhorts the audience, 'Come on everybody we've got quilting to do', a humorously belittling reference to the NAMES Project AIDS Memorial Quilt. Here the quilt, like the epidemic itself, is trivialised and reduced to fuel for spectacle.

'Everyone Has AIDS', rather than directly imitate any particular song from *Rent*, functions as an overall stylistic parody. Still, the song is comparable to numbers featuring the entire *Rent* company, such as 'Finale B', 'La Vie Bohème' or the title song, 'Rent', compositions relying upon stock-in-trade rock 'n' roll progressions such as the cyclical, pentatonic Eb/F/C/// progression in 'Rent'. Even more musically biting is the interminable, repetitive, prolonged ending, a spot-on parody of *Rent*'s musical style. 'AIDS, AIDS, AIDS, AIDS', sings the cast of *Lease*, reminiscent of 'No day but today' from 'Finale B', an endlessly repeating slogan cheapened to meaninglessness, a musical fragment orphaned from any larger melody.

While Parker and Stone lampoon *Rent* as a sacred cow, the parody serves to establish a duplicitous politic that simultaneously supports and undermines the notion of Gary as a 'top gun actor', as praised by Spottswoode. A problem with *Rent* was that while the show worked as an East Village, Off-Broadway, New York Theatre Workshop production that hit home with gritty and edgy rock music, a clever current-day homage to Puccini's *La Bohème*, when it was put up on a large stage for mainstream audiences, the magnification made it trite, cloying and maudlin. The sincerity of *Lease* is effusively saccharine, implying that the audience has been manipulated by the script, rather than by the quality of Gary's acting.

The puppet audience's tearful reaction to *Lease* lampoons problems with *Rent*. It was socially unacceptable to dislike *Rent*. Crying was the expected response; it showed that the audient was in the know and consequently moved by a show about themselves or their peers, or alternatively that one had learned about the tragedy of AIDS through watching the show. In either case, the problem of having a deadly crisis reduced to a piece of middling (if hit) musical theatre and forcing a requisite response demanded parody. The inclusion of the racial epithet 'spades' in 'Everyone Has AIDS' further incorporates Parker and Stone's own brand of humour: racist jokes embedded within a seemingly liberal context. Hypothetically, someone truly conservative would be incapable of parodying *Rent*, because either they would never have seen it, or would avoid grappling with the emotional subtext.

Mockery of actors

Parker and Stone's relentless mockery of actors and acting is part comedy, part serious cultural commentary, and part personal crusade. Gary Johnston is a parody of the actor as hero: the man of special talent who will save the day for Team America. The oppositional 'FAG' actors (affiliated with the 'Film Actors Guild') are parodies of the actor as self-appointed political pundit. Opines the puppet Janeane Garofalo, 'As actors, it is our responsibility to read the newspapers, and then say what we read on television like it's our own opinion'. *Team America* critiques the sexuality, gender characteristics and liberal politics of outspoken Hollywood actors, particularly those who aspire to direct or influence foreign policy (Sean Penn's 2002 well-publicised visit to Iraq wins special mention). Furthermore, as public figures, these actors can be inserted into the film as puppets, and then mockingly and gruesomely dispatched. As Trey Parker states,

> The main reason we wanted to do puppets was just because we *hate* actors. Anytime you bring an actor in, they're just like, 'oh, how should I say this?' Like it's written? Like it's funny? Not like an idiot, like you're saying it? No matter how big or small the actor, they always just have such an attitude and think they're all rad. There's no lamer thing you can be in the world than an actor. It's the most self-serving [thing . . .]. We just wanted to do a show that ripped on celebrities and how much people love celebrities because now we can have all the celebrities made into puppets, and then we can kill them.[9]

Whilst the film uses Gary Johnston to mock the notion of the actor himself as hero – to save the day, Team America must recruit the right *actor* – it goes further in killing off the celebrity actors. These are cathartic destructions, one of the audience 'payoffs' of the film. Outspoken celebrity director Michael Moore is parodied and killed off as a suicide bomber who blows himself up. Moore took it in his stride.

> I loved it. What I really loved was the mustard stain on my shirt, because I had gone to an In-N-Out Burger with Matt [Stone]. And we were sitting outside there in L.A., at the In-N-Out Burger, and literally it happened: the mustard came out of the burger and onto my shirt. The fact that he would remember that little detail, I was just very amused by it. I like any kind of satire that's good, and I think you have to be able to also laugh at yourself, and the left has to be able to laugh at itself, and not take things too seriously. I don't know really what Matt and Trey's politics are. I don't even know if they *have* politics. They're certainly not of the left. But it doesn't mean that [*Team America*] is not good simply because they don't necessarily share my politics. And he was very good about being in *Bowling for Columbine,* so I appreciated that.[10]

Moore's idea that Stone and Parker might not even 'have politics' is echoed elsewhere; cultural studies scholar Sean Nye pinpoints a *South Park* episode 'I'm a Little Bit Country' (S7E1) that features a song with the line, 'For the war? Against the war? Who cares! 100 episodes!'[11] The implication is that political posturing is secondary to, or in direct support of, building a fan-base and thereby increasing personal revenue in show business.

There is an inescapable irony here that Stone and Parker gleefully mock celebrities who try to be politically engaged while being politically engaged themselves. Why not have *their own* cameos in the film? That would have shown a fanciful meta-critique of their own cultural critique. Their 'hatred' of actors eclipses their own self-recognition.

Joe, one of the World Police puppets, does not like actors either, so Parker and Stone's hatred of actors is encapsulated within the film, dramatised by Joe's dislike of Gary. The backstory of Joe's hatred of actors is revealed: as a teenager, Joe went backstage after seeing the musical *Cats* – 'When I got back there, they were drunk and out of control' – and was raped by Mr Mistoffelees. This ties in yet another musical reference; Joe's rape would have been backstage at another musical, *Cats*, within the musical *Team America*. *Cats* similarly employs the upbeat rock sound and instrumentation espoused by *Rent* and *Lease*.

Team America, as it began, will end as a backstage musical again, albeit this time in a much larger theatre: the immense outdoor auditorium in North

Korea, for the 'International World Peace Ceremony' spectacular hosted by Kim Jong-il. This is not pure absurdity; Kim has established connections to musical films, and has hosted politically messaged musical stage events in the past.

'I'M SO RONERY'

Kim Jong-il's signature song, 'I'm So Ronery,' which occurs mid-film, is a central set piece and structural tent-pole of the film.[12] According to Trey Parker, who wrote and performs the song,

> We always had this idea of Kim Jong-il singing a song about him being lonely. I'd written it really early on, and we just really liked the song. I actually think if the real Kim Jong-il ever sees that, he'll probably start crying. Pretty sure it's exactly how he feels.[13]

The song establishes the complexity of Kim's character and shifts the film into solid musical theatre territory, functioning as a traditional 'hopes and dreams' number. 'I'm So Ronery' raises three significant cultural issues that I wish to dissect: the real life North Korean dictator Kim Jong-il, the film's problematic and duplicitous depiction of race and deployment of racist humour, and the music as it creates Kim's character in *Team America*.

The actual dictator Kim

While racist and facile on its surface, occasionally reductive to a stock Bond villain, the portrait of Kim Jong-il created by Parker and Stone was carefully researched and accurate in certain salient aspects. *Team America*'s Kim is an aesthete, composer, singer, and a mastermind not only of political intrigue and world destruction but of the arts as well.

The real life Kim's education was rich in theatre, film and music.[14] Matt Stone remarked of North Korea's dictator: 'He is a huge movie buff. He has a personal library of 25,000 movies. He probably will see this movie, and cry.' Trey Parker recalled that Kim 'kidnapped a director in South Korea, brought him to North Korea, and forced him to teach him how to direct movies'.[15] South Korean director Shin Sang-ok and his wife, Choi Eun-hee, were separately abducted in 1977, and brought to North Korea. They escaped in 1989. Shin helped Kim to make films; Kim's films included 'an extravagant musical reminiscent of Busby Berkeley, with fantasy creatures, expensive costumes, and underwater scenes, *The Tale of Shim Chong*' (1985).[16]

The real life Kim composed music, encouraged the State Symphony Orchestra, and was interested in opera and grand spectacle. Kim gave speeches and wrote a book-length treatise on opera, arguing that North Korea 'must free ourselves from the Western style of opera and create a new style which accords with the characteristics of our nation and suits the aesthetic tastes of our people today'.[17]

Kim's artistic bent provided inspiration for the film's 'World Peace Conference'. Matt Stone explains, 'When Madeline Albright went to North Korea in 1998, I think it was, he put on a big show for her in this big stadium in Pyongyang. He choreographed it all and wrote the music.' Parker continues, 'So that's what we based the third act on, was basically like him having this big show.'[18] Hence, *Team America* picks up again as a backstage musical in the third act; where in the first act, *Lease* was the foreground, in the third act Kim's 'World Peace Conference' takes centre stage.

Depiction of race

It must be acknowledged that Parker and Stone's racial parodies are highly problematic. A flimsy argument can be made that they invoke deliberate hyper-stereotypes, a critical concept of the exaggerated stereotype intended to mock racism itself. This does not seem to be the real motivation. An overarching context of excessively juvenile humour – fart jokes, poop jokes, barf jokes, foul or idiotic language – cannot excuse the racist humour, either.

The racist humour must be seen as inherently duplicitous: while *Team America* overall can be read as attacking American exceptionalism and racist foreign policy, thereby adopting or simulating a 'liberal' posture, this position is exploited as a cushion to soften overtly racist humour and race baiting. In this manner, a 'liberal' posture can be seen as having an enabling function for racism: by appearing to advocate certain leftist policies, the filmmakers seem to be angling for a pass to be racist. By extension, liberal fans of the movie are given a pass to enjoy and partake in racist humour.

It should be noted that Parker and Stone are white, heterosexual, cisgender men from the central mountain state of Colorado.[19] Furthermore, Parker and Stone's target demographic is white males ages eighteen to thirty-four.[20] Sean Nye notes that Parker and Stone's 'aesthetics of negativity and irony at times turns into the disparaging of others from the position of the hetero-normative macho male'.[21] Parker and Stone's negotiations with network executives on *South Park*, as seen in the documentary *6 Days to Air: The Making of South Park* (Arthur Bradford, 2011), show their awareness of the push–pull of the marketplace and the need for trade-offs in content.[22] Racist jokes, poop jokes and political posturing all exist within a calculus between creators, the public, advertisers, and studio and network executives.

Parker and Stone have a long fascination with racist humour and how it is enabled or presented. In particular, they have discussed how Archie Bunker, the racist patriarch of the sitcom *All in the Family* (1971–9), was a model for *South Park*'s Cartman. Parker recalls,

> We were big fans of *All in the Family*. In time of the early 90s, we were sitting there going, you know, a show like that couldn't be on the air right now. You couldn't do it. Because things were so PC, you couldn't have an Archie Bunker. And we used to talk about how if Archie Bunker was eight years old, I bet you could do it.[23]

Bunker, played by Carroll O'Connor, was musical too, crooning the opening theme song 'Those Were The Days' with a warbly Jean Stapleton. But tracing *Team America*'s racist humour to the beloved *All in the Family* provides little excuse either. What Parker and Stone saw in Archie Bunker was a challenge and a way to bring that humour back using the safety of animated school kids.

Sean Nye notes the problematic conventionality of stereotypes in *South Park*, notably Chef, 'who parodies the stereotype of the oversexed black man by combining sexual and musical soul food'.[24] The only African American kid at South Park Elementary is named Token Black. Nye recollects how Cartman insists that because Token is black, he is able to play bass, which he does.

> This moment admits the common, though often unstated, assumption that there is an element of truth to all stereotypes, a twisted but effective logic for maintaining prejudice. In such moments, *South Park* challenges viewers to examine the twisted logic of stereotypes themselves and their roles in truth, lies, and prejudice. At the same time, the show demands that viewers acknowledge and reflect upon the comedic resources and pleasure that caricatures and stereotypes can provide. In such ways, *South Park* works against the popular belief that racial caricature in Hollywood and prejudice in American culture is something of the past.[25]

The lack of depth and complexity of African American characters reduces blacks to tokens and stereotypes, and if this approach works for Parker and Stone, one can expect it might be extended to other races, ethnicities and various subcultures.

Parker and Stone perform most of the roles in *South Park* and *Team America* themselves (given their distaste for actors), rendering it expected that a white man would perform the role of the Korean dictator; nevertheless, Trey's caricature performance of Kim Jong-il is a reprisal of historic Hollywood racism, a re-enactment of Hollywood at its worst, even as the film attempts to lampoon Hollywood. Film and media scholar Karla Rae Fuller notes, 'The most well known Oriental figures on the Hollywood screen were almost always non-Asian actors made up to look Asian'.[26] While Parker and

Stone mock Hollywood celebrities and their self-righteous sensibilities, they simultaneously participate in Hollywood's oldest racist transgressions. Fuller elaborates:

> The 'Oriental' performance by the non-Asian actor [. . .] keenly exposes the artificial foundations in Hollywood's depiction of race. [. . .] Like any masquerade, the artificiality of the impersonation is apparent, and yet this performance practice operates with a high degree of complexity, promoting certain qualities while effacing others.[27]

Parker's impersonation of the Korean strongman promotes selected qualities: Kim as musical, Kim as sensitive, alienated and lonely, Kim as powerful and impatient. What is effaced, of course, in Parker's demonising caricature, is Kim's very humanity; the parody of his accent is a racist accentuation of the Other. At the end of the film, Kim turns out to be a cockroach from outer space, making the erasure of his humanity complete, much as his ability to pronounce an 'l' phoneme.

This maladroit handling of race has especial salience in connection with a reading of *Team America* as a musical film that exploits traditional musical conventions. Regrettably, one of those conventions is having white or non-Asian actors portray Asian characters; consider Yul Brynner in *The King and I* (Walter Lang, 1956), and Juanita Hall as Bloody Mary performing 'Happy Talk' (sung in the film by Muriel Smith) in *South Pacific* (Joshua Logan, 1958). The casting of non-Asians in Asian roles also added controversy to the London production of the musical *Miss Saigon*. In this light, Parker's performance of Kim Jong-il fits into a tradition of the mishandling of race and troublesome casting that has plagued musicals historically.

The music as it creates the Kim character

Taken as a piece of music, regardless of cinematic context, 'I'm So Ronery' (Figure 3.2) is absolutely beautiful. The song begins with a delicious appoggiatura on the first syllable, 'lone', of 'lonely': a non-chord tone G against the tonic chord F major, resolving upwards to A. Appoggiaturas repeat, adding similar spice to 'only', giving the major-key song a wistfulness inherent in the dissonant, stressed beats.

The melody is decorated with tasty chromatic passing tones, painting the dictator as delicate, refined and sophisticated. My transcription of measures 9-14 of the tune (the second period of the melody) shows chromatic lower neighbours via the accidentals in 'make up great plans' and 'understands' (Figure 3.3). (To document the underlying composition, I am not transcribing the racist mispronunciations.)

Figure 3.2 *Team America*, 'I'm So Ronery'.

My transcription does not accurately reflect Parker's performance on 'understands'; Parker does not actually sing the G#, but rests on A. I argue that to satisfy the demands of the sequence established in 'make up great plans', the G# is the true underlying melody, and Parker, given the job of affecting Kim's ridiculous accent, simply lets it slide. (Once you have heard this with the implied G#, it is difficult to hear it any other way.) The rise in the melody pushes the performance into falsetto, heightening the drama and the emotional strain. Those fascinated by key symbolism will be delighted: the song is in F major, with one solitary flat in the key signature.

The beauty and tenderness of this music codes Kim Jong-il as a sympathetic character, even if he is the antagonist, in the same way the baritone aria 'Up There' coded Satan sympathetically in the *South Park* movie. These movies are influential in part because they do not espouse a monochromatic approach; there is not a black-and-white, good guy/bad guy dichotomy. In *Team America*, our World Police heroes destroy Paris at the outset of the film, and it is Michael Moore who blows up the team's Mount Rushmore hideaway, not anyone from Derkaderkastan.[28] In casting Kim as a sympathetic character

Figure 3.3 'I'm So Ronery' by Trey Parker, transcribed by the author.

through music, whilst having the World Police wreak havoc on the world to the refrain of 'America, Fuck Yeah', *Team America* acknowledges that we ourselves might be the bad guys.

This layered approach is reprised in *The Interview,* where Kim Jong-un is a decadent playboy who eloquently critiques the failures of the American capitalist and political system. While in all these films it is clear America will win the day, greater complications of the system are exposed. In the *South Park* movie aria 'Up There', Satan sings a telling line: 'Without evil there can be no good, so it must be good to be evil sometime'. This argument against a monochromatic, binary politic reflects Parker and Stone's own humour. By extension, they might be trying to say that it is good to be racist sometimes; without racism there can be no struggle for justice, so the inclusion of racist humour propels the entire vehicle. This is one possible reading; it may be equally valid to say that these films sugarcoat racism in a digestible liberal politic so that audiences can feel entitled to enjoy it without compromising their self-identities as good people.

POLITIC AND FORMULA

Team America's fanciful humour exposes an absurdist political reality: attempting to police the world does not work, giving actors credibility as pundits does not further political discourse, and extending white colonialism does not create freedom. All brought to you by singing puppets in a world at one-third scale.

Music moderates the film's pacing, and softens characters like Kim Jong-il into a lovable villain. The film adopts musical theatre traditions, including the conventions of the backstage musical, problematic racist casting and the clichéd 'hopes and dreams' number. There may be an underlying guiding philosophy or aesthetic behind how these techniques are deployed: Trey Parker has described a 'simple formula' which places extremes in opposition, creating humour from how they interact. It is possible that to Parker and Stone the musical and the action adventure film represent two extremes, and by placing them together, the resultant dissonances create a pleasurable artefact. Says Parker:

> To some degree, *South Park* has a simple formula that came from the very first episode. There was Jesus on this side and there was Santa on this side, there's Christianity here and there's Christmas commercialism here, and they're duking it out. And there are these four boys in the middle going, 'Dude, chill out'. It's really what *Team America* is as well: taking an extremist on this side and an extremist on that side. Michael Moore being an extremist is just as bad, you know, as Donald Rumsfeld. It's like they're the same person. It takes a fourth-grade kid to go, 'You

both remind me of each other.' The show is saying that there is a middle ground, that most of us actually live in this middle ground, and that all you extremists are the ones who have the microphones because you're the most interesting to listen to, but actually this group isn't evil, that group isn't evil, and there's something to be worked out here.[29]

By using music to partake in the creation of these oppositions and resulting messages, *Team America* does not pander to the audience. It does not preach, and allows dissonances and disjunctures to communicate or suggest whatever 'middle ground' message the filmmakers wish to impart. The film, given its broad success, may be more centrist than it appears on the surface, not by advocating a particular position, but by lampooning various postures from country western nationalism to celebrity anti-corporatism. The film actively debates the notion of American exceptionalism; when Spottswoode declares 'There is no 'I' in Team America', the team's computer replies, 'Yes there is'. The joke is not just a commentary on spelling, but on the way American nationalism is promoted by self-interest.

The importance of Parker and Stone's work has been proven through award recognition, box office receipts, and influence upon later political action adventure comedies such as *The Interview* and *OSS 117 Le Caire: nid d'espions*. Parker and Stone have influenced the Broadway musical genre itself, incorporating much of the extremism, foul language, sex, AIDS references and political humour from their television and film work into *The Book of Mormon*. But what is especially interesting and promising is the way they seamlessly and effortlessly, if shockingly at times, inject musical conventions into all their work. This cross-pollination is not a subversion of the musical per se, but rather an adherence to conventions of the musical, largely leaving musical structures faithfully intact, while subverting the territory around them.

NOTES

1. Andy Greene, 'Flashback: animated short "The Spirit of Christmas" births "South Park"', *Rolling Stone*, 9 July 2015, available at <http://www.rollingstone.com/tv/videos/flashback-animated-short-the-spirit-of-christmas-births-south-park-20150709> (last accessed 3 January 2017).
2. Ibid.
3. Matt Stone, in *Making the Movie: Team America: World Police*, MTV Networks, 2004, 'Team America: World Police – MTV Making The Movie – Trey Parker & Matt Stone – 2004', posted 21 September 2014, available at <https://youtu.be/aUmD8EYQU9s> (last accessed 3 January 2017).
4. David Laderman, *Punk Slash Musicals* (Austin: University of Texas Press, 2010), p. 2.
5. Ibid. pp. 2–3.
6. Martin Rubin, 'Busby Berkeley and the backstage musical', in Steven Cohan (ed.),

Hollywood Musicals The Film Reader (New York: Routledge, 2002, reprinted 2008), p. 57.

7. Richard Barrios, *Dangerous Rhythm: Why Movie Musicals Matter* (New York: Oxford University Press, 2014), p. 16.

8. Broadway.com Staff, '*Hairspray* Tony winner Marc Shaiman marries partner Louis Mirabal', posted 28 March 2016, *Broadway.com* blog, available at <http://www.broadway.com/buzz/184288/hairspray-tony-winner-marc-shaiman-marries-partner-louis-mirabal/> (last accessed 3 January 2017).

9. Trey Parker, in *Making the Movie: Team America: World Police*, MTV Networks, 2004,'Team America: World Police – MTV Making The Movie – Trey Parker & Matt Stone – 2004', posted 21 September 2014, available at <https://youtu.be/aUmD8EYQU9s> (last accessed 3 January 2017).

10. Michael Moore, interviewed by the author, 4 November 2016.

11. Sean Nye, 'From Punk to the musical: *South Park*, music, and the cartoon format', in James Deaville (ed.), *Music in Television: Channels of Listening*, (New York: Routledge, 2011), p. 159.

12. For discussion of 'tent-poles' as elements of cinematic structure and planning, see Jack Curtis Dubowsky, 'The evolving "temp score" in animation', *Music, Sound, and the Moving Image*, Spring 2011, 5(1): 6; Jack Curtis Dubowsky, 'Interview: Jack Curtis Dubowsky on live music for film', in *Experinautas*, 14 February 2016, available at <http://experinautas.com/interviews/jack-curtis-dubowsky-live-music-for-film/> (last accessed 3 January 2017); and Tasha Robinson, 'Pete Docter interview', *The Onion*, A. V. Club, 2009, 45:22:20.

13. Trey Parker, in 'Up close with Kim Jong-il', *Team America* DVD special feature (Paramount Pictures, 2004).

14. Brian Wise, 'The strange musical world of Kim Jong Il: weird orchestral tributes and epic tracts on opera', *WQXR Blog*, 19 December 2011, available at <http://www.wqxr.org/#!/story/176557-strange-musical-world-kim-jong-il/> (last accessed 3 January 2017).

15. Parker and Stone, in 'Up close with Kim Jong-il', *Team America* DVD special feature (Paramount Pictures, 2004).

16. Paul Fischer, *A Kim Jong-Il Production: The Extraordinary True Story of a Kidnapped Filmmaker, His Star Actress, and a Young Dictator's Rise to Power* (New York: Flatiron Books, 2015).

17. Kim Jong-il, *On the Art of Opera: Talk to Creative Workers in the Field of Art and Literature, September 4–6, 1974* (Pyongyang: Foreign Languages Publishing House, 1988) (University Press of the Pacific, 2001).

18. Parker continues, 'My dream is that if we can get I'm So Ronery nominated for an Oscar, is that he comes and performs it at the Oscars'. Parker and Stone, in 'Up close with Kim Jong-il', *Team America* DVD special feature (Paramount Pictures, 2004).

19. Stone was born in Texas; his mother is Jewish.

20. Sean Nye, 'From Punk to the musical', pp. 144–5.

21. Ibid. p. 160.

22. *6 Days to Air: The Making of South Park*, directed by Arthur Bradford (television documentary) (Comedy Partners, 2011).

23. Trey Parker on Steve Kroft, 'Interview, Parker and Stone', *60 Minutes*, CBS News, uploaded 26 September 2011, available at <https://www.youtube.com/watch?v=0KppaxFfPNw> (last accessed 3 January 2017). See also Trey Parker, in 'Speaking freely: South Park's Trey Parker & Matt Stone with Larry Divney', S03 E06, posted 27 July 2015, available at <https://youtu.be/7oXk0EhF450> (last accessed 3 January 2017).

24. Sean Nye, 'From Punk to the musical', p. 154.
25. Ibid. p. 155.
26. Karla Rae Fuller, 'Creatures of good and evil: Caucasian portrayals of the Chinese and Japanese during World War II', in Daniel Bernardi (ed.), *Classic Hollywood, Classic Whiteness* (Minneapolis: University of Minnesota Press, 2001), p. 281.
27. Ibid. pp. 281–2.
28. *Team America* features two notable references to *North by Northwest* (directed by Alfred Hitchcock, 1959): the use of Mount Rushmore as a locale, and the flying limo's entrance into Washington's mouth, a phallic entry that echoes the train entering the tunnel at the end of Hitchcock's thriller.
29. Trey Parker, in Nick Gillespie and Jesse Walker, 'South Park libertarians: Trey Parker and Matt Stone on liberals, conservatives, censorship, and religion', *Reason.com* blog, 5 December 2006, available at <http://reason.com/archives/2006/12/05/south-park-libertarians/print> (last accessed 3 January 2017).

BIBLIOGRAPHY

Barrios, Richard, *Dangerous Rhythm: Why Movie Musicals Matter* (New York: Oxford University Press, 2014).
Broadway.com Staff, '*Hairspray* Tony winner Marc Shaiman marries partner Louis Mirabal', posted 28 March 2016, *Broadway.com* blog, <http://www.broadway.com/buzz/184288/hairspray-tony-winner-marc-shaiman-marries-partner-louis-mirabal/> (last accessed 3 January 2017).
Dubowsky Jack Curtis, 'Interview: Jack Curtis Dubowsky on live music for film', in *Experinautas*, 14 February 2016, <http://experinautas.com/interviews/jack-curtis-dubowsky-live-music-for-film/> (last accessed 3 January 2017).
Dubowsky, Jack Curtis, 'The evolving "temp score" in animation', *Music, Sound, and the Moving Image*, Spring 2011, 5(1).
Fischer, Paul, *A Kim Jong-Il Production: The Extraordinary True Story of a Kidnapped Filmmaker, His Star Actress, and a Young Dictator's Rise to Power* (New York: Flatiron Books, 2015).
Fuller, Karla Rae, 'Creatures of good and evil: Caucasian portrayals of the Chinese and Japanese during World War II', in Daniel Bernardi (ed.), *Classic Hollywood, Classic Whiteness* (Minneapolis: University of Minnesota Press, 2001).
Gillespie, Nick and Jesse Walker, 'South Park libertarians: Trey Parker and Matt Stone on liberals, conservatives, censorship, and religion', *Reason.com* blog, 5 December 2006, <http://reason.com/archives/2006/12/05/south-park-libertarians/print> (last accessed 3 January 2017).
Greene, Andy, 'Flashback: animated short "The Spirit of Christmas" births "South Park"', *Rolling Stone*, 9 July 2015, <http://www.rollingstone.com/tv/videos/flashback-animated-short-the-spirit-of-christmas-births-south-park-20150709> (last accessed 3 January 2017).
Jong-il, Kim, *On the Art of Opera: Talk to Creative Workers in the Field of Art and Literature, September 4–6, 1974* (Pyongyang: Foreign Languages Publishing House, 1988) (University Press of the Pacific, 2001).
Laderman, David, *Punk Slash Musicals* (Austin: University of Texas Press, 2010).
Making the Movie: Team America: World Police, MTV Networks, 2004,'Team America: World Police – MTV Making The Movie – Trey Parker & Matt Stone – 2004', posted 21 September 2014, <https://youtu.be/aUmD8EYQU9s> (last accessed 3 January 2017)
Nye, Sean, 'From Punk to the musical: *South Park*, music, and the cartoon format',

in James Deaville (ed.), *Music in Television: Channels of Listening*, (New York: Routledge, 2011).

Parker, Trey and Matt Stone, 'Interview, Parker and Stone', *60 Minutes*, CBS News, uploaded 26 September 2011, <https://www.youtube.com/watch?v=0KppaxFfPNw> (last accessed 3 January 2017).

Robinson, Tasha, 'Pete Docter interview', *The Onion*, A. V. Club, 2009, 45:22:20.

Rubin, Martin, 'Busby Berkeley and the backstage musical', in Steven Cohan (ed.), *Hollywood Musicals: The Film Reader* (New York: Routledge, 2002, reprinted 2008).

'Speaking freely: *South Park*'s Trey Parker & Matt Stone with Larry Divney', S03 E06, posted 27 July 2015, <https://youtu.be/7oXk0EhF450> (last accessed 3 January 2017).

'Up close with Kim Jong-il', *Team America* DVD special feature (Paramount Pictures, 2004).

Wise, Brian, 'The strange musical world of Kim Jong Il: weird orchestral tributes and epic tracts on opera', *WQXR Blog*, 19 December 2011, <http://www.wqxr.org/#!/story/176557-strange-musical-world-kim-jong-il/> (last accessed 3 January 2017).

4 THE ANTI-MUSICAL OR GENERIC AFFINITY: IS THERE ANYTHING LEFT TO SAY?

Beth Carroll

Though the film musical has experienced peaks and troughs in its popularity over the years, the stage musical, rather than straightforward drama, appears to be dominating London's West End and New York's Broadway, with hits such as *Chicago* (John Kander and Fred Ebb, 1975) and *Miss Saigon* (Claude-Michel Schonberg and Alain Boublil, 1980) running for years and still managing to bring in audiences.[1] The longevity of these shows and their success is increasingly dependent on international tourists.[2] Going to a performance in the West End or on Broadway is about more than the musical; it is an almost essential part of the city break experience, an experience shared by millions of people every year.[3] There appears to be a joy in the familiar, in the collective experience of well-known stage plays, in the conservative, both generically and financially. Originality is dead, and tourism killed it. It is no surprise that the film industry has sought to replicate the success of the stage. As Ian Sapiro, K. J. Donnelly and Catherine Haworth explore in their chapters for this collection, musical theatre's triumph has led to some of the biggest stage shows being adapted into film musicals, with varying degrees of accomplishment: *The Phantom of the Opera* (Joel Schumacher, 2004), *Chicago* (Rob Marshall, 2002), *Dreamgirls* (Bill Condon, 2006) and *Into the Woods* (Rob Marshall, 2014) are but a few recent examples.

Whilst the stage musical adaptation is, economically, going from strength to strength, cinema audiences still experience the rare treat of an original film musical. For instance, Ryan Bunch discusses Disney's success, epitomised by *Frozen* (Chris Buck and Jennifer Less, 2013). Other examples include the recent successes *Pitch Perfect* (Jason Moore, 2012) and *Pitch Perfect 2* (Elizabeth Banks, 2015), *The Muppets* (Jason Bobin, 2011), or the rather less acclaimed *Burlesque* (Steven Antin, 2010). Indeed, although the musical heyday of classical Hollywood has passed, the film musical, 'original' or stage adaptation, is buoyant. Should we be pleased? Should we look to the steady flow of new film musicals, or indeed, the stream of films being turned into stage shows (for instance: *Shrek* in 2008, *Mary Poppins* in 2004, and *Legally Blonde* in 2007) with a sense of pleasing satisfaction ringing the bells of musical originality? My instinct is to pause when asking these questions; to ask myself what it is I want from the contemporary film musical. And whether what I want is even possible: can the musical genre be at the forefront of creativity or does its inherent conservatism consume and cast out all that is inventive and ground-breaking? What would an imaginative and novel musical even look or sound like?

What primarily interests me in this chapter is whether the original film musicals are offering something different to the stage adaptations or remakes; the latter including such films as *Fame* (Kevin Tancharoen, 2009), *Hairspray* (Adam Shankman, 2007), *Annie* (Will Gluck, 2014) and the upcoming *A Star is Born* (to be directed by Bradley Cooper, 2017).[4] Whilst it is pleasing to have so many original film musicals to choose from, not all of them make claims for 'pioneering' takes on the genre. For these we need to refine the film musical further, namely to film musicals directed by 'non-musical' auteurs – undoubtedly a problematic term loaded with erroneous meaning. Since 2000, cinema audiences have had the chance to experience musicals by filmmakers such as Lars von Trier with his film *Dancer in the Dark* (2000), François Ozon's *8 Femmes* (2002) and Baz Luhrmann's *Moulin Rouge!* (2001) amongst others. In short, musicals by filmmakers who are not known for the musical genre, but instead best understood as auteurs.[5] My aim is deliberately somewhat at odds with the auteurist approach arguably still dominant in academia, and certainly in marketing material and popular discourse. Indeed, my contention is that the perceived innovation of these auteurs is lost when the films are surveyed through a generic lens, when the films are considered as musicals first and foremost. Have these filmmakers made singular interventions into the genre or have they replicated what has gone before? My assertion is that the stage musical form has become so dominant, in both the public imaginary and on screen, that any film musical that does not follow this form is deemed 'innovative', thus erasing the genre's nuanced history.

Although von Trier's *Dancer in the Dark* was perhaps the first film to make me question the strength of the genre, it was John Turturro's *Romance & Cigarettes* (2005) that provided the text that made me want to explore more deeply. As a fan of musicals, I am constantly at an impasse: wanting something novel and different, but simultaneously seeking the comfort of the known and familiar. In part, I have taken Dyer's utopianism to heart, hiding behind the musical as a form of coping mechanism that only hides, and never eradicates.[6] Analysing my own enjoyment of the genre, the recent films that stand out, such as Turturro's *Romance & Cigarettes*, the aforementioned *8 Femmes* and Rufus Norris' *London Road* (2016), force me to confront the genre's limitations and question whether these films are extraordinary in *any* way. Has the genre been so diluted that this is no longer possible? Have the boundaries between film musical and musical film become so indistinct as to make us ask: in extremis, outside of stage musical adaptations, do we have a film musical genre at all?

ROMANCE & CIGARETTES AS MUSICAL AFTERTHOUGHT

John Turturro's time behind the camera has shown him to be an interesting and engaging filmmaker gaining critical acclaim.[7] With a close connection to the Coen brothers, who are widely held to be auteurs, Turturro's films have been described as audacious.[8] Focusing predominantly on the working classes, and often with overt biographical references, Turturro's films have had mixed commercial success.[9] Though directing only six films, one of which is a segment of *Rio, I Love You* (2014), he has had a long acting career.[10] Both his acting and his directorial output demonstrate a desire to represent Italian American men experiencing degrees of hardship. *Mac* (1992), for instance, oscillates between the problems of becoming the family patriarch and attempting to run a business. *Passione* (2010), meanwhile, uses the documentary form to explore the lasting impact of the Neapolitan musical heritage. Like the aforementioned films, Turturro's *Romance & Cigarettes* uses influences from his own life; for instance, his mother was an inspiration for the lead female character. It is clear from Turturro's output that he is willing to move between genres even if his narrative or diegetic focus is narrower. However, what makes *Romance & Cigarettes* specifically more interesting for my work here is that Turturro did not intend the film to be a musical:

> I had some ideas for scenes – the first scene with the toe, into the first Engelbert Humperdinck song. At that time, I hadn't planned for people to burst into song yet, but I knew I wanted that song to come on there.[11]

Turturro's *Romance & Cigarettes* is a good example of a film that straddles different musical conventions and provides an opportunity to approach a discussion on the tension that exists in the genre, between innovation and formal conservatism. As Todd Decker's chapter on the *Fast and the Furious* (2001–) franchise makes clear, the conventions of the musical are now perhaps all-encompassing. The 'traditional' musical, defined in numerous ways by theorists such as Rick Altman, Steve Cohan, Jane Feuer and others, is no longer broadly restricted to the integrated or the backstage.[12] Films such as *Sucker Punch* (Zack Snyder, 2011) and *Juno* (Jason Reitman, 2007) incorporate music into the narrative to be engaged with by characters and provide degrees of spectacle, both visual and aural. These 'musicals by any other name' force us to question the nature of the genre: a broad church or distilled? What is the difference between film musical and musical film?

If we wished to further question the limits of the musical genre we might note that the action and horror genres have long appeared to hold strong parallels with the musical. The emphasis on excess, often coupled with narrative subversion or suspension, in these genres is similar to that of the musical. The musical's seemingly difficult generic cataloguing often sees it with an absence of iconography so distinctive of genres such as the Western or gangster film. Perhaps it is better understood as a form or synthesis: a contract between audience and film, a hybrid.[13] Attempts at musical delineation often fall short or prove deficient, creating too many exceptions to the rule. Must a musical have people singing? What of films such as *Honey* (Bille Woodruff, 2003), the *Step Up* film series (2006–14) or *Save the Last Dance* (Thomas Carter, 2001), where dancing is the focus?[14] What of films such as *Drumline* (Charles Stone III, 2002), where the focus is on the performance of musical instruments? In films with song sequences, must there be a certain number to qualify as a musical? Would *Volver* (Pedro Almodóvar, 2006) count? Is a close correlation between image and sound necessary, and if so what of the martial arts genre where choreography and cinematography are so instrumental? This is not my attempt to create a new taxonomy of the musical, but rather to highlight the potential porosity of the genre both in terms of influences, but perhaps more pertinently, with regards to how it is engaged with by audiences. Though we should celebrate the breadth of the musical genre, there are two key consequences. First, that stage musicals tend to stand out as a separate group, often consolidating an understanding of the musical in the public imagination as fixed. Secondly, that such an extensive genre, particularly as I suggest it to be above, is difficult to theorise with any level of comprehension.

By not starting life as a musical, *Romance & Cigarettes* arguably throws weight behind the idea that the genre is not its defining component, at least not using Turturro's overt references to singing and dancing. The musical genre was not at the forefront of the director's thinking when he began fleshing out the narrative. This is particularly interesting when you consider the importance of song sequences or musical numbers, in whatever form they may take, to the musical; one might contend that they are more important than the 'narrative' components.[15] Turturro's emphasis on the importance of songs during the development stage of the film does suggest, however, a strong musical bent. Indeed, the final version of *Romance & Cigarettes* is populated by well-known songs, including: Engelbert Humperdinck's 'A Man Without Love', Tom

Jones's 'Delilah', Dusty Springfield's 'Piece of my Heart', Bruce Springsteen's 'Red Headed Woman', and Connie Francis's 'Scapricciatiello (Do You Love Me Like You Kiss Me?)' amongst others.

When exploring *Romance & Cigarettes*' status as a musical there are two essential components worthy of discussion: the musical as community and the musical as a potentially problematic marketing strategy. These two factors converge into one essential issue, namely the use the musical genre is put to and whether *Romance & Cigarettes* is unusual in any way.

The musical has long engaged with discourses connected to a feeling of community. Richard Dyer's seminal piece 'Entertainment and Utopia' famously argues that musicals epitomise entertainment when conceived of from capitalist structuring principles. This entertainment involves a contract between audience and professional performer; a contract based on the deliverance of pleasure. This pleasure, as well as the form of the entertainment, is in a constant tension between what Dyer describes as 'capital (the backers) and labour (the performers) for the control of the product'.[16] In many respects, Dyer elucidates the very tension between innovation and conservatism that is inherent to the musical, indeed entertainment more widely. Dyer writes:

> The fact that professional entertainment has been by and large conservative in this century should not blind us to the explicit struggle within it. [. . .] Just as it does not simply 'give the people what they want' (since it actually defines wants), so, as a relatively autonomous mode of cultural production, it does not simply reproduce unproblematically patriarchal-capitalist ideology.[17]

My interest in the ambivalent tension between innovation and conservatism that Dyer highlights is in no small part due to an instinctual feeling of dissatisfaction at the genre's current balance between the two. Claims of innovation in the genre are shown to be fallacious, exposed as a facade upon reflecting on the films through the lens of genre rather than auteurism.

Dyer's work on the necessary connection in entertainment between performer and audience is vital to understanding the musical's association with discourses on community, and more particularly how it is evoked in *Romance & Cigarettes*. Dyer is not alone in his belief in the essential connection between audience and performer in the musical. Indeed, Jane Feuer has famously noted the role of the creation of a proscenium arch in musical numbers not performed on traditional stage settings (the backstage musical will often see musical numbers performed as part of a stage show).[18] The creation of a faux proscenium arch will essentially surreptitiously reposition the 'amateur' performers within the musical numbers as professionals, thus redressing any potential unbalance in relationship between audience and performer and reconfiguring the binary that causes the tension that Dyer speaks of, between backers, labour and audiences. In short, the musical number provides a site for the consolidation in relationship between audiences and performers. And it is this relationship that is at the heart of the genre.

Feuer argues that musicals are a mythic form, whereby they are perceived to have excessive value. The 'myth of entertainment' in the musical happens through an 'oscillation between demystification and remythicization'.[19] Put simply, musicals provide pleasure by giving away backstage secrets into the entertainment process, whilst simultaneously revalidating the entertainment process.[20] The myth of entertainment has three components: myth of spontaneity, myth of integration, and myth of the audience. The myth of spontaneity, as the name suggests, is a performance that appears to suddenly burst forth from 'a joyous and responsive attitude to life'.[21] The myth of integration, meanwhile, may be broadly defined as the integration of the individual's personal life with the musical performance. This may be through an evocation of a romantic relationship through song and dance or through an individual's integration into a cultural sphere or group. In short, musical numbers become sites of possibility, where, as Feuer states, 'the audience [is given] a sense of participation in the creation of the film itself'.[22] This is possible due to the blending of folk art with mass consumption, musicals self-reflexively using a sense of community to encourage audience identification.

Like the myth of spontaneity and myth of integration, the myth of the audience is what completes the audience's sense of participation in a performance and all but guarantees pleasure. This might be done through an onscreen audience to inspire mimicry in the cinema audience; the onscreen audience shows pleasure at a performance, thus indicating what we, the cinema audience, should feel. These point of view shots will be accompanied by more privileged camera positions, for instance from the point of view of the performer.[23]

The trinity of myths that make up the myth of entertainment combine in a film such as *Romance & Cigarettes* to evoke a feeling of community: both on screen and off. My use of the term 'community' is deliberately broad. It is both the diegetic bringing together of characters on screen and the feeling of audience 'immersion'. It is the coping mechanism that the musical number provides, Dyer's 'utopia', as well as references to the role music plays in our lives. Turturro's film provides unabridged community. Certainly there is a clear intention in his choice of music. He states: 'My idea was to use an everyday person's connection to popular music.'[24]

In a nuanced twist on Feuer's amateur/performer dichotomy, Turturro has chosen to have his actors sing alongside the 'professionals'. Almost every song in *Romance & Cigarettes* is sung to the 'original' pop record, be it Engelbert Humperdinck's 'A Man Without Love', Tom Jones's 'Delilah', or, as Turturro particularly highlights, Dusty Springfield's 'Piece of my Heart'. The audience hears competing voices on the soundtrack, often balanced in favour of the pop record. This raises a number of interesting issues, many of which can be seen in the film's opening song, the aforementioned 'A Man Without Love'.

James Gandolfini plays Nick Murder, the patriarch of a disintegrating family. His wife, Kitty Kane (Susan Sarandon), has discovered he has been having an affair with a British woman named Tula, played by Kate Winslet. When his wife confronts Nick, their three daughters join the conversation, clearly siding with Kitty. It does not take long for Nick to feel outnumbered and unwanted. He leaves the house, lights a consolatory cigarette and steps out on to the porch. He starts to sing without any musical support, merely the background sound of disinterested birds; life is going on. Nick has started to sing Humperdinck's 'A Man Without Love'. He does not sing the opening lines, but rather starts on the second verse that reads: 'I cannot face this world that's fallen down on me'. After singing solo for two lines, Nick is joltingly joined by Humperdinck's voice with the song's attached music. Nick, previously in close-up, leaves the porch with a slight flourish. The camera cuts to a close-up of a waste disposal lorry with its associated men now accompanying Nick, belting out the lyrics with arms wide whilst the lorry rides along. The camera shortly reveals other blue-collar workers joining in the song. The song is set up as a battle of the sexes, with women dressed in pseudo-baseball attire throwing baseballs at the men. Nick (and one can assume the same is true in the lives of the other singing men) has lost his place in the home, his blue-collar work is coming under threat, and women have even taken over the sporting world; the oppression of man is complete. Indeed, the film has a clear undercurrent of working class representation, with music playing the leading role. As Aida Edermariam writes, 'Music [Turturro] suddenly realised, was key to a film about the working class – "music, for people who don't have a lot, is essential".'[25]

It is a variant of what Claudia Gorbman calls 'artless singing', normally reserved for moments when film characters sing in 'non-musical' numbers.[26] Though, unlike with 'artless singing', there is orchestral accompaniment for Nick, his blend of speech and singing does draw parallels with Gorbman's description:

> the imperfections of voice – the breathiness, faltering and quavering, false notes, singing out of comfortable range, pauses, forgotten or mistaken lyrics – that equate amateurishness with authenticity, and that make of the singing a natural and sincere expression of the character.[27]

At this time of loneliness and isolation for Nick, there is solace and community in the musical performance. He is not alone the song says, it is not his fault; society has gone wrong. There is more than this though; there is also the connection to Humperdinck. Humperdinck's voice merging with Nick's parallels that which happens each time we sing along to our favourite tunes, we become the performer. However tunelessly we sing along, Humperdinck's voice will carry us through, it will be forgiving, and it will improve us. In these moments, the amateur and the professional merge, as Feuer so nicely elucidates. Nick is not just Nick, he is the successful Humperdinck and every other person who has tried to sing along to 'A Man Without Love'.

Kitty Kane's key musical number, 'Piece of my Heart', works in a similar way but with subtle differences. Seeking comfort after her falling out with Nick, she attends church where she is encouraged to participate in the choir. Intercut with scenes of her second daughter's burgeoning relationship and contrasted with the extramarital antics of Nick, Kitty stands at the front of the choir and nervously begins singing. Springfield's music has already begun in the background and her singing is high in the mix, clearly overpowering Sarandon's voice. Kitty becomes increasingly engaged in the performance and with the choir that is accompanying her. Here, again, we have music as support mechanism. Based in the community, the church provides a venue for both lost souls and budding singers.

The use of well-known songs in *Romance & Cigarettes* illustrates the centrality of music in our lives. Music is simultaneously social and personal: you can go to a concert or listen on a personal stereo. The importance of pop music, despite the changes it has undergone over the years, can in part be found in its commercial appeal. Questions of quality aside, there is little denying the universal success of pop music. Musicals, as Catherine Haworth discusses in her chapter, have capitalised on its appeal, and jukebox musicals are now ubiquitous. As K. J. Donnelly describes, pop music has iconic status.[28] This iconic status leads to songs having clear associations and communal understandings attached to them. Resultantly, pop music, whilst often also being cheaper, can act as a shorthand.[29] Springfield's 'Piece of my Heart' not only acts as a shared experience on screen for Kitty, but for all of those who have heard the song over the years. Equally, Tom Jones's 'Delilah', performed by Christopher Walken, acts as a wry performance of (camp) excess. These well-known songs act as musical clichés familiar to all.

What is clear throughout *Romance & Cigarettes* is that despite the merging of voices, the actors are clearly not professional singers, with the exception of Mandy Moore. Although several of the actors have sung in film before, it is clear that Sarandon, Winslet and Gandolfini are neither the most confident nor able of musical performers. This was an important and deliberate factor in Turturro's casting choices. When interviewed by *Filmmaker Magazine* he stated:

> I wanted people who were very grounded and not cerebral actors, and I
> didn't want people who were so great musically. I wanted really earthy

people [. . .]. I sent them all to singing lessons, and I figured that they would all sing along, like you would sing along with the radio. James was a little nervous, but James actually has a very nice voice. Everyone just embraced it. We had two choreographers and then I would come in and rechoreograph it because I wanted it to be more like regular movements and not Broadway choreography.[30]

There is a clear attempt by Turturro to position the film away from more recent discourses on the musical, specifically those developed on the stage and in filmic adaptation of stage musicals. One can infer from his comment about 'regular movement' that part of his issue with stage musicals is connected to the issue of 'realism'. Though any use of the word realism is fraught with both ambiguity and often contradiction, it is an issue that Turturro himself and critics of the film have frequently referred to. Turturro has justified the perceived lack of quality of the singing in the following way:

You can watch a movie where an actor has trained for a year to sing, and they're okay, but they're never going to be as expressive as Dusty Springfield or Tom Jones. That was always my idea, that they would be the dominant voices. But James sings along, Kate sings along. That's what people do in real life, and that's what I thought would be appropriate for the film.[31]

In several respects this appears to confuse the professional/amateur dichotomy. Turturro is creating a distinction between different types of people who sing for a living; perhaps a valid point if a reason had been given. What is clear, however, is that the director did not want clarity of sound or a precision of voice, but rather for it to sound mundane. Instances of this, of highlighting the amateur nature of the performances – examples might include *London Road*, *Rocky Horror Picture Show* (Jim Sharman, 1975), *Dancer in the Dark*, or *Once More With Feeling* (Joss Whedon, 2001) – make an attempt at incorporating the audience into the performance; of encouraging the audience to project themselves onto the performer and their situation. Mundanity is enticing; perfection can be jarring or limiting to absorption. 'A character singing artlessly', as Gorbman states, 'is normally indulging in an intimacy, conveying a truth, externalising a subjectivity. It is a performance that participates in the codes of realism [. . .].'[32]

Critics too appeared to pick up on the quality of singing, often lauding it as an innovative aspect of *Romance & Cigarettes*. Nick Dawson, for instance, describes the film in the following way:

Like *Illuminata* [John Turturro, 1998], *Romance & Cigarettes* combines moments of broad comedy and bawdy humor with ones of soulful loneliness; as a musical, it breaks the mold by both embracing the surreal nature of the genre and adding a stark realism which is alien to the form [*sic*].[33]

When reading statements such as Dawson's, it is tempting to accompany them with a sigh. There appears to be an inherent assumption that the musical is static, unproblematic, and known by all. That 'realism', though always amorphous, cannot exist in the genre unless a risky auteur 'breaks the mold'. Here again we have 'innovation' by an individual attempting to combat the essential conservatism of the genre. 'In the film', Dawson writes, '[Turturro] really embrace[s] the surreal aspects of musicals, even more than the classical Hollywood model, and then juxtapose[s] that with very realistic elements.'[34] Musicals are surreal; it is Turturro who provides 'realism'.

What is problematic about such statements appears to be the ubiquity of this understanding of the musical. The musical form seems to be an obstacle for general audiences, something that must be overcome and treated carefully in promotional and marketing material. Stephen Holden of *The New York Times* describes *Romance & Cigarettes* as risky and a 'commercial liability'.[35] This commercial liability, as Franz Lidz highlights, is due to the film's genre.[36] Lidz's article for *The New York Times* details the interesting background to *Romance & Cigarettes*. He explains how Turturro was given the deal with United Artists to make the film, with $4.5 million being given for the rights in North America and select other foreign territories. The rest of the budget, $4 million from Turturro himself and another $4 million from Icon productions, was found, but Sony bought MGM, who owned United Artists, in 2005. Sony deemed the film lacking in commercial appeal and refused to provide finances to market and distribute the film, instead preferring a direct to DVD release. Turturro took the film onto the festival circuit but Sony's buy out price of $3 million proved to be too high for investors. Rather than a broad cinema release, *Romance & Cigarettes* was eventually exhibited in foreign countries such as the UK, Italy and other European countries in particular. In 2007 it made its US debut in New York thanks to Adam Sandler, due to act alongside Turturro in *You Don't Mess with the Zohan* (Dennis Dugan, 2008), making it part of his contract negotiations with Sony.[37] Nepotism and Turturro's persistence permitted a film deemed too risky by studios to be released in cinemas. This despite the influx of musicals on cinema screens around the world: *Moulin Rouge!* had been released in 2001, *Chicago* in 2002, and *The Phantom of the Opera* in 2004.

Is *Romance & Cigarettes* so very different from the musicals that have preceded it? Are stage musical adaptations so dominant and different as to not allow space for original film musicals? Are musicals rigid in structure and form? In short, is *Romance & Cigarettes* too innovative? Though the short answer seems to me to be without a doubt, no, there are other considerations that the capitalist entertainment product must pay attention to. Whilst the essential economic argument from Sony is a strong one – their main goal is making money after all – I want here to draw attention to aesthetic and structural components of *Romance & Cigarettes*. Despite my enjoyment of *Romance & Cigarettes*, its innovation is but a facade, a distraction that prevents us from seeing the changes that the musical has undergone.

Like many integrated musicals, both stage and original film, *Romance & Cigarettes* focuses on a heterosexual couple's relationship.[38] Despite the dour and somewhat despairing tone of the film, the eventual reconciliation between Nick and Kitty is not in doubt. If genre tropes for the musical exist, perhaps that is one of the most persistent: the 'happy' ending. There is no innovation there for *Romance & Cigarettes*. Even if it had subverted the trend (*Dancer in the Dark* – another dreary musical – comes to mind here), would this be a subversion of the musical as a form? Is narrative variance enough to constitute novelty, especially when a cursory examination of historic musical examples demonstrates evidence of the same? Dennis Potter's *The Singing Detective* (Jon Amiel, BBC, 1986) comes to mind in more ways than one. The use of pre-existing music, not only popularised by jukebox musicals in general, but as accompaniment to the actors, is also present in Potter's drama. *Romance & Cigarettes* offers us nothing new in this regard.

Indeed, perhaps the defining characteristic of the musical genre is not one of narrative, but of form: the musical number. The palimpsestic nature of the musical numbers in *Romance & Cigarettes*, the layering of the actor's singing with that of the original pop songs, provides a space for multiple interpretations: for nostalgia from the audience as well as new interpretations. Whether it is the feeling of being part of a larger group or being able to bridge the gap between audience and performer, *Romance & Cigarettes* demonstrates how music alleviates pain and provides coping mechanisms; a key factor of the musical.

Romance & Cigarettes continues the engagement with long-held discourses of the musical: the balance between professionalism and amateurism, engagement with the audience, and the connection between musical number and intimacy. The integrated nature of the numbers, whilst akin to the popularised stage musical of recent years, extends the form that has long existed in film genre and is found in such films as *On the Town* (Gene Kelly and Stanley Donen, 1949) and *Gigi* (Vincente Minnelli, 1958). There is no innovation in the film's use of popular music; indeed it too is harking back to the musical's long history and seen in films from *King Creole* (Michael Curtiz, 1958) to *Footloose* (Herbert Ross, 1984).

There is nothing innovative about *Romance & Cigarettes*, merely the appearance of it. Such claims of originality are easy to make and result in no overt questioning, especially in the face of the dominance of the West End and Broadway. The stage musical has become the de facto musical form at the expense of understanding the more nuanced aspects of the film musical genre. The genre's varied history, its ability to alter in the face of changing tastes and filmic literacy, to move between the backstage and the integrated, to incorporate shifting tastes in music, should be considered in a discussion of the modern musical. If we permit a broader, more thoughtful consideration of the genre, one that also sees the symbiotic relationship with the action and horror genre for instance, it becomes clear that the musical does not need the help of auteurs or auteurist discourse to be innovative; it has been so for decades.

Notes

1. *Chicago* is Broadway's second longest running musical, *Miss Saigon* is currently number thirteen.
2. Judd Hollander, 'Broadway's reliance on tourist trade increases – report', *The Stage*, 13 January 2014, available at <https://www.thestage.co.uk/news/2014/broadways-reliance-tourist-trade-increases-report/> (last accessed 20 July 2016).
3. Broadway League, 'Grosses – Broadway in NYC', *The Broadway League*, available at <https://www.broadwayleague.com/research/grosses-broadway-nyc/> (last accessed 21 July 2016).
4. *Movieweb*,available at <http://movieweb.com/movie/a-star-is-born-2017/> (last accessed 25 July 2016).
5. These directors are arguably primarily understood and discussed in terms of auterism. See: Jack Stevenson, *Lars von Trier* (London: British Film Institute, 2002); Andrew Asibong, *François Ozon* (Manchester: Manchester University Press, 2008); Pam Cook, *Baz Lurhmann* (Basingstoke: Palgrave Macmillan, 2010).
6. Richard Dyer, 'Entertainment and Utopia', in *Only Entertainment* (London: Routledge, 2002), pp. 19–35.
7. Examples of awards and nominations include John Turturro's debut film, *Mac* (1992), which won the Caméra d'Or at Cannes and was nominated for an Independent Spirit Award. *Illuminata* (1998) was nominated for the Palme d'Or and *Romance & Cigarettes* was nominated for the Golden Lion at the Venice Film Festival.
8. Stephen Holden, 'Blue collar guy loses his heart and ruins his lungs', *New York Times*, 7 September 2007, available at <http://www.nytimes.com/2007/09/07/movies/07roma.html?ref=movies&_r=1> (last accessed 20 July 2016).
9. Data from <http://www.boxofficemojo.com/>.
10. The anthology film *Rio, I Love You* has segments by ten different directors.
11. Mark Kermode and John Turturro, 'John Turturro', interview, *The Guardian*, 23 March 2006,available at <https://www.theguardian.com/film/2006/mar/23/features> (last accessed 5 August 2016).
12. For examples of seminal texts on the musical genre see: Rick Altman, *The American Film Musical* (Bloomington: Indiana University Press, 1989); Steve Cohan (ed.), *Hollywood Musicals: The Film Reader* (London: Routledge, 2002); Jane Feuer, *The Hollywood Musical*, 2nd edn (London: Macmillan Press, 1993).
13. Rick Altman, *Film/Genre* (London: British Film Institute, 1999), pp. 14–15.
14. *Step Up* (Anne Fletcher, 2006); *Step Up 2: The Streets* (Jon M. Chu, 2008); *Step Up 3D* (Jon M. Chu, 2010); *Step Up Revolution* (Scott Speer, 2012); *Step Up: All In* (Trish Sie, 2014).

15. See Beth Carroll, *Feeling Film: A Spatial Approach* (London: Palgrave Macmillan, 2016).
16. Dyer, 'Entertainment and Utopia', p. 20.
17. Ibid. p. 20.
18. Feuer, *The Hollywood Musical*.
19. Jane Feuer, 'The self-reflexive musical and the myth of entertainment', in Barry Keith Grant (ed.), *Film Genre Reader II* (Austin: University of Texas Press, 1995), pp. 441–55.
20. Ibid. p. 443.
21. Ibid. p. 443.
22. Ibid. p. 449.
23. Ibid. p. 450.
24. Kermode and Turturro, 'John Turturro', *The Guardian*.
25. Aida Edemariam, 'Burning desire', *The Guardian*, 21 March 2006, available at <https://www.theguardian.com/film/2006/mar/21/1> (last accessed 5 August 2016).
26. Claudia Gorbman, 'Artless singing', *MSMI*, Autumn 2011, 5(2): 157–71.
27. Ibid. p. 159.
28. K. J. Donnelly, 'Tracking British television: pop music as stock soundtrack to the small screen', *Popular Music*, 2002, 21(3): 331–43, esp. 333.
29. Ibid. p. 339.
30. Nick Dawson, 'John Turturro, *Romance & Cigarettes*', *Filmmaker Magazine*, 7 September 2007, available at <http://filmmakermagazine.com/1280-john-turturro-romance-cigarettes/#>, V3OxIfkrKUl (last accessed 5 August 2016).
31. Kermode and Turturro, 'John Turturro', *The Guardian*.
32. Gorbman, 'Artless singing', p. 159.
33. Dawson, 'John Turturro', *Filmmaker Magazine*.
34. Ibid.
35. Holden, 'Blue collar guy loses his heart and ruins his lungs'.
36. Franz Lidz, 'The actors sing, the director suffers, the film survives', *New York Times*, 2 September 2007, available at <http://www.nytimes.com/2007/09/02/movies/02lidz.html> (last accessed 5 August 2016).
37. Ibid.
38. Altman, *The American Film Musical*.

Bibliography

Altman, Rick, *The American Film Musical* (Bloomington: Indiana University Press, 1989).
Altman, Rick, *Film/Genre* (London: British Film Institute, 1999).
Asibong, Andrew, *François Ozon* (Manchester: Manchester University Press, 2008).
Broadway League, 'Grosses – Broadway in NYC', *The Broadway League*, <https://www.broadwayleague.com/research/grosses-broadway-nyc/> (last accessed 21 July 2016).
Carroll, Beth, *Feeling Film: A Spatial Approach* (London: Palgrave Macmillan, 2016).
Cohan, Steve (eds), *Hollywood Musicals: The Film Reader* (London: Routledge, 2002).
Cook, Pam, *Baz Lurhmann* (Basingstoke: Palgrave Macmillan, 2010).
Dawson, Nick, 'John Turturro, *Romance & Cigarettes*', *Filmmaker Magazine*, 7 September 2007, <http://filmmakermagazine.com/1280-john-turturro-romance-ciga rettes/#>, V3OxIfkrKUl (last accessed 5 August 2016).
Donnelly, K. J., 'Tracking British television: pop music as stock soundtrack to the small screen', *Popular Music*, 2002, 21(32): 331–43.

Dyer, Richard, 'Entertainment and Utopia', in *Only Entertainment* (London: Routledge, 2002).

Edemariam, Aida, 'Burning desire', *The Guardian*, 21 March 2006, <https://www.theguardian.com/film/2006/mar/21/1> (last accessed 5 August 2016).

Feuer, Jane, *The Hollywood Musical*, 2nd edn (London: Macmillan Press, 1993).

Feuer, Jane, 'The self-reflexive musical and the myth of entertainment', in Barry Keith Grant (ed.), *Film Genre Reader II* (Austin: University of Texas Press, 1995), pp. 441–55.

Gorbman, Claudia, 'Artless singing', *MSMI*, Autumn 2011, 5(2): 157–71.

Holden, Stephen, 'Blue collar guy loses his heart and ruins his lungs', *New York Times*, 7 September 2007, <http://www.nytimes.com/2007/09/07/movies/07roma.html?ref=movies&_r=1> (last accessed 20 July 2016).

http://www.boxofficemojo.com/

Hollander, Judd, 'Broadway's reliance on tourist trade increases – report', *The Stage*, 13 January 2014, <https://www.thestage.co.uk/news/2014/broadways-reliance-tourist-trade-increases-report/> (last accessed 20 July 2016).

Kermode, Mark and John Turturro, 'John Turturro', interview, *The Guardian*, 23 March 2006, <https://www.theguardian.com/film/2006/mar/23/features> (last accessed 5 August 2016).

Movieweb, <http://movieweb.com/movie/a-star-is-born-2017/> (last accessed 25 July 2016).

Lidz, Franz, 'The actors sing, the director suffers, the film survives', *New York Times*, 2 September 2007, <http://www.nytimes.com/2007/09/02/movies/02lidz.html> (last accessed 5 August 2016).

Stevenson, Jack, *Lars von Trier* (London: British Film Institute, 2002).

5 'IS THIS REAL ENOUGH FOR YOU?': LYRICAL ARTICULATION OF THE BEATLES' SONGS IN *ACROSS THE UNIVERSE*

Stephanie Fremaux

Julie Taymor's *Across the Universe* (2007) presents an array of hits spanning the Beatles' relatively brief career, loosely tying together the 'boy meets girl, girl meets [radical activist], boy gets girl back' plot commonly associated with the musical. Unlike previous musicals however, Taymor's focus on the film's thirty-three musical sequences that make up the linear narrative emphasises *Across the Universe*'s 'hybrid of long-form music video and movie musical' that highlights the resonance of the Beatles' lyrics to contemporary audiences.[1] Because the Beatles' canon is so well established within popular music culture and the band's music studied in great detail by scholars, arguably any visual representation of those well-known songs would need to offer a coherent narrative based on one possible interpretation while still allowing space for the audience to project their own, often personal meanings onto those songs.[2] With songs so familiar, it becomes a difficult undertaking to offer a new and challenging film musical that does not recycle the same formulaic structure, while still attempting to appeal to a mainstream cinema-going audience. In regards to these issues, the film's innovation then is to eschew the classic film musical formula of using the music sequence to address and counter the moments within the film's narrative where disruptions or problems are presented.[3]

For Taymor, it was important not to create a film that '[regurgitated] the same old, same old' in order to contribute a piece of art that would enable the audience to 'grow as a culture'.[4] However, in a recent interview with Jodie Foster at the Tribeca Film Festival in New York, Taymor recalled how the production company Revolution Studios not only tried to have the film cut to a more audience friendly length, but also kept trying to influence changes to make the film more like Kenny Ortega's *High School Musical* (2006). In Taymor's words, she was pressured to 'get rid of the black people, the lesbians, the politics, the Vietnam war [. . .]'.[5] By being uncompromising in her artistic vision, Taymor delivers a musical, partly influenced by the aesthetical approaches of 1950s integrated musicals where moments of dance and song merge into non-musical sequences, to *challenge* audiences rather than retread mainstream musical ground ensuring that *Across the Universe* is 'unlike *Hairspray*, or *Dreamgirls*, or *Chicago*' in terms of narrative presentation and unrealistic moments of breaking out into song.[6] Arguably, by constructing a film musical that creates a sung narrative from Beatles' songs Taymor uses the music as moments of realism rather than escape to confront the timeless themes of innocence, exploration, and chaos/war in order to liberate cinema, theatrical convention, and the established meanings of songs.

As the film is two hours long with only half an hour of spoken dialogue, a sung narrative allows Taymor to develop characters around what she felt were not only key Beatles' songs but that also captured the fearful and uncertain mood in the aftermath of the 11 September 2001 terrorist attacks and in the ensuing war in Iraq. This approach works in two specific ways that counter generic convention. First, rather than creating distinct musical moments that abruptly break from the narrative, Taymor more naturally develops moments where it 'feels as if the songs emerge from the characters' and where pieces transition from one into the next.[7] For instance, the majority of the principal cast were relative unknowns with the exception of Evan Rachel Wood (Lucy), and all of the cast were asked to sing live rather than lip-synch to a recorded track as is common practice. To add a further sense of realism to the film and authenticity to the vocal performances, some cast members were also experienced musicians, including Jim Sturgess (Jude), Joe Anderson (Max), Dana Fuchs (Sadie) and Martin Luther McCoy (JoJo). These casting choices make sense when considering Taymor's background in theatre to select a cast that would be able to approach acting for cinema similarly to acting for stage by bringing a competency to performing musical theatre live.

Second, by creating the narrative from the songs chosen, Taymor is able to 'juxtapose simple, absolute naked songs' like 'Something' against 'big extravagant sequences' like 'Being for the Benefit of Mr. Kite!'[8] In creating both stark, simple moments and highly stylised hyperreal numbers, Taymor draws once again upon her artistic sensibilities and theatre background to create textures that develop characters and move the narrative forward in the absence of the traditional musical narrative structure of conflict/musical number solution or relief. Rather than present straightforward cover versions, many of the songs, including 'Girl' and 'If I Fell', deconstruct the Beatles' original arrangements to instead present 'echoes of friendly ghosts in the arrangements',[9] while the more complex and stylised numbers such as 'I Want You (She's so Heavy)' and 'Strawberry Fields Forever' transcend spectacle and pop hit mash-ups prevalent in contemporary musicals such as Baz Luhrmann's *Moulin Rouge!* (2001) and Phyllida Lloyd's *Mamma Mia!* (2008) in order to present more natural responses inspired by the songs' lyrics. Through this approach, Taymor has arguably, if inadvertently, presented a film musical that redresses some of the shortcomings of previous scholarship on the relationship between film and music on screen. For example, Goldmark et al. note the need to 'consider film as representing music, not simply as adding music as a supplement to a cinematic representation formed via image or narrative'.[10] Music functions as an element that is just as vital as the characters, themes and the narrative itself, and to isolate music from the analysis of these elements is to overlook the way music is used to construct meaning and represent identity. Similarly, Donnelly's most recent work on studying popular music in film argues that rather than 'pulling apart "the music" and the "images"', research should not consider music and images as '"two discourses" but a merged unity'.[11] These approaches to film analysis set the foundation for this chapter's methodological approach in order to understand how Taymor's fusion of the Beatles' songs and narrative work to problematise previous understandings of the narrative/musical sequence binary commonly found both in traditional Hollywood musicals and in the majority of scholarship on film musicals.

Further problematising an analysis of *Across the Universe* is the way in which the film does not neatly sit within the existing definitions or analyses proposed by scholarship to date. While Altman, Mundy, and Romney and Wootton offer definitions and discussions of a range of subgenres and types within the film musical, Neale calls it for what it is: 'The musical has always been a mongrel genre'.[12] He continues by explaining, 'In varying measures and combinations, music, song, and dance have been its only essential ingredients'.[13] Even when interviewed or speaking on the film's commentary track, Taymor herself muddies the terminology. For example, Taymor comments that on the one hand she wanted to create 'a musical that didn't exist' inspired by the Beatles' songbook, but that her approach in using the music in order to 'forward action, emotions' was like working on 'a very old fashioned musical'.[14] While Taymor does not mention specific influences, similarities can be drawn most closely with the integrated musicals of the 1950s including films such as Vincente Minnelli's post Second World War *An American in Paris* (1951) and Fred Zinnemann's screen adaptation of *Oklahoma!* (1955), which begin to use choreography in non-musical number scenes and also begin to break down the utopian, burst into song musical sequences and spectacles characteristic of the 1930s musicals.[15] For example, at the beginning of *An American in Paris*, Gene Kelly's protagonist, Jerry Mulligan, performs a subtle dance routine as he wakes up, hoists his bed up to the ceiling in his comically small apartment, and sets up a small table and chair from hidden spaces. Throughout this scene, the non-diegetic orchestral score guides Kelly's movements around the cramped space as he prepares his breakfast. In addition, the musical numbers do introduce characters and at times help to move the plot forward. However, these examples still rely primarily on spoken dialogue to advance the plot and develop characters, whereas Taymor's approach almost exclusively does this with music and sung song lyrics.

In an interview with *Variety* journalist Anne Thompson, Taymor argues that the film 'doesn't have to make sense. We're liberated because it's a musical', but also notes, 'the movie is so unusual that it will challenge most audiences'.[16] Taymor's statement suggests that while some may see the musical number as a moment of liberation, for Taymor the genre itself is liberating because those rules and definitions are so contested. Similarly, *New York Times* journalist Sylviane Gold's review of the film begins by stating, 'Call it a jukebox musical, or a rock opera, or a long-playing music video. All of those labels fit – and don't.'[17] It is not the purpose of this chapter to contest definitions or to propose a new definition, for as Neale notes, many esteemed colleagues have themselves 'disagreed about the meanings [. . .] some invent their own'.[18] Instead, this research aims, through a textual analysis of key numbers such as 'Let it Be', 'I Want You (She's so Heavy)' and 'Strawberry Fields Forever', to work through the ways in which, in Collins's words, the musical is 'multifaceted, hybrid, and complex'.[19]

Previous musicals have most commonly utilised the musical number to provide utopian relief from the troubles presented in the narrative[20] or to 'reconcile tensions and dichotomies',[21] often emphasising white-centric, heteronormative depictions of love and life. Specifically, Mundy drawing upon Altman's work explains that the classical Hollywood musical was reliant upon a series of dichotomies – 'dualities, of contradictions and oppositions, which, within the text, need to be recognised, commented upon, and resolved'.[22] Mundy notes that these arising problems or issues were commonly addressed and resolved in the musical sequences.[23] He goes on to further point out that the conventional narration, typically featuring spoken dialogue, was where the 'real' was placed, while the musical sequences where dialogue and lyrics are sung represents the idealised, potential solutions being considered outside 'reality'.[24] Mundy does acknowledge that once songs and their lyrics 'are constrained and determined by the images which contextualize them', it becomes more difficult for them to be 'appropriated by [viewers]'.[25] Perhaps *Across the Universe* was not a success at the box office because mainstream film audiences are so used to expecting more traditional narrative/musical sequence binaries. However, *Across the Universe* arguably explores the idea of complex, multi-layered 'enacted life narrations' also reflected in the Beatles' own song writing style.[26] Both of Womack's[27] key pieces of scholarship on the Beatles' music investigate the role of narrative, selfhood and identity through the lens of Jerome Bruner's[28] concept of 'life as narrative'.[29] In exploring this strong theme of how reflecting upon the self and identity is used in the band's lyrics, one can start to see a strong parallel to the emphasis Taymor places on the Beatles' songs through the unusual narrative structure. With this in mind, the thirty-three songs that make up the film's soundtrack are no longer merely a greatest hits selection, for as Womack notes, the whole of the Beatles' output represents 'the very act of life-writing itself: by authoring the text of their lives via their music [. . .], The Beatles engaged in a self-conscious effort to tell their own stories about the inherent difficulties that come with growing up and growing older'.[30] This process Womack goes on to describe is a very complex process of recollections, reflecting and critical evaluation that eventually leads to greater self-awareness and self-understanding to the question of 'who am I?'

Before Taymor could tell these characters' stories through the Beatles songs, however, she had to obtain the necessary licence. The two main licences to use songs in film, television or advertising are a synchronisation licence and a master licence. A master licence allows the use of the original version of a song. A synchronisation licence allows that song or a cover version (if no master licence can be secured) to be 'synched up' to the moving image.[31] As the Beatles and their company Apple Corps own the rights to any master licensing, obtaining this type of licence is extremely rare because the surviving members and the estates of the deceased members must be in agreement.[32] In order to obtain a synchronisation licence, Taymor had to approach the owners of the publishing rights to the Beatles catalogue, Sony/ATV Music Publishing. In a 2009 interview with *Billboard* magazine, executives Ron Broitman and Rob Kaplan, who oversee synch licences, discussed the process. They explained that a committee at Sony/ATV consider the requests 'to evaluate each of the uses' in order to 'make sure it's the right use'.[33] With a production budget of US$45 million and a cast of largely unknown actors and musicians, a substantial (though undisclosed) amount of money would have been spent on obtaining synchronisation licences for each of the thirty-three songs, which were rear-ranged by Elliot Goldenthal and sung entirely by the cast.[34]

In developing her characters, trying to make sense of the political and social landscape, and those characters' places within this time of uncertainty and turmoil, Taymor is drawing upon a body of work that, as Womack's work points out, provides strong templates in helping to guide the listener/viewer through these questions. This template is then used to create a seamless narrative reflecting Polkinghorne's argument that 'we achieve our personal identities and self-concept through the use of the narrative configuration, and [we] make our existence into a whole by understanding it as an expression of a single unfolding and developing story'.[35] The literal depiction of the Beatles' lyrics that create the film's narrative visually underpins the ways in which music has always had the ability to move audiences, reflect current issues and challenge established ideologies. Taymor reinforces these themes through motifs reliant on militarised choreography and other jarring visual juxtapositions between coming of age relationship issues and war footage. In order to draw parallels between the mood and events of the 1960s again encapsulated around the themes of innocence, experimentation and chaos/war, Taymor was adamant that she 'didn't want the movie to be dance-y. I wanted the choreography to come out of natural movement.'[36] In exploring Taymor's unorthodox approach, this chapter argues that the literal depiction of the Beatles' lyrics reposition the musical's emphasis not on utopian escapism, but instead reimagines those lyrics and familiar arrangements to offer new interpretations of the Beatles' songs through natural movements, using the music to invoke a sense of realism, and re-work arrangements to better align music with dramatic function around universal themes such as unrequited love, loss of innocence and the effects of war on a young generation.

ACT I: INNOCENCE – 'LET IT BE'

Throughout her career, Taymor has established a visual language that borrows from art, theatre and cinematic traditions – a hybrid approach to storytelling that favours an emphasis on an emotional journey represented in vibrant, immersive spectacle often presented with dark and poignant undertones to anchor a social commentary. In addition, Taymor's work often inverts classical approaches to casting and directorial choices when these functions risk jeopardising the integrity of the narrative and character development. For example, *Frida*'s (2002) mixture of animation, cut outs, slow motion and live action helped to invite the audience into the traumatic and artistic journey of surrealist Frida Kahlo. Taymor's direction earned the American Film Institute's (AFI) 'Movie of the Year: Official Selection' award with the AFI commenting: 'The film's unique visual language takes us into an artist's head and reminds us that art is best enjoyed when it moves, breathes, and is painted on a giant canvas, as only the movies can provide.'[37]

Again, Taymor eschewed classic form by casting Helen Mirren (as Prospera) in the role of Prospero in her film adaptation of William Shakespeare's *The Tempest* (2010), as no male lead in the casting call could match Mirren's performance. Taymor's best known and most successful theatre work has been directing the stage version of Disney's *The Lion King* (1994), which opened on Broadway in 1997. The *New York Times* opening night review commented on the effectiveness of the visual style throughout, observing the way the journey of Simba, from cub to king, is linked to the spectacle Taymor creates. Brantley specifically points to the 'maverick artist's [. . .] bold multicultural experiments [and] her own distinctive vision' in this theatrical experience.[38] Furthermore,

The Lion King reflects Taymor's work in that it characteristically features 'singular, and often haunting, visual flourishes'.[39]

It is this 'singular' and 'haunting' approach that Taymor opens *Across the Universe* with as the audience hears the opening whispers of 'Girl' being sung wistfully by Jude as he sits slouched on the beach in a wide angle establishing shot. The diegetic sound of the waves breaking on the shore set the tempo for the faint sound of strings and wind instruments sustaining long chords. Sturgess sings the song's opening lyrics slowly, and naturally rhythmic with the waves and the instruments seemingly on the breeze highlighting not only Taymor's realistic and more natural approach to the musical sequence, but also reinforcing the trope of emotional storytelling. Jude, framed left of centre, breaks the fourth wall to implore the audience to listen to his 'story all about the girl who came to stay'. The camera slowly, again in rhythm to the sonic and visual movement on screen, zooms until Jude is in an extreme close-up, looking now beyond the camera/audience. A dissolve in black and white leads to waves crashing in close-up and images of said girl (Lucy) are interspersed with images of protest, clashes and violence. Kramer argues, 'Musical meaning does not depend on being decoded; it depends on being lived.'[40] Jude's story seems to be one of heartache but without regret – the framing and lyrical familiarity the audience brings cues an understanding that this will be a lived experience rather than the saccharin sweetness of previous attempts to bring the Beatles' song book to screen.[41] This opening device to establish tone and narrative is not uncommon in the theatre as similar approaches have been used in well known plays such as *Amadeus* (1979), *Rent* (1996) and Taymor's own *The Lion King*. In this way, Taymor also makes an emotional connection early on between the protagonist, Jude, and the audience, whom Taymor is trying to guide towards parallels between the unrest in the 1960s and post 9/11.

If the prelude of 'Girl' establishes a tone of frustration and heartache at pursuing what the song's primary author, John Lennon, described as a 'recurring fantasy' of a 'dream girl',[42] framed by Jude's naivety, then the film's opening flashback establishes a time of innocence, carefree love and a search for one's self against the rock 'n' roll, 'Hold Me Tight' backdrop of the late 1950s sock hop in the US and the early 1960s Cavern Club in the UK. (It should be noted that Taymor does incorporate the film's chronology into the narrative very loosely.) Within this section, characters' individual storylines are introduced, begin to intersect, and finally converge upon the countercultural, inclusive utopia of 1960s New York City. Jude leaves Liverpool for the US to search for a father he has never met and runs (literally) into Max – a 'frat boy' jokester. Jude is introduced to Max's high school aged sister Lucy at Thanksgiving dinner and the two explore an initially platonic but flirtatious friendship despite Lucy's engagement to her high school sweetheart – a US serviceman away at war. The innocence of new friendships, young love and moving out of the suburbs to the big city forces an abrupt confrontation of grown up, adult issues when Lucy receives news that her boyfriend, Daniel, has been killed serving in Vietnam.

The end of Act I comes to a close with the segue from Max and Jude arriving at a flat in New York City, meeting their landlord 'Sexy' Sadie in one of the few scenes with spoken dialogue, to a minimalist audio track of children playing in a front yard, and the clacking of Lucy's bicycle chain and creaking bike frame as she pedals towards Daniel's parents' house. The scene of Lucy approaching the house cuts to a close-up of two US servicemen walking down the front porch steps in slow motion in time to the low drone of a passing airplane. Still in slow motion, Lucy pushes past the expressionless soldiers as Daniel's mother lets out a low sob as she collapses. Again using slow motion, the camera cuts to an extreme close-up of Daniel's identity tags falling from the hand of his mother, the sound amplified to focus solely on the sound of the metal tags. Taymor uses this sound to connect sonically to the next scene – an extreme close-up of an African American man's hand grasping onto a metal chain link fence, again amplifying the sound of the metal to create a juxtaposition between Daniel's war and the violent and explosive diegetic clashes of the 'war' between the US national guard and the predominantly African American community of Detroit.

An unnamed young boy (Timothy T. Mitchum) hides crouched against a burnt out car singing a gospel version of 'Let it Be' as the sequence cuts to images of white soldiers beating up black men and women. Initially the boy's singing is a slow and steady tempo *a cappella* style, punctuated by an explosion, shouts of 'get down' by a soldier, a glass bottle smashes against a wall, and a thud as the butt of a rifle connects with the body of a black man. The boy pleads for calm as he sings 'And in my hour of darkness, she is standing in front of me, speaking words of wisdom, "let it be"', his words drowned out with a cut to a solider shooting from a roof top. A low level tracking shot focuses solely on the boy singing 'let it be' as a low organ can be heard playing only the central identifying chords of the arrangement, silencing the diegetic cacophony as the camera tracks in on a tighter shot. As the sequence climaxes there is a juxtaposition of Daniel's military honours funeral and the young boy's funeral in an inner city church, punctuated by the voices of a full gospel choir singing the chorus – war has indiscriminately united these two young men from different class and ethnic backgrounds just as the Beatles' song has, and the message of abusive power and racial tension is as poignant today as it was during the Civil Rights movement of the 1960s around which this scene is contextualised. Taymor ends this act with an introduction to a new character, the boy's musician older brother Jojo, laying a handful of dirt over his brother's grave, and a cut to Lucy lying on her bed alone, before fading to black.

Act II: Experience – 'I Want You (She's So Heavy)'

Act II opens with the cast exploring a variety of new and unknown experiences in gurus, drug culture, love, life and commitment to a cause. The music cues to a slinky, minimal blues infused version of 'Come Together' sung by Joe Cocker as Jojo makes his way to New York City. Musical arranger Elliot Goldenthal strips the song back to essential kick drum and bass to punctuate a natural seediness that greets Jojo as he arrives in the city at night. There are slight twangs of guitar note sustain to underline the 'weird' encounters of the homeless man, the pimp and the drugged-up freak dancing around the street. The tempo of the backing track aligns with the movement of the characters on screen to create a surreal uncertainty that is both nightmarish and claustrophobic. An aerial shot of the New York City skyline turns out to be a distorted perspective painted on a wall as the camera pans to reveal Jojo walking past the mural and Cocker's pimp walks ever closer to the camera, singing the chorus directly to the audience in a wide angle, centre framed close-up. The choreography, as the dizzying night turns into an ever dizzying day, features Jojo caught amongst the hustle and bustle of ad men and Wall Street types (all Caucasian) in identical suits, trilby hats and briefcases performing choreography based on natural movements with the sound of their movements acting as musical accompaniment punctuating the down beats of the song's rhythm track. Jojo starts to fit into the rhythm of the city when he reaches Greenwich Village, in advertently crossing paths with both Max and Jude, before fully 'tuning in' to the city during an audition for Sadie's band – his guitar solo becoming the diegetic guitar solo so well known in the original song.

The natural choreography and literal depiction of lyrics is used to its most hyperreal effect in the 'I Want You (She's So Heavy)' sequence where Max undertakes his army recruitment interview and evaluation. The sequence is the furthest from Dyer's utopian musical number as a close-up of the large, masculine block of the recruitment centre building is paired with the slow, heavy minor notes from the brass section.[43] As Max enters the building, there is a cut to a close-up of Max's feet weighing heavily upon each step in the darkened hallway as the bass and kick drum is cued in. The guitar line, as in the original arrangement, is repetitive and hypnotic. Max is surrounded by large posters of the Second World War recruitment image of 'Uncle Sam' featuring the slogan 'I Want You'. The poster comes alive with Uncle Sam singing 'I want you, I want you so bad'. He is grabbed by two soldiers and forced onto a conveyor belt where he is stripped of his clothes and his identity, and 'processed' by expressionless, almost faceless masks the soldiers are costumed in. This processing is done in a mechanical fashion to the heavy beat of the music. During the guitar solo that plays the main theme, a military drum line replaces Ringo Starr's original drum break as Max enters a hall with other awkward recruits standing in their underwear, where a militaristic choreographed routine starts, by Sergeants First Class. These soldiers' parade movements are again underscored by the marching drum line, manipulating their arm movements to force a perfectly aligned salute. The collective footwork stomps sound like gun fire. Sliding panels on the floor move the recruits into place, perfectly paired with a Sergeant First Class as a network of cubicles descends from the ceiling above. The recruits are boxed, tested and prodded, all in time to the masculine, short, sharp stomping and stamping of the process. A partially animated sequence of Joseph Cornell style boxes opening to reveal specific body parts being tested – eyes, chest, feet, arms – compartmentalises whatever remained of the individual. When the song enters the bridge to the 'She's So Heavy' segment, Max and the other recruits are being aggressively manipulated by the soldiers into the same choreographed marching/saluting routine demonstrated moments ago, the down beat again being echoed by the loud stomping of the movements. MacDonald described the musical shift between the song's two parts (while referring to Lennon's obsession with and dependency on then lover Yoko Ono) as,

> the sickening plunge from E7 to B flat 7; the augmented A that drags [Lennon's] head up to make him go through it all again; the hammering flat ninth that collapses, spent, on the song's insatiable D minor arpeggio. Nightmarishly tormented, this is a musical tryst with a succubus.[44]

This passage is an apt description of the tone Taymor is trying to replicate in this musical number in charting Max's defiant swagger up the steps, to one of nervousness and apprehension, to that of compliance. Now Max is in Vietnam and he and his fellow soldiers literally carry a large Statue of Liberty – Taymor emphasising the weight and the burden of freedom and liberty marking a parallel with the Iraq war. The recruits are still in their underwear, exposed and naive, each boot stomp in the mud heavy and sluggish, while they sing in chorus 'she's so heavy' repeatedly. The image of the large statue is match mixed with Max back in the recruiter's office placing a smaller version of the statue back on the desk. This moment of spoken dialogue between SFC Richards and Max is a brief comedic reprieve inverting the traditional formula; Max states he should not be recruited because he is 'a cross dresser, homosexual pacifist with a spot on [his] lungs'. The recruiter replies, 'as long as you don't have flat feet', cutting back into the musical number where Max is wrapped in cling film and stamped 1A like a piece of meat. A reprise of the number begins back at the flat where Jojo and Sadie dance together while Prudence (T. V. Carpio) watches on from the fire escape outside, singing her unrequited love for Sadie.

Act II ends after experiencing Bono's guru Dr Robert ('I am the Walrus') and the ensuing psychedelic drug trip courtesy of Eddie Izzard's Mr Kite ('Being for the Benefit of Mr. Kite!'). The group wake up in a field, having come down from their trip singing the multi-harmony of 'Because' *a cappella*. This is the briefest of respites from the disturbing hallucinations in the Mr Kite sequence as the group are all together for one last time before their various wars tear them apart in Act III. The 'Because' sequence once again shows off what a 'generously inventive choreographer' Taymor is as the 'underwater sequences [. . .] approach ballet'.[45] Within moments the beauty and stillness of the scene comes to a jarring end as Max floats to the surface of a murky lake with the shadow of a military helicopter cast upon him from above.

ACT III – CHAOS – 'STRAWBERRY FIELDS FOREVER'

Chaos comes in many forms in Act III and the following musical numbers are reinterpreted to reflect the frustration and breakdown of Jude and Lucy's relationship, as well as Jojo and Sadie's relationship. Lucy becomes more involved with a revolutionary protester and a television brings the Vietnam War into the friends' flat. Both 'Something' and 'Oh! Darling' become break-up songs and 'Strawberry Fields Forever', stripped back of its iconic Mellotron and electric slide guitar to mere echoes, becomes a stark reminder of the complexities of the original lyric – 'on the one hand, a study in uncertain identity, tinged with the loneliness of the solitary rebel [. . .]' while on the other hand 'an eerie longing for' childhood.[46] The sequence begins with Jude slowly exhaling smoke, key lighting from the left of centre obscuring his face in dark shadow. The audio track is initially silent until the diegetic sound of the news report filters through. The haunt of the Mellotron melody played by a wind section becomes more prominent as a close-up of a bowl of strawberries provides a trigger to the opening lines. Fill lighting emerges and the drums are cued in as Jude starts pinning 'bleeding' over-ripe strawberries onto the white back wall. As he sings 'nothing is real, and nothing to get hung about' the camera pans across the wall to reveal what looks like a field of bleeding bodies/hearts – an image that closely resembles the many crosses in the Second World War cemeteries in Normandy, France. As Lucy opens the door to reveal Jude standing in front of a large canvas of strawberries, Jude sings, 'living is easy with eyes closed, misunderstanding all you see' and the camera cuts to a close-up of Lucy's face, her eyes suddenly open to what the war means – it is real. As Taymor explains, Lucy reflects the concrete, rationalising of war and chaos, not understanding what Jude sees, which is reflected in abstract images of the strawberries he pins up.[47] For Taymor, the lyrics, again taken literally, inspire the imagery and the actors' responses.[48] The sequence focuses on Jude's introspective development as a central character that becomes a duet between Max in Vietnam and Jude, who has tried to avoid thinking about the war. The duet is symbolised in creating a collage of Max filmed in 16mm superimposed on Jude singing in his studio.

As bombs drop in Vietnam, Jude throws strawberries at the canvas, making the pinned strawberries 'explode'. A pressure and intensity builds – there are cuts to footage of actual strawberries dropping from the sky to the town below and then a jump cut back to the jungle where archive footage is used to show a gas like explosion of napalm 'strawberry bombs'. Jude and Max keep exchanging the lines of 'there's nothing to get hung about, strawberry fields forever', almost hypnotically, as the music crescendos, Jude becoming more violent, stepping on strawberries and slashing red paint around, splattering across the superimposed images of Max in close-up – to the point where, as Goldenthal describes, it feels like being in a crashing B52 bomber to create the loudest sonic moment in the movie. The arrangement becomes militaristic with the drum beats in time to the explosions and each swipe of Jude's paint brush. Taymor cuts back and forth between Jude and the archive footage, increasingly becoming more saturated in red. The music becomes further drowned out by the drum cadence and a crashing plane. This surreal intensity is match mixed into the banality of an extreme close-up on a washing machine in a Laundromat – the sounds of war becoming the diegetic sound of the rinse cycle – again creating small moments of relief. The film continues to navigate 'a true to life love story with all its problems'[49] until the final musical number, which finally functions in the more traditional sense of providing a utopian moment where the friends are reunited to sing 'All You Need is Love' in the closing moments of the film, first in *a cappella* and then in a rock style harmony without the familiar horn arrangement. The film finishes just as the Beatles finished, on a rooftop, yet where the Beatles went their separate ways, the film is resolved with the classic Hollywood happy ever after.

CONCLUSION

Across the Universe is problematic as a pop musical in the traditional sense.[50] In inverting the classic Hollywood musical formula, the film creates a difficult binary whereby it tries to be both authentic in its musical delivery through the use of song lyrics as dialogue and in its literal depiction of those lyrics, but also tries to evoke a sense of fantasy in that the majority of the film is sung and relies heavily on a variety of visual styles and collage of techniques. Unlike previous traditional film musicals, *Across the Universe* uses the lyrics and new, sometimes sparser arrangements of Beatles' songs to explore emotion through moments of realism throughout the narrative, rather than reserve such moments merely within the spectacle of a short musical number situated between plot developments. Interestingly, Donnelly notes the ways in which non-musicals have begun to create 'a convergence between incidental musical in films [. . .] and the modes of the film musical', and yet, *Across the Universe* uses such an 'aesthetic convergence' to develop a film's narrative from the music of the Beatles by visually transcribing the lyrics onto the screen.[51] As the film moves from one musical narrative sequence to the next, there is only one abrupt fade to black as the sequences instead segue using visual cues such as matched mixes, dissolves, rainfall that turns into snow fall, etc. When visual cues are not used, the director relies on Goldenthal's arrangements and the sound design to create these seamless transitions – a guitar that sounds like a ticking clock or an accordion that represents a heart beat in order to create 'musical textures that serve as an introduction to the next song'.[52] Despite taking some of these visual and audio cues from theatre and Classical Hollywood musicals, the film creates unsettling moments of truth where the viewer may expect to find the moment of musical relief. Dyer argues that 'the stuff of utopia' is the 'sense that things could be better, that something other than what is can be imagined and maybe realized'.[53] But these alternatives and hopes are not present in the normal way – the musical sequences do not afford us such hopes and dreams. The audience may be familiar with the Beatles' songs and nostalgia may evoke more upbeat feelings associated with that music but Taymor's approach reintroduces audiences to the complexities, the seriousness and the forlorn emotions contained within the lyrics. It jars the viewer by creating strange juxtapositions of the meditative 'Across the Universe' with a stark reality – images of dead Vietnamese women dancing on water before falling back to their watery grave, or the hopefulness of 'Something' with that of a pained Jude unable to fully win Lucy over. Where Dyer feels that though 'we are moved by music, [. . .] it has the least obvious reference to "reality"',[54] Taymor is able to illustrate this reality by deconstructing the arrangements and weaving these songs together to present a cohesive narrative that ties together both musical and non-musical elements. The parallels between the 1960s nuclear threats of the Cold War and Vietnam echo the uncertainty and discourses of fear politicians and news media broadcast in a post 9/11 world. In these desperate times of war both overseas and at home where ethnic and racial divides are ever present, and the social and political unrest so common in the 1960s mirrors today's headlines, *Across the Universe*'s challenging delivery demonstrates the depth of the Beatles' lyrics and that their music may still be a uniting force fifty years on.

NOTES

1. Stephen Holden, 'Lovers in the '60s take a magical mystery tour', *New York Times*, 14 September 2007, available at <http://www.nytimes.com/2007/09/14/movies/14univ.html?pagewanted=all&_r=0> (last accessed 8 December 2014).
2. See Walter Everett, *The Beatles as Musicians:* Revolver *through the* Anthology (New York: Oxford University Press, 1999); Walter Everett, *The Beatles as Musicians: The Quarry Men through* Rubber Soul (New York: Oxford University Press, 2001); Ian MacDonald, *Revolution in the Head*, 2nd edn (London: Pimlico, 2005); Ian Inglis (ed.), *The Beatles, Popular Music, and Society* (Basingstoke:

Macmillan Press, 2000); Michael Frontani, *The Beatles: Image and the Media* (Jackson, MS: University of Mississippi Press, 2007); Bob Neaverson, *The Beatles Movies* (London: Cassell, 1997).

3. John Mundy, *Popular Music on Screen: From Hollywood Musical to Music Video* (Manchester: Manchester University Press, 1999), p. 57.

4. Joey Nolfi, 'Julie Taymor: studio wanted to cut minorities from "Across the Universe" to make it like "High School Musical"', *Entertainment Weekly*, 21 April 2016, available at <http://www.ew.com/article/2016/04/21/julie-taymor-jodie-foster-tribeca-talk> (last accessed 30 April 2016).

5. Ibid.

6. Anne Thompson, 'Julie Taymor flies *Across the Universe*', *Variety*, 6 September 2007, available at <http://variety.com/2007/film/columns/julie-taymor-flies-across-the-universe-1117971531/> (last accessed 12 May 2016).

7. 'Creating the Universe' featurette, 2008, *Across the Universe*, 2007 [DVD], directed by Julie Taymor (USA: Revolution Studios), 06:00.

8. *Across the Universe*, 2007 [DVD], directed by Julie Taymor (USA: Revolution Studios), director's commentary track, 1:13:50.

9. 'All About the Music' featurette, 2008, *Across the Universe*, 2007 [DVD], directed by Julie Taymor (USA: Revolution Studios), 08:25.

10. Daniel Goldmark, Lawrence Kramer and Richard Leppert (eds), *Beyond the Soundtrack: Representing Music in Cinema* (Ann Arbor, MI: University of Michigan Press, 2007), pp. 4–5.

11. K. J. Donnelly, *Magical Musical Tour: Rock and Pop in Film Soundtracks* (New York: Bloomsbury Academic, 2015), p. 2.

12. Steve Neale, *Genre and Hollywood* (London: Routledge, 2001), p. 105. See also Rick Altman, *The American Film Musical* (London: British Film Institute, 1989); John Mundy, *Popular Music on Screen: From Hollywood Musical to Music Video* (Manchester: Manchester University Press, 1999); Jonathan Romney and Adrian Wootton (eds), *Celluloid Jukebox: Popular Music and the Movies Since the 50s* (London: British Film Institute, 1995).

13. Neale, *Genre and Hollywood*, p. 105.

14. 'Creating the Universe', 05:25.

15. James Chapman, *Cinemas of the World: Film and Society from 1895 to the Present* (London: Reaktion Books, 2004), available at <https://books.google.co.uk/books?id=SMYo4Abel2EC&lpg=PT189&dq=1950s%20integrated%20musicals&pg=PT189#v=onepage&q=1950s%20integrated%20musicals&f=false> (last accessed 23 August 2016).

16. Thompson, 'Julie Taymor flies *Across the Universe*'.

17. Sylviane Gold, 'Re-meet the Beatles through the voices of a new narrative', *New York Times*, 9 September 2007, available at <http://www.nytimes.com/2007/09/09/movies/moviesspecial/09Gold.html?_r=1> (last accessed 12 May 2016).

18. Neale, *Genre and Hollywood*, p. 105.

19. James M. Collins, 'The musical', in Wes D. Gehring (ed.), *Handbook of American Film Genres* (Westport: Greenwood Press, 1988), p. 269.

20. See Richard Dyer, *Only Entertainment*, 2nd edn (London: Routledge, 2002); Rick Altman (ed.), *Genre: The Musical* (London: Routledge and Kegan Paul in association with the British Film Institute, 1981); Rick Altman, *The American Film Musical* (London: British Film Institute, 1989).

21. Mundy, *Popular Music on Screen*, p. 63. See Altman, *The American Film Musical*.

22. Mundy, *Popular Music on Screen*, p. 63. See Altman, *The American Film Musical*, p. 56.

23. Mundy, *Popular Music on Screen*, p. 63. See Altman, *The American Film Musical*, p. 56.
24. Mundy, *Popular Music on Screen*, p. 63. See Altman, *The American Film Musical*, p. 57.
25. Mundy, *Popular Music on Screen*, p. 63. See Altman, *The American Film Musical*, p. 62.
26. Kenneth Womack, 'Reconsidering performative autobiography: life-writing and the Beatles', *Life Writing*, 2005, 2(2): 51.
27. Womack, 'Reconsidering performative autobiography'; Kenneth Womack, '"Nothing's going to change my world": narrating memory and selfhood with the Beatles', *Style*, 2010, 44(1/2): 261–88.
28. Jerome S. Bruner, *Acts of Meaning* (Cambridge, MA: Harvard University Press, 1990).
29. Womack, 'Reconsidering performative autobiography', p. 49.
30. Womack, '"Nothing's going to change my world"', p. 262.
31. Jeffrey P. Fisher, *Soundtrack Success: A Digital Storyteller's Guide to Audio Post-Production* (Boston, MA: Course Technology Cengage Learning, 2012), p. 259.
32. In one of the more recent examples, AMC drama *Mad Men*'s creator Matthew Weiner pursued obtaining a master licence from Apple Corp for 'a few years' and was asked to share storylines and script pages with Apple Corp before a decision to use the band's song 'Tomorrow Never Knows' in the show. Where most master licences for television are usually around US$100,000 and below, the master licence for this track cost US$250,000. Dave Itzkoff and Ben Sisario, 'How "Mad Men" landed the Beatles: all you need is love (and $250,000)', *New York Times*, 7 May 2012, available at <http://artsbeat.blogs.nytimes.com/2012/05/07/how-mad-men-landed-the-beatles-all-you-need-is-love-and-250000/> (last accessed 13 August 2016).
33. Ed Christman, 'Commercial potential: Sony/ATV execs explain how they pick Fab Four synch deals', *Billboard*, 12 September 2009, p. 21.
34. '*Across the Universe*', IMDb.com, available at <http://www.imdb.com/title/tt0445922/> (last accessed 11 August 2016).
35. Donald E. Polkinghorne, *Narrative Knowing and the Human Sciences* (Albany: State University of New York Press, 1988), p. 150.
36. Gold, 'Re-meet the Beatles'.
37. 'AFI awards 2002', American Film Institute, available at <http://http://www.afi.com/afiawards/AFIAwards02.aspx> (last accessed 10 June 2016).
38. Ben Brantley, 'Theater Review. Cub comes of age: a twice-told cosmic tale', *New York Times*, 14 November 1997, available at <http://www.nytimes.com/1997/11/14/movies/theater-review-cub-comes-of-age-a-twice-told-cosmic-tale.html?pagewanted=all> (last accessed 10 June 2016).
39. Ibid.
40. Lawrence Kramer, *Why Classical Music Still Matters* (Berkeley and Los Angeles: University of California Press, 2007), p. 6.
41. Other such examples include the box office flop *Sgt. Pepper's Lonely Hearts Club Band* (1978), in which musicians the BeeGees and Peter Frampton played the eponymous band, and the Beatles' very own animated *Yellow Submarine* (1968) a decade earlier. *Sgt. Pepper*'s plot is situated around the band's attempt to recover their instruments in order to restore peace and morality to their fair town of Heartland. Along the way, the band encounter the evils of greedy managers, rival bands, false gurus and music industry executives, each played by popular musicians and actors of the day including Donald Pleasence, Frankie Howerd, Steve Martin, Alice Cooper and Aerosmith. *Yellow Submarine*, though an authorised

Apple Corps product, did not achieve the box office success or critical acclaim of the Beatles' previous two films, *A Hard Day's Night* (1964) and *Help!* (1965), both directed by Richard Lester, arguably due to its psychedelic animation style and the use of voice actors standing in for the actual Beatles. The Beatles do appear in a brief live action token cameo. The film has since gone on to attract child audiences with its remastered release on DVD in 1999.

42. MacDonald, *Revolution in the Head*, p. 181.
43. Dyer, *Only Entertainment*.
44. MacDonald, *Revolution in the Head*, pp. 343–4.
45. Roger Ebert, 'Across *the Universe* Movie Review', RogerEbert.com, 13 September 2007, available at <http://www.rogerebert.com/reviews/across-the-universe-2007> (last accessed 10 June 2016).
46. MacDonald, *Revolution in the Head*, p. 216.
47. *Across the Universe*, director's commentary track, 1:22:06.
48. Ibid. 1:22:19.
49. Ibid. 1:14:30.
50. Barry Keith Grant, 'The classic Hollywood musical and the "problem" of rock 'n' roll', *Journal of Popular Film and Television*, 1986, 13(4): 195–205.
51. Donnelly, *Magical Musical Tour*, p. 8.
52. *Across the Universe*, director's commentary track, 1:12:00.
53. Dyer, *Only Entertainment*, p. 20.
54. Ibid. p. 21.

BIBLIOGRAPHY

Across the Universe, film, directed by Julie Taymor, 2007. London: Sony Home Pictures Entertainment, 2008. DVD.
'All about the music' featurette, *Across the Universe*, film, directed by Julie Taymor, 2007. London: Sony Home Pictures Entertainment, 2008. DVD.
Altman, Rick, *The American Film Musical* (London: British Film Institute, 1989).
Altman, Rick (ed.), *Genre: The Musical* (London: Routledge and Kegan Paul in association with the British Film Institute, 1981).
American Film Institute, 'AFI Awards 2002', <http://www.afi.com/afiawards/AFIAwards02.aspx> (last accessed 10 June 2016).
Brantley, Ben, 'Theater Review. Cub comes of age: a twice-told cosmic tale', *New York Times*, 14 November 1997, <http://www.nytimes.com/1997/11/14/movies/theater-review-cub-comes-of-age-a-twice-told-cosmic-tale.html?pagewanted=all> (last accessed 10 June 2016).
Bruner, Jerome S., *Acts of Meaning* (Cambridge, MA: Harvard University Press, 1990).
Collins, James M., 'The musical', in Wes D. Gehring (ed.), *Handbook of American Film Genres* (Westport: Greenwood Press, 1988), pp. 269–84.
Chapman, James, *Cinemas of the World: Film and Society from 1895 to the Present* (London: Reaktion Books, 2004), <https://books.google.co.uk/books?id=SMYo4Abel2EC&lpg=PT189&dq=1950s%20integrated%20musicals&pg=PT189#v=onepage&q=1950s%20integrated%20musicals&f=false> (last accessed 23 August 2016).
Christman, Ed, 'Commercial potential: Sony/ATV execs explain how they pick Fab Four synch deals', *Billboard*, 12 September 2009, p. 21.
'Creating the universe' featurette, *Across the Universe*, film, directed by Julie Taymor, 2007. London: Sony Home Pictures Entertainment, 2008. DVD.
Donnelly, K. J., *Magical Musical Tour: Rock and Pop in Film Soundtracks* (New York: Bloomsbury Academic, 2015).
Dyer, Richard, *Only Entertainment*, 2nd edn (London: Routledge, 2002).

Ebert, Roger, 'Across the Universe movie review', RogerEbert.com, 13 September 2007, <http://www.rogerebert.com/reviews/across-the-universe-2007> (last accessed 10 June 2016).

Everett, Walter, The Beatles as Musicians: Revolver through the Anthology (New York: Oxford University Press, 1999).

Everett, Walter, The Beatles as Musicians: The Quarry Men through Rubber Soul (New York: Oxford University Press, 2001).

Fisher, Jeffrey P., Soundtrack Success: A Digital Storyteller's Guide to Audio Post-Production (Boston, MA: Course Technology Cengage Learning, 2012).

Frontani, Michael, The Beatles: Image and the Media (Jackson, MS: University of Mississippi Press, 2007).

Gold, Sylviane, 'Re-meet the Beatles through the voices of a new narrative', New York Times, 9 September 2007, <http://www.nytimes.com/2007/09/09/movies/moviesspecial/09Gold.html?_r=1> (last accessed 12 May 2016).

Goldmark, Daniel, Lawrence Kramer and Richard Leppert (eds), Beyond the Soundtrack: Representing Music in Cinema (Ann Arbor, MI: University of Michigan Press, 2007).

Grant, Barry Keith, 'The classic Hollywood musical and the "problem" of rock 'n' roll', Journal of Popular Film and Television, 1986, 13(4): 195–205.

Holden, Stephen, 'Lovers in the '60s take a Magical Mystery Tour', New York Times, 14 September 2007, <http://www.nytimes.com/2007/09/14/movies/14univ.html?pagewanted=all&_r=0> (last accessed 8 December 2014).

IMDb.com, 'Across the Universe', <http://www.imdb.com/title/tt0445922/> (last accessed 11 August 2016).

Inglis, Ian (ed.), The Beatles, Popular Music, and Society (Basingstoke: Macmillian Press, 2000).

Itzkoff, Dave and Sisario, Ben, 'How "Mad Men" landed the Beatles: all you need is love (and $250,000)', New York Times, 7 May 2012 <http://artsbeat.blogs.nytimes.com/2012/05/07/how-mad-men-landed-the-beatles-all-you-need-is-love-and-250000/> (last accessed 13 August 2016).

Kramer, Lawrence, Why Classical Music Still Matters (Berkeley and Los Angeles: University of California Press, 2007).

MacDonald, Ian, Revolution in the Head, 2nd edn (London: Pimlico, 2005).

Mundy, John, Popular Music on Screen: From Hollywood Musical to Music Video (Manchester: Manchester University Press, 1999).

Neale, Steve, Genre and Hollywood (London: Routledge, 2001).

Neaverson, Bob, The Beatles Movies (London: Cassell, 1997).

Nolfi, Joey, 'Julie Taymor: studio wanted to cut minorities from Across the Universe to make it like High School Musical', Entertainment Weekly, 21 April 2016, <http://www.ew.com/article/2016/04/21/julie-taymor-jodie-foster-tribeca-talk> (last accessed 30 April 2016).

Polkinghorne, Donald E., Narrative Knowing and the Human Sciences (Albany: State University of New York Press, 1988).

Romney, Jonathan and Adrian Wootton (eds), Celluloid Jukebox: Popular Music and the Movies Since the 50s (London: British Film Institute, 1995).

Thompson, Anne, 'Julie Taymor flies Across the Universe', Variety, 6 September 2007, <http://variety.com/2007/film/columns/julie-taymor-flies-across-the-universe-1117971531/> (last accessed 12 May 2016).

Womack, Kenneth, '"Nothing's going to change my world": narrating memory and selfhood with the Beatles', Style, 2010, 44(1/2): 261–88.

Womack, Kenneth, 'Reconsidering performative autobiography: life-writing and the Beatles', Life Writing, 2005, 2(2): 47–70.

6 'LOVE IS AN OPEN DOOR': REVISING AND REPEATING DISNEY'S MUSICAL TROPES IN *FROZEN*

Ryan Bunch

When it comes to the animated film musical, the Disney formula dominates like no other. Although there are some notable alternatives, such as the films of Don Bluth, it is the Disney canon that overwhelmingly defines this subgenre of film musical, its conventions and its themes.[1] Disney animated features have always included songs, but since the so-called Disney Renaissance of the late 1980s and 1990s, Disney's animated features have both modelled their songs and forms on the contemporary Broadway musical and influenced it in turn. The tropes and conventions deployed in these influential animated musicals are recognisable to audiences and deliberately referenced in each new film.

Frozen (Chris Buck and Jennifer Lee, 2013) has been widely acknowledged for devising a departure from, or variation on, Disney's animated musical tropes – specifically those associated with the Disney Princess franchise, which are faulted (fairly or not) for portraying inactive princesses who find their heart's desire through marriage to a prince. In the common view, *Frozen* commits an inversion of gendered tropes by emphasising a relationship between sisters rather than a heterosexual couple, producing, for many, a more feminist Disney princess musical.[2]

For several months after the movie was released in late 2013, a flood of articles appeared on the Internet and in the popular press debating critical questions surrounding *Frozen,* including whether or not *Frozen* was a feminist or conceivably queer film.[3] These commentaries produced an invigorating debate but often emphasised certain aspects of the film over others – in many cases privileging narrative over musical affect or, in others, showing a preoccupation with the physical appearance of the animated characters. One commentator complained of female characters' eyes being unrealistically bigger than their wrists, while another protested that a film genre with a talking snowman need not be held to such standards of realism.[4] This latter position might be reactionary, but it is a reminder that an animated film musical does have its own genre conventions, which should be taken into account.

It might be more productive, therefore, to see *Frozen* as fitting into a tradition of Disney films in which recognisable tropes are communicated through complex interactions of music and animation, along with narrative. These tropes, repeated and revised from one film to the next, come from the fairy tale, the musical and the established practices of Disney films themselves. My hope is that directing our attention to these tropes can contribute some nuance to discussions of *Frozen*'s gender politics. Where *Frozen* either replicates or revises these existing patterns, it brings their contradictions and complexities to the surface.

Among the tropes employed in *Frozen* and other animated Disney musicals, those with roots in the fairy tale tradition are perhaps most fundamental. Fairy tale and musical theatre conventions have been central to the Disney cinematic canon, starting with Disney's first animated feature, *Snow White and the Seven Dwarfs* (David Hand, 1937). Prominent among these is the fairy tale romance, which Disney critics blame for regressive gender politics in the films. The trope of heterosexual coupling or marriage is also pervasive in the musical genre as described by scholars such as Rick Altman and Raymond Knapp.[5] For Altman, film musicals follow a dual-focus narrative in which thematic binaries are reconciled by the romantic pairing of the musical's male and female leads in an alternative to traditional linear narrative. This dual focus involves pairs of scenes or songs in a musical that characterise the male and female leads as opposites to be reconciled by the end of the film. Knapp further identifies the reconciling of different values represented by the leading couple in this type of narrative – for example, Maria's spontaneity and the Captain's severity in *The Sound of Music* (Richard Rogers and Oscar Hammerstein II, 1959) – by what he terms the marriage trope.[6] The fulfilment of this trope at the end of a musical in literal or symbolic marriage may lead to a healing of the community, whether a family (as in *The Sound of Music*), town or nation, as, for example, when the marriage of Laurie and Curlie in *Oklahoma!* (Richard Rogers and Oscar Hammerstein II, 1943) coincides with the extermination of the outside threat, Judd Frye, and the entry of Oklahoma as a US state. A similar trope in fairy tales and myths involves the healing of the land and breaking of a spell with the conclusion of a quest.[7] Examples of the restoration of society accompanied by a royal union in the Disney canon include the waking of the kingdom after Prince Philip rescues Aurora in *Sleeping Beauty* (Clyde Geronimi, 1959), the restoration of Ursula's imprisoned mer-folk after Prince

Eric impales her in *The Little Mermaid* (Ron Clements and John Musker, 1989), and the disenchantment of the palace staff when the Beast-Prince earns Belle's love in *Beauty and the Beast* (Gary Trousdale and Kirk Wise, 1991). All of this is to say nothing of the fact that the kingdom gets a future queen and assurance of the royal lineage out of these unions.

These heterosexual marriage plots and their power to restore social order can easily be seen as upholding existing ideologies – and here we might think of how 'Disneyfication', with its mostly cautious corporate agenda, meshes with what Jane Feuer views as the film musical's culturally conservative tendencies.[8] It might be said that, in musicals of recent times, these conservative and heteronormative representations have shared the stage with more progressive narratives in musicals explicitly treating themes of queerness and homosexuality or in more ostensibly feminist musicals. Nonetheless, the basic structures of musicals tend to privilege the heterosexual marriage or romance plot, and since Disney has not yet ventured to produce any films with openly queer characters, the format remains the traditional one, with any queer readability relegated to subtext. The prominence of marriage plots in the Disney fairy tale musical provides the basis for *Frozen*'s attempt to reinvent the genre by replacing the romantic couple with two sisters. As we will see, Anna's relationship with Elsa, rather than with either of her male love interests, is easily readable as the 'couple' relationship for purposes of the dual-focus narrative in *Frozen*.[9]

The more immediate influences on *Frozen*'s tropes come from the films of the Disney Renaissance, a period of resurgence in Disney animation beginning with 1989's *The Little Mermaid*. The most common type of story told by these films is of young people longing to escape from undesirable circumstances. Ariel wants to leave her undersea world to explore the human world above, Belle wants adventure far from her provincial town, Aladdin wishes to escape a life of poverty, Pocahontas an arranged marriage, Quasimodo the isolation of the cathedral, and Mulan the gender roles of a traditional society into which she does not seem to fit. To express their aspirations, these young people turn to the most liberating convention of the musical – they burst into song. As Jennifer Fleeger notes, in contrast to the vague dreams of love and happiness expressed by the more passive early Disney princesses of *Snow White, Cinderella* (Clyde Geronimi, Wilfred Jackson, Hamilton Luske, 1950) and *Sleeping Beauty,* princesses of the Disney Renaissance sing about exactly what they want (usually not initially a prince), in the specific terms of the modern musical theatre 'I Want' song.[10] These songs express the protagonists' central motivating desires, and are a specialty of young women throughout the repertoires of both musicals and Disney films. In these moments of empowering excess, the characters sometimes seem to float or fly in their animated environments as though the desire to escape the narrative limitations imposed on them makes them want to defy the boundaries of the body itself. Ariel floats upward in her underwater grotto as she dreams of life on the land, Pocahontas floats off the ground on the 'Colors of the Wind,' and Quasimodo swings from the spires of Notre Dame Cathedral.

These animated musical numbers rely on the ability of animation to represent plasticity in the bodies of their characters, a quality Sergei Eisenstein described as *plasmatic*, and which he saw as disrupting realist narrative and ideology.[11] Plasmatic characters are most radically in evidence in the early cartoon shorts of Disney, but even in the relatively realist feature films, plasmatic moments and characters still occur, and may be significant when they do. The achievement of the special register of song for which musicals strive is a challenge in animation, because, as Daniel Goldmark notes, animation is already in a special register.[12] In recent Disney film musicals this shift into a higher register of feeling is achieved through a combination of selectively plasmatic animation and the expressive style of contemporary belted Broadway singing.

Music and animation are thus both capable of breaking the narratives of musical films, and one way to assess Disney's animated musicals is to see the liberating *jouissance* of music and animation in competition with linear, patriarchal narratives. For Stacy Wolf, songs in musicals give young women access to affective powers in spite of narratives in which their agency may be suppressed.[13] For Elizabeth Bell, on the other hand, the affects of animation and music are insufficient to overcome what she sees as the dominating narratives.[14] In *The Little Mermaid* and *Beauty and the Beast*, the protagonists' desires for freedom and adventure, strongly expressed in song at the beginning of the movie, are narratively diverted into heteronormative romance by the end of the film. Ariel's general fascination with humans is eventually overshadowed by her more particular infatuation with Prince Eric. This change in the object of her desire is musicalised in the change from 'Part of That World,' to 'Part of *Your* World' in the song's reprise, sung after she rescues Eric from a shipwreck.

This binary choice between momentary affect and crushing narrative is not the only one we have, however. More nuanced analyses taking careful account of both music and technologies of animation have been offered by Susan Smith and Jennifer Fleeger, among others.[15] Referencing Altman, Fleeger notes that the dual-focus narratives in Disney film musicals are not strictly between the princesses and their princes, who are often rather vaguely sketched, but more often between the young women and their oppressive environments.[16] For example, Ariel and Belle long to escape the sea and the village respectively, and their 'I Want' songs are in a duality with songs that reveal the dangers of those spaces – Ursula's collection of 'Unfortunate Souls' and the provincial scapegoating of the villagers' 'Mob Song'. Even Altman's theory, though based in binary distinctions of gender, gives the female protagonist rather equal time and attention with the male lead. This together with the fact that women tend to be the focal point, vocally, in musicals give them a great deal of significance. No single aspect of a film, then – narrative, music, or animation – is reducible to a single agenda.

By taking a more multifaceted approach to Disney's animated musicals, we might discover that in any Disney film there is already a range of possibilities arising from the complex interplay of words and music, animated plasticity and realism, narrative and affect. I would like to keep these operations in mind in exploring the gendered dynamics of *Frozen* by paying attention to the ways in which all of these elements repeat and revise the existing tropes.

The first few scenes and songs in *Frozen* signal the use of familiar musical and narrative tropes while also introducing variations on them. The film begins with 'Frozen Heart', a standard opening song of a type common in musicals and Disney films. These songs, much like overtures, set the tone and often express a theme of the film. A classic example is 'When You Wish Upon a Star', sung by Jiminy Cricket over the opening credits of *Pinocchio* (Hamilton Luske and Ben Sharpsteen, 1940). Closer in style to 'Frozen Heart' is 'Fathoms Below', which opens *The Little Mermaid*. Like this song, which is a sea shanty, 'Frozen Heart' is a faux folk song with a melody that slides between the melodic and harmonic versions of the minor scale, vaguely evoking a stereotype of European folk music opposed to the major key sonorities associated with either the refined tradition of classical music or the mainstream of commercial popular music. Sung by icemen as they work, it foreshadows the story of Anna and Elsa's frosty relationship:

> Born of cold and winter air
> And mountain rain combining
> This icy force both foul and fair
> Has a frozen heart worth mining
>
> Cut through the heart, cold and clear
> Strike for love and strike for fear
> There's beauty and there's danger here
> Split the ice apart
> Beware the frozen heart

'Frozen Heart' signals that this will be a film in which we can expect to encounter some established Disney musical tropes, and following this musical opening, a number of familiar narrative tropes are presented. Elsa, the princess and soon-to-be-queen of Arendelle, has magical freezing powers that accidentally harm her sister Anna during their childhood play. In order to keep this dangerous power a secret, both sisters are confined to the palace and denied contact with each other or the outside world. This trope of a princess imprisoned is a standard of fairy tales, one strengthened in the contemporary imagination by Disney's habitual choice of stories that include princesses not allowed to leave the house or its environs, among them, *Cinderella* (1950), *Sleeping Beauty* (1959), *Beauty and the Beast* (1991), *The Little Mermaid* and *Tangled* (Nathan Greno and Byron Howard, 2010), based on the story of Rapunzel. Doors and windows symbolise the separation between the sisters, their condition of being shut in, and Elsa's inability to love because of her fear that she will hurt someone, especially Anna. Like their predecessors, Elsa and Anna are trapped, but the themes of restraint and freedom are more complicated because of the two sisters' character arcs – Anna is open and ready to meet the world while Elsa seeks security in confinement and isolation.

The next two songs show Anna and Elsa to be differently embodied in animation and music, with Anna given sung material from the tradition of 'I Want' songs and love duets for which Disney princesses are known and having the more plasmatic physical constitution, while Elsa is more bodily contained and given a more constrained range of vocal expression. 'Do You Want to Build a Snowman?' establishes the relationship between Anna and Elsa during the period of their separation, collapsing time to show them growing up and depicting the death of their parents. Over the course of several verses, each at a different stage of growth for the girls from childhood to adolescence, Anna tries to convince Elsa to come out and play. During this sequence, Anna is bursting with physical excess and plasmatic animation, running and sliding across the floor to knock on Elsa's door. Elsa repeatedly tells her to go away. Although 'For the First Time in Forever' might seem a more obvious choice as *Frozen*'s major 'I Want' song, 'Do You Want to Build a Snowman' establishes for the audience Anna's deepest desire, to be close to her sister:

> Please, I know you're in there
> People are asking where you've been
> They say 'have courage', and I'm trying to
> I'm right out here for you, just let me in
> We only have each other
> It's just you and me
> What are we gonna do?
>
> Do you want to build a snowman?

There is no response from Elsa to this final plea. The unanswered question and Anna's unfulfilled desire are underscored by the accompaniment, which ends the song on the subdominant harmony of an incomplete cadence.

'For the First Time in Forever' continues this delineation of the two characters as high-spirited princess and cautious queen. On her eighteenth birthday, Elsa is about to have her coronation, and for the first time since Anna's accident, the palace doors will be opened. 'For the First Time in Forever' and its reprise introduce a type of song rare, if not unheard of, in previous Disney films – the fully formed musical scene with characters in different psychological states singing in counterpoint with each other. Anna sings the bulk of the song as a Broadway-style number with a pulsating accompaniment resembling that of 'Don't Rain on My Parade', from *Funny Girl* (Jule Styne and Bob Merrill, 1964), in anticipation of gaining her freedom and finding true love. Anna's physical lightness in this performance signals her kinship to the traditional Disney princess. She displays a good deal of plasmatic quality, sliding down a spiral banister, lingering in mid-air to pose with the paintings on the walls, and indulging again in her signature move, sliding across the floor of the palace, garments fluttering. We also see her doing traditional Disney princess things like talking to animals – she shares her secret romantic longing with the birds, in this case some baby ducks: 'Maybe I'll meet *the* one!' By contrast, Elsa is the picture of agony – staid, earthbound and afraid to move, crossing her gloved hands in front of her tightly fitting frock with its high collar and singing her mantra, 'conceal, don't feel', as she tries not to freeze the orb and sceptre she must hold without gloves at the coronation. She is in both musical and animated counterpoint to Anna.

The song is packed with 'I Want' tropes, linking Anna's desire to escape confinement with her desire for romantic love. As noted, in many earlier Disney films, the heroines sing about their longing for adventure before that desire gets diverted into heteronormative romance. *Frozen* collapses this process into one song. At first, Anna sings about the excitement of the open doors and windows and of generally being around people, but soon she is fantasising about meeting her true love. Because of the way 'For the First Time in Forever' focuses on these two themes, which have been the motivations for such songs in earlier Disney films, it is not surprising that many would, at first viewing, take this for the main 'I Want' song. Indeed, the song is composed to make us think of it as such, setting us up to believe we are watching another formula Disney film so that the filmmakers can pull the rug from under us later, when Anna's desire for romantic love turns out to be less the key to *Frozen* than her desire to be reunited with Elsa. 'For the First Time in Forever' thus combines and compresses the tropes of earlier Disney films while also introducing an ironic inversion in which Elsa seeks security and isolation rather than exposure and contact.

Anna does indeed meet someone as soon as she steps outside the palace. Prince Hans of the Southern Isles is among the foreign dignitaries who have arrived in Arendelle for Elsa's coronation. During the party that follows, he and Anna sing 'Love Is an Open Door', a song that replicates and parodies the cliché, common to fairy tales, musicals and Disney films, of love at first sight, expressed in a song immediately after meeting. However, 'Love Is an Open Door' is different from 'Once Upon a Dream' or 'A Whole New World'. The song is playful, silly ('we finish each other's' – sandwiches!') and superficial – not like a true love duet or ballad. Anna and Hans's comedic and anachronistic robotic movements on the lines 'our mental synchronization can have but one explanation / you and I were just meant to be' serve as a subtle metacommentary in animation on the absurdity of their belief in instant love. While the narrative suggests one thing about the budding romance of Anna and Hans, the musical and animated affect of the song betray a different story, the one that we will see at the end of the film when we learn that Hans is only using Anna to seize the throne. Taken at face value on first viewing, 'Love Is an Open Door' is a superficial and somewhat insincere misdirection of our expectations. The eventual unravelling of the narrative thread allows us on re-watching to see the ruse being played, so the interplay of narrative, visual and song is important in our reception of events on screen.

Anna accepts Hans's offer of marriage at the end of the song, and they immediately express their intentions to Elsa, who, just in case we in the audience have missed it, calls out the absurdity of the cliché: 'You can't marry a man you just met.' This leads to a confrontation in which Elsa, in a moment of passion, loses control of her powers, revealing her secret to the assembled guests. When the scheming Duke of Weselton accuses her of being a sorceress and a monster, she is compelled to flee, freezing the entire kingdom in her wake.

Still frightened by her own power, but alone and unburdened of her secret, Elsa sings the song that most defines her. 'Let It Go' is unusual in the Disney repertoire in its particular hybridisation and revision of existing tropes. As Elsa trudges up the snow-covered North Mountain, 'Let It Go' opens with a minor-key piano introduction. The style is noticeably pop, and unlike Ariel's motive in 'Part of That World', which strives upward like floating bubbles, Elsa's instrumental introduction turns back on itself, swirling around like the magic snowflakes that materialise from her hands. The combination of the pop-influenced piano music and the distant visual at the beginning of the song cause the scene to feel more like a music video than a musical number, as though a pre-existing pop song in the soundtrack has come to the foreground to give us a glimpse into Elsa's interior subjectivity.[17] As the song moves into its major-key chorus, Elsa's 'swirling storm inside' becomes more and more externalised, and she begins to let her power go. She removes her gloves and allows the snow to swirl out of her body, releasing and diffusing her emotional excess into the environment. The words echo this externalisation of pent up power ('Let it go, let it go, can't hold it back anymore'), but paradoxically mix these sentiments with images of slamming doors shut, as Elsa declares, 'I'm never going back' and 'I'm alone and free'. She lets her cape fly on the wind on the words 'The cold never bothered me anyway'. Stomping the ground and singing 'here I am and here I'll stay', Elsa magically creates the ice castle in which she will isolate herself from the community. In a dramatic ending, the camera pulls back to show the castle from a distance, but instead of staying in flight in the open air, we suddenly pull in tight again, and Elsa confidently slams the door on us. The emotional heart of a Disney musical is usually an 'I Want' song, but this one is more 'I Am'. In contrast to the traditional princess, Elsa has chosen her form of freedom by isolating herself and shutting herself in, and the pop style of the music, with its exhilarating groove and motoric rhythm, gives the sequence a feeling of inevitability rather than the expectant yearning of the Broadway-style 'I Want' song.

At this point, it is worth mentioning that Elsa is technically the villain of the movie. In the film's long production history, her character evolved from that of the wicked Snow Queen in Andersen's fairy tale, on which *Frozen* was loosely based. When the songwriters composed 'Let It Go', the song prompted a rewrite of the character.[18] Nonetheless, Elsa contains vestiges of the Disney villainess, admired for her power, independence and agency. Her embodiment and carriage reflect these origins by more closely resembling those of Disney queens and villains than those of Anna and the plasmatic princesses, who float on ocean currents or levitate on the wind.[19] Elsa remains bodily planted during her most liberating song, while her magic swirls about her. Princesses are limited by their environment, but Elsa, like Disney villainesses, can manipulate it. Her pose at the end of 'Let It Go', with arms outstretched, recalls a similar characteristic posture associated with *Sleeping Beauty*'s Maleficent.

In its projection of power and competency, 'Let It Go' is the kind of song usually given to Disney's antagonistic divas like Ursula ('Poor Unfortunate Souls' from *The Little Mermaid*) and Mother Gothel ('Mother Knows Best' from *Tangled*), but with a twist, in that Elsa is a sympathetic character, and the style of the music suits her combination of power and relatability. Fleeger notes that the pop style of singing heard in recent Disney films fits into a twenty-first century musical aesthetic in which prerecording and spectacle are not antithetical to liveness or authenticity.[20] The pop style of 'Let It Go' might therefore be experienced as having more intimacy and honesty than the more musical-theatre derived style it resides alongside in *Frozen*. The song's resemblance to a pop anthem makes Elsa sympathetic and allows fans to take on her empowering embodiment as a heroine rather than a villainess. Indeed, with 'Let It Go', we even have the strong suggestion that Elsa, not Anna, is the most important character in *Frozen*. It is the only powerful solo and the musical centrepiece of the movie, whereas all of Anna's songs are in scenes shared with either Elsa or Hans.

With this amount of focus placed on Elsa, we now might want to reconsider any notions we had of Anna and Hans forming the central couple of the musical. Dispensing with a linear assumption of narrative and instead following Altman's model of the dual-focus narrative, we can look to the songs for clues about the central relationship. If we trust what the songs are telling us, 'Do You Want to Build a Snowman' and 'For the First Time in Forever' have signalled from the beginning that Elsa and Anna are the important characters, and their dualistic characterisations only strengthen this view according to the conventions of the musical. The next song, 'Love Is an Open Door', seems to point in a different direction, suggesting a relationship between Anna and Hans, but if we have already seen the movie, we know that Hans is really a distraction. If we instead think of 'Love Is an Open Door' as Anna's song (since Hans's part in it is insincere) and pair it in juxtaposition to the next song, 'Let It Go', we can see again the duality of the sisters' characters, showing Anna in one song to be open, trusting, and naive, and Elsa in the other happily isolated and closed off from the world.

This emphasis on Anna and Elsa as the central 'couple' in the film is further confirmed by the trivial nature of the songs given to the remaining male characters. When Anna sets off to find Elsa, along the way she meets three male companions – the iceman Kristoff, who guides her up the North Mountain, his reindeer Sven, and the snowman Olaf. Whereas Elsa, with her secret powers and apparent lack of interest in male companionship is easily read as queer, the next few scenes seem designed to deny any gender deviance on the part of Kristoff or Anna. Kristoff first appears as a gruff and burly stranger who is dismissive towards Anna. By convention, we immediately know he is the guy she is really going to wind up with. In a series of battle-of-the-sexes interactions, Anna bargains for his help, overcoming her gendered disadvantage with the class and wealth privilege that enables her to buy the supplies Kristoff needs. In delivering these, she interrupts Kristoff's 'duet' with Sven, 'Reindeers Are Better Than People'. This brief comic charm song, in which Kristoff sings the mute Reindeer's part in a character voice, is Kristoff's only number, as though to sing in earnest would compromise his brand of masculinity. His homosocial bond with Sven, expressed in this song, is undercut by its humour and triangulated by Anna's intrusion as a possible love interest. Throughout this section of the film, Anna and Kristoff carry on in gender-stereotyped roles, as Kristoff displays the kind of overprotection towards his sled that a young man might show for an automobile. Meanwhile, Anna babbles, expresses emotion, and feigns independence with comic results as Kristoff shows his know-how. Olaf provides some comic relief by disrupting these heteronormative goings-on. When he pinches Sven's cheeks and calls him 'my cute little reindeer', Kristoff snaps, 'Don't talk to him like that'. He seems offended by this show of affection between Olaf and Sven, but Olaf has also touched a nerve regarding Kristoff's own attachment to Sven. Later, the trolls sing of Kristoff's 'thing with the reindeer/that's a little outside of nature's laws'. Olaf's own song,

'In Summer', is another comic charm song, evocative of any classic soft-shoe number such as 'Singin' in the Rain' or Lumiere's introduction to 'Be Our Guest', rendering Olaf's rather queer personality harmless through humour and infantile innocence. That the male characters get such throwaway songs gives further emphasis to the two sisters, and notably, Anna and Kristoff never sing together.

Anna and Elsa, however, have another duet, and it is a strong musical expression of their predicament. On arrival at Elsa's ice palace, Anna, while trying to convince her sister not to shut her out again, transitions from speech into song for a reprise of 'For the First Time in Forever'. This reprise is especially striking in its overt, stagey theatricality and is the best evidence yet that *Frozen* has been written with a Broadway production already in mind. Here, Anna and Elsa are in direct conversation (before, their counterpoint was not addressed to each other). Again singing in counterpoint to Anna, Elsa learns that she has frozen all of Arendelle and because of her fearful emotions is unable to reverse the spell. Realising that she has not learned to control her power, she is overcome with fear and accidentally strikes Anna again, this time freezing her heart. Elsa creates a monstrous snowman to throw Anna and her friends out before more harm is done.

Anna's condition is serious, and her heart will completely freeze if something is not done in time. Kristoff takes her to consult with his adoptive family of trolls, whom he describes as 'love experts'. The trolls, who can see where things are going between the two of them, sing 'Fixer Upper', which is no mere diversion or conditional love song – it also contains the key to all of Anna's, Elsa's and Arendelle's problems, extolling love of family as much as love of significant other.

> Everyone's a bit of a fixer upper
> That's what it's all about
> Father, sister, brother
> We need each other
> To raise us up and round us out

'Fixer Upper' encapsulates the theme of family love – compressing the film's shift of focus from romance to family into one song. At the end of the song, Anna takes a turn for the worse, and Grand Pabbie troll declares that only an 'act of true' love can cure her frozen heart and save her from death. Everyone assumes this means a kiss of true love from Hans.

At this point, the film does what many film musicals, even Disney ones, often do – it stops being a musical and resolves its remaining issues, including the overturning of the expected conventions, through narrative action. Anna races back to the castle to be kissed by Hans, and here is where the tables are turned. Hans turns out to be the true villain, revealing that he does not love Anna and plans to have Elsa executed so he can take the throne. It then seems that Kristoff will be Anna's true love, but before she can kiss him, she sees Hans about to kill Elsa, so she intervenes to save her sister, just as her frozen heart spreads and she turns into solid ice. There is silence as plasmatic Anna has now become the frozen one. This is Elsa's worst fear come true, but it turns out that Anna has just committed an act of true love for her sister. The spell is broken and Anna comes back to life. Elsa now realises that love is the solution and is able to thaw the kingdom, bringing about a healing of the land, which takes place not in a standard musical number, but to the purely affective choral singing of Frode Fjellheim's 'Vuelie'. This is the completion of the dual focus narrative, with the two sisters resolving their differences and restoring the kingdom.

Meanwhile, the false marriage trope between Anna and Hans has been subverted, but importantly, the true romance between Anna and Kristoff remains. They kiss at the end of the film – and in Disney terms is this not essentially a consummating act signalling an inevitable marriage? Even a revision of the traditional marriage trope still requires its repetition, which reinforces its potency by its mere presence. Earlier Disney princesses seek adventure but find romance. Anna seeks romance, but finds adventure, but then also finds romance again. In the end, the narrative does not simply reverse or negate the traditional romance, but offers it as one relationship among many that matter.

In the end, *Frozen* both upholds and provides an alternative to the conventional fairy tale narrative. The songs, interestingly, help to set up both possibilities, but do not participate in their resolutions – neither Anna and Elsa nor Anna and Kristoff sing in musical expression of their relationship at the end. Nor does *Frozen* so much eliminate patriarchal narratives as add alternative voices by doubling down with its two heroines on what has always been the affective heart of the Disney princess musical – feminine vocal energy and power. Elsa in her ambivalence and Anna in her selflessness do in some measure rewrite older stereotypes of the Disney princess, and both are available as role models. Although free-spirited Anna is meant to appeal to modern girls, sales of merchandise and other evidence suggest that Elsa is more popular – after all, she is the one with magic powers and the best song. Indeed, there was a crisis of supply and demand in 2014 when Disney sold out of Elsa dresses.[21] As Sean Griffin suggests, audiences are capable of making their own meanings and uses of Disney films, revising the intended or dominant readings of them.[22] The many elements that go into an animated musical contribute to an open text that, because of its own complexities, imperfections, and contradictions, is big enough to accommodate our own. Like the open doors symbolising personal connection in *Frozen*, the musical provides a space for active participation, debate and negotiation with its critically engaged audiences.

NOTES

1. Examples of Don Bluth's musical films include *An American Tail* (1986) and *Anastasia* (1997).
2. Michael Macaluso, 'The postfeminist princess: public discourse and Disney's curricular guide to feminism', in Jennifer A. Sandlin and Julie C. Garlen (eds), *Disney, Culture and Curriculum* (New York and London: Routledge, 2016), Kindle edition.
3. For examples, see Macaluso as well as Dani Colman, 'The problem with false feminism (or why "Frozen" left me cold)', *Medium*, 1 February 2014, available at <https://medium.com/disney-and-animation/the-problem-with-false-feminism-7c0bbc7252ef> (last accessed 20 May 2015); Melissa Leon, 'Disney's sublimely subversive *Frozen* isn't your typical princess movie', *The Daily Beast*, 29 November 2013, available at <http://www.thedailybeast.com/articles/2013/11/29/disney-s-sublimely-subversive-frozen-isn-t-your-stereotypical-princess-movie.html> (last accessed 6 January 2017); and R. Kurt Osenlund, 'Frozen', *Slant*, 13 November 2003, available at <http://www.slantmagazine.com/film/review/frozen-2013> (last accessed 6 January 2017).
4. Philip N. Cohen, '"Help, my eyeball is bigger than my wrist!": gender dimorphism in Frozen', *Huffington Post*, 18 December 2013, available at <http://www.huffingtonpost.com/philip-n-cohen/gender-dimorphism-frozen_b_4467178.html> (last accessed 6 January 2017); Kara Wahlgren, 'For the love of Olaf, can we stop dissecting Frozen?', *Huffington Post*, 4 March 2014, available at <http://www.huffingtonpost.com/kara-wahlgren/for-the-love-of-olaf-can-we-stop-dissecting-frozen_b_4893806.html> (last accessed 6 January 2017).
5. Rick Altman, *The American Film Musical* (Bloomington: Indiana University Press, 1987), pp. 16–58; Raymond Knapp, *The American Musical and the Formation of National Identity* (Princeton, NJ: Princeton University Press, 2005), p. 9. As discussed by Jennifer Fleeger, *Mismatched Women: The Siren's Song Through the Machine* (New York: Oxford University Press, 2014), p. 107, the Disney Princess franchise is part of a marketing strategy, largely aimed at girls, that extends beyond the films to other merchandise.
6. Knapp, *The American Musical*, p. 9.
7. In his discussion of the subgenre of the fairy tale musical, Altman, *The American Film Musical*, p. 149, puts special emphasis on the marriage trope and the welfare of the kingdom.
8. Jane Feuer, *The Hollywood Musical*, 2nd edn (Bloomington: Indiana University Press, 1993), p. x.
9. This same-sex narrative coupling is also evident in the Broadway musical *Wicked* (2003), as noted by Stacy Wolf, *Changed for Good: A Feminist History of the Broadway Musical* (Oxford and New York: Oxford University Press, 2011), pp. 197–218.
10. Fleeger, *Mismatched Women*, p. 120.
11. On Eisenstein, plasmaticness, and the animated musical see Susan Smith, 'The animated musical', in Raymond Knapp, Mitchell Morris and Stacy Wolf (eds), *The Oxford Handbook of the American Musical* (New York: Oxford University Press, 2011), pp 170–3.
12. Daniel Goldmark, *Tunes for 'Toons: Music and the Hollywood Cartoon* (Berkeley: University of California Press, 2005), p. 93.
13. Wolf, *Changed for Good*, pp. 6–7, 12.
14. Elizabeth Bell, 'Somatexts at the Disney shop: constructing the pentimentos of women's animated bodies', in Elizabeth Bell, Lynda Haas and Laura Sells (eds),

From Mouse to Mermaid: The Politics of Film, Gender, and Culture (Bloomington and Indianapolis: Indiana University Press, 1995), p. 114.

15. Smith, 'The animated musical', pp. 167–78; Fleeger, *Mismatched Women*, pp. 106–36.

16. Fleeger, *Mismatched Women*, pp. 120–1.

17. Robin Stilwell, 'The fantastical gap between diegetic and nondiegetic', in Daniel Goldmark, Lawrence Kramer and Richard Leppert (eds), *Beyond the Soundtrack: Representing Music in Cinema* (Berkeley: University of California Press, 2007), pp. 190–7.

18. Kristen Anderson-Lopez and Robert Lopez, 'Songwriters behind *Frozen* let go of the princess mythology', transcript of interview by Terry Gross, *NPR Music*, 10 April 2014, available at <http://www.npr.org/templates/transcript/transcript. php?storyId=301420227> (last accessed 6 January 2017).

19. See Bell, 'Somatexts at the Disney shop', pp. 107–20, on the three feminine archetypes in Disney fairy tales: dancing girls, *femmes fatales* and grandmothers. Sean Griffin, *Tinker Belles and Evil Queens: The Walt Disney Company from the Inside Out* (New York: New York University Press, 2000), pp. 67–77, 141–2, 146–7, 211–13, discusses both princesses and villains in the performance of gender.

20. Fleeger, *Mismatched Women*, pp. 129, 133.

21. Lisa Liddane, 'Most-wanted dress in the U.S.: "Frozen's" Elsa frock', *The Orange County Register*, 11 April 2014, available at <http://www.ocregister.com/articles/costume-609376-costumes-stores.html> (last accessed 10 January 2017); Ellen Byron and Paul Ziobro, 'Elsa dominates Anna in *Frozen* merchandise sales', *Wall Street Journal*, 4 November 2014, <http://www.wsj.com/articles/elsa-dominates-anna-in-frozen-merchandise-sales-1415131605> (last accessed 10 January 2017).

22. Griffin, *Tinker Belles and Evil Queens*, pp. 48–89.

Bibliography

Altman, Rick, *The American Film Musical* (Bloomington: Indiana University Press, 1987).

Anderson-Lopez, Kristen and Robert Lopez, 'Songwriters behind *Frozen* let go of the princess mythology', transcript of interview by Terry Gross, *NPR Music*, 10 April 2014, <http://www.npr.org/templates/transcript/transcript.php?storyId=301420227> (last accessed 6 January 2017).

Bell, Elizabeth, 'Somatexts at the Disney shop: constructing the pentimentos of women's animated bodies', in Elizabeth Bell, Lynda Haas and Laura Sells (eds), *From Mouse to Mermaid: The Politics of Film, Gender, and Culture*, (Bloomington and Indianapolis: Indiana University Press, 1995), pp. 107–24.

Byron, Ellen and Paul Ziobro, 'Elsa dominates Anna in *Frozen* merchandise sales', *Wall Street Journal*, 4 November 2014, <http://www.wsj.com/articles/elsa-dominates-anna-in-frozen-merchandise-sales-1415131605> (last accessed 10 January 2017).

Cohen, Philip N., '"Help, my eyeball is bigger than my wrist!": gender dimorphism in *Frozen*', *Huffington Post*, 18 December 2013, <http://www.huffingtonpost.com/philip-n-cohen/gender-dimorphism-frozen_b_4467178.html> (last accessed 6 January 2017).

Colman, Dani, 'The problem with false feminism (or why "Frozen" left me cold)', *Medium*, <https://medium.com/disney-and-animation/the-problem-with-false-feminism-7c0bbc7252ef> (last accessed 20 May 2015).

Feuer, Jane, *The Hollywood Musical*, 2nd edn (Bloomington: Indiana University Press, 1993).

Fleeger, Jennifer, *Mismatched Women: The Siren's Song Through the Machine* (Oxford and New York: Oxford University Press, 2014).

Goldmark, Daniel, *Tunes for 'Toons: Music and the Hollywood Cartoon* (Berkeley: University of California Press, 2005).

Knapp, Raymond, *The American Musical and the Formation of National Identity* (Princeton, NJ: Princeton University Press, 2005).

Leon, Melissa, 'Disney's sublimely subversive *Frozen* isn't your typical princess movie', *Daily Beast*, 29 November 2013, <http://www.thedailybeast.com/arti cles/2013/11/29/disney-s-sublimely-subversive-frozen-isn-t-your-stereotypical-prince ss-movie.html> (last accessed 6 January 2017).

Liddane, Lisa, 'Most-wanted dress in the U.S.: "Frozen's" Elsa frock', *The Orange County Register*, 11 April 2014, <http://www.ocregister.com/articles/costume-609376-costumes-stores.html> (last accessed 10 January 2017).

Macaluso, Michael, 'The postfeminist princess: public discourse and Disney's cur-ricular guide to feminism', in Jennifer A. Sandlin and Julie C. Garlen (eds), *Disney, Culture and Curriculum* (New York and London: Routledge, 2016). Kindle edition.

Osenlund, R. Kurt, 'Frozen', *Slant*, 13 November 2003, <http://www.slantmagazine. com/film/review/frozen-2013> (last accessed 6 January 2017).

Sells, Laura, 'Where do the mermaids stand? Voice and body in *The Little Mermaid*', in Elizabeth Bell, Lynda Haas and Laura Sells (eds), *From Mouse to Mermaid: The Politics of Film, Gender, and Culture* (Bloomington and Indianapolis: Indiana University Press, 1995), pp. 175–92.

Smith, Susan, 'The animated film musical', in Raymond Knapp, Mitchell Morris and Stacy Wolf (eds), *The Oxford Handbook of the American Musical* (Oxford and New York: Oxford University Press, 2011).

Stilwell, Robynn, 'The fantastical gap between diegetic and nondiegetic', in Daniel Goldmark, Lawrence Kramer and Richard Leppert (eds), *Beyond the Soundtrack: Representing Music in Cinema* (Berkeley: University of California Press, 2007).

Wahlgren, Kara, 'For the love of Olaf, can we stop dissecting Frozen?', *Huffington Post*, 4 March 2014 <http://www.huffingtonpost.com/kara-wahlgren/for-the-love-of-olaf-can-we-stop-dissecting-frozen_b_4893806.html> (last accessed 6 January 2017).

Wolf, Stacy, *Changed for Good: A Feminist History of the Broadway Musical* (Oxford and New York: Oxford University Press, 2011).

PART TWO

STAGE TO SCREEN

7 STAR QUALITY? SONG, CELEBRITY AND THE JUKEBOX MUSICAL IN *MAMMA MIA!*

Catherine Haworth

Reviews of the 2008 film adaptation of 'jukebox' stage musical *Mamma Mia!* ranged from wild enthusiasm to outright embarrassment, with many critics expressing confusion at the film's unusual mixture of slick professionalism and cheery, improvisatory exuberance.[1] Despite this lack of critical consensus, *Mamma Mia!* was a huge commercial success, performing well in US and European markets and becoming one of the highest-grossing films of all time at the UK box office.[2] The film's success points towards its broad audience demographics, a mainstream appeal that is often partially attributed to the trio of women at its helm: screenwriter Catherine Johnson, producer Judy Craymer and director Phyllida Lloyd.[3] But this particular understanding of authorship and appeal is of course only half the story in a film structured around the music of Swedish superstars ABBA, and with leading roles performed by recognisable A-list stars in a cinematic, and musical, environment that is often far outside their usual context.

The potential for simultaneous pleasure and discomfort engendered by the film's pedigree of musical and personal celebrity is a key way in which *Mamma Mia!* destabilises conventional registers of 'quality'. It embraces ideas of performativity and literal role-play whilst also fostering the appearance of genuine and unfiltered (although sometimes uncomfortable) realism. The film intensifies the musical's oft-noted juxtaposition of artifice and transparency, using the shimmering Europop of ABBA's familiar hits as a backdrop to the 'imperfections' of highly personal vocal performance. Its deliberate aesthetic of enthusiastic amateurism provides a forum in which individualised modes of engagement are actively fostered: musical performance is an axis around which shifting character, star and audience subjectivities can be both constructed and celebrated. This is facilitated by the strength of the genre conventions underpinning the film (and stage) musical – and whilst *Mamma Mia!*'s jukebox format challenges some of these conventions, it also embraces and exploits them.

MONEY, MONEY, MONEY: *MAMMA MIA!* AS JUKEBOX MUSICAL

The jukebox film musical uses pre-existing material for all or most of its numbers – a broad and flexible definition that can encompass anything from revue and variety shows, crossover pop-star vehicles such as *Yellow Submarine* (George Dunning, 1968) and *Spice World* (Bob Spiers, 1997), the film-of-the-album (The Who's *Tommy* [Ken Russell, 1975], *Pink Floyd – The Wall* [Alan Parker, 1982]), through to the biographical story of *Walk The Line* (James Mangold, 2005), and the multiple-artist approaches of *Singin' in the Rain* (Gene Kelly, Stanley Donen, 1952), *Rock of Ages* (Adam Shankman, 2012), and *Moulin Rouge!* (Baz Luhrmann, 2001). Written by Catherine Johnson with input from ABBA's Benny Andersson and Björn Ulvaeus, *Mamma Mia!* combines several of these strategies, working an original, fictional plot and characters around a selection of hits drawn from the output of a single group. Like its later film adaptation, the stage show has been enormously successful, playing in over forty countries and grossing in excess of $2 billion worldwide.[4] This hybrid original-story/familiar-soundtrack approach has provided a template for other successful shows, and jukebox musicals have been an increasingly significant presence in the live theatre market over the past 20 or so years. Hit musicals that follow the *Mamma Mia!* model include *We Will Rock You* (based on the music of Queen), *Jersey Boys* (Frankie Valli and the Four Seasons), and *Our House* (Madness).

Mamma Mia!'s musical formula is simple: it plunders the biggest hits from ABBA's internationally-successful back catalogue, and crams as many of them as possible into its runtime. Whilst there are occasional changes to lyrics, style or structure in order to accommodate or emphasise the storyline (often to remove some of the less palatable gendered stereotypes of ABBA's lyrics), these editorial changes are minor.[5] The emphasis is on recognisability and enjoyment of the familiar, to the point where guessing how various tracks might be (often tenuously) linked into the storyline becomes pleasurable in itself. Almost all of ABBA's most well-known songs are present, and the film's soundtrack closely resembles the content of *Gold*, the band's greatest hits album, originally released in 1992. *Gold* is one of the most successful compilation albums ever, selling over 30 million copies across multiple releases, and credited with bringing ABBA's music to newer, younger listeners – an appeal to both nostalgic and new audiences that prefigures the success of *Mamma Mia!*[6]

The theatrical and screen versions of *Mamma Mia!*, although not identical, are largely similar in their approach to plot, structure, tone and scoring; a synchronicity that might be partially explained by a desire to replicate a successful model, but also by a continuity of personnel (Johnson, Lloyd and Craymer all reprised their stage positions for the film). The film takes place amid the final preparations for the marriage of Sky and Sophie. Sophie's mother, Donna, will host the wedding at her Greek island guesthouse, and her lifelong friends Tanya and Rosie arrive to help. Another trio of faces from Donna's distant past also appear on the island: Sam, Harry and Bill, all invited secretly by Sophie, who has realised that one of them is her father. Unsurprisingly, chaos ensues, with a variety of set pieces and soul-searching leading to an ultimate resolution where Donna and Sam take the place of Sophie and Sky at the altar, and the younger couple agree to live for the moment without tying themselves into marriage.

Mamma Mia! is very much an ensemble vehicle, and one that enjoys various symmetries and points of comparison within its characters. As well as the obvious focus on the mother–daughter relationship suggested by its title, the film also makes much of ideas about past and present, youth and ageing and – as we might expect in a musical – gender differences and their reconciliation via romance. As many have noted, these issues are frequently dealt with in progressive ways (Naomi Graber's characterisation of the film as nostalgically feminist in a postfeminist landscape is a convincing one), but *Mamma Mia!*'s feminism is layered upon a solid foundation of traditional genre structures and attitudes that can be somewhat challenging to unravel.[7] This complexity is heightened by the familiar faces, as well as musical material and genre conventions, that are found throughout the film. Although *Mamma Mia!* was an early major film role for both Amanda Seyfried (Sophie) and Dominic Cooper (Sky), the six adult leads are all played by established stars with long film, stage and television careers. Meryl Streep (Donna), Christine Baranski (Tanya), Julie Walters (Rosie), Pierce Brosnan (Sam) and Colin Firth (Harry) are all instantly recognisable to US and UK cinema audiences, and although a majority of Stellan Skarsgård's (Bill) earlier work was in Swedish-language films, by 2008 he was appearing regularly in mainstream Hollywood productions.[8]

EVERYONE LISTENS WHEN I START TO SING: VOICE, IDENTITY AND STARDOM IN THE MUSICAL

These layers of familiarity raise interesting questions about how *Mamma Mia!*, and the jukebox musical in general, works. Any film is laden with the potential for extra-textual associations, either deliberately invoked or more subjective, but *Mamma Mia!*'s all-star approach to the presentation of such well-known and autonomously circulated musical material pushes these associations to the fore. Literature on performance within the musical most commonly stresses its potential to create the feeling of unfiltered emotional transparency, a heightened articulation of character subjectivity that is attractive within and outside the diegesis. In a move that both embraces the trickery of film production and effaces it, song and dance not only articulate problems but also solve them, show us the supposed reality behind the facade, bring couples and communities together, and showcase familiar, all-singing, all-dancing famous names.[9] That they manage to do this whilst simultaneously showcasing the spectacular is perhaps the key to the special place the musical genre holds, sitting both within and outside the discourses of dominant cinema.

Featuring well-known – but 'non-musical' – stars singing the hits of an internationally famous band challenges ideas about authenticity, specificity and virtuosity in the musical genre; all values that imbue the ideas of transparency, emotional realism and subjectivity outlined above. The jukebox musical is therefore particularly prone to criticism that it has sold out to rampant commercialism, is a money-making exercise rather than a creative one, or, to invoke an idea that simmers under the surface of much discussion of musicals – that it is unabashedly 'entertainment', rather than 'art'. Even with an increasing awareness of and respect for the work of cinematic music supervisors, arrangers and editors, there is still often a perception that the compiled score is somehow second best to an original one – lazy musical wallpaper, rather than a crafted, made-to-measure approach. Despite the potential for feelings of familiarity and connection, 'actors-who-sing' or reality star cast members can be treated with similar suspicion: non-specialists cast because they will make money, or television-friendly faces who can belt it out for a studio audience, but cannot cut it live on stage for eight shows a week. If big stars are shipped in to sing big songs that we already know, how might this square with the idea of the genuine, unfiltered emotional subjectivity of the utopian musical number?

Of course there is a flip side to these issues. The very recognisability of stars and songs in musicals like *Mamma Mia!* has the potential to increase subjective engagement with the act of performance and all that it signifies. As Anahid Kassabian notes, personal recognition, remembrance and association can provide an intensely powerful connection to a text, and the idea that this recognition – in some form or other – might be shared with a majority of the watching audience has the additional potential to invoke a sense of solidarity, where perceivers are drawn together into socially unfamiliar positions.[10] Similarly, the presence of the star-who-sings might also provide additional layers of pleasure and personal authenticity, especially in their moments of musical performance. Their recognisability outside their character adds an extra sense of realism, of on-the-line-ness to their performances that comes from their lack of 'fit' within the musical genre. Stars have of course always been important in the world of the film musical, but they have most commonly been specialists within that genre – all-singing, all-dancing professionals. The non-musical A-list actor who appears in a singing role (regardless of any prior training or experience) takes risks by performing outside their established persona, an idea that might mirror and intensify the emotionality and subjectivity of the musical number itself.

This potential for star-initiated engagement is particularly heightened in the physical and musical act of singing. One of the most important communicators of the musical's transparent emotional appeal is the voice, an instrument that implicates the whole body of the singer in their musicianship. To use Michel Chion's term, our listening practices are 'vococentric', and in the musical's performance-centred world, singing's ability to unite the vocal, the musical, and the physical gives it a particularly special status.[11] Jane Feuer argues that song transfigures speech – it lifts it up into a more expressive realm, one where words have weightier meanings, an intensity of expression in their combination with music that sets it apart from everyday speech, no matter how heartfelt.[12] When we combine singing's special qualities with *Mamma Mia!*'s all-star casting, another route into subjective identification becomes clear: star voices are in themselves recognisable, and the film's transatlantic cast makes sure that is especially the case here, featuring the Birmingham regional accent of Walters, clipped and proper pronunciation of Firth (UK) and Baranski (US), Brosnan's Irish and Skarsgård's Nordic inflections, and the more drawn-out American vowels of Streep.

These vocal accents and personalities are also audible during sung performance: there is a deliberate aesthetic of 'realism' in the recording and mixing of lead vocals, and care is taken to distinguish between individual voices in ensemble numbers. For example, 'Chiquitita', sung by Tanya and Rosie as they try to cheer up a distraught Donna, starts tentatively with rhythmic, cadenced speech that foregrounds accent and delivery style, paving the way for a continuing recognisability of sung voice in a number that features a large amount of unison singing and close harmony. As the visuals cut between close-ups of the two women, their respective voices are slightly raised in the mix: ownership of voice is never in doubt, and fidelity and realism are firmly established (though of course through highly artificial means). All these stars are competent singers, and several of them have had extensive training – but they are not professional vocalists, and production techniques are not used to disguise this. Instead, *Mamma Mia!* showcases an aesthetic of audible imperfection – its songs sound polished but not flawless, and most importantly, they sound 'real'. This intensifies the slippage between character and star that is always latently present, and heightens the sense of risk-taking and realness in the film's casting. It brings stars closer to audiences, and potentially to audience experiences of singing along to these songs as well, almost a 'quality karaoke' approach that emphasises the familiarity of the music – and the performer delivering it – even further. Rather than communicating ideas of 'inauthenticity' or 'selling out', the presence of big stars and big hits may instead result in an intensification of some of the musical's appeal to audience engagement, emotional transparency, and other feel-good factors.

When You're Near Me, Darling Can't You Hear Me? Stardom, Sincerity and the Celebrity Couple

As a jukebox musical, *Mamma Mia!* needs to revel in its star cast and greatest hits soundtrack whilst ensuring that their familiarity does not overemphasise the commercial over the artistic, or act as too much of a distancing factor. The film achieves this through the use of three distinct, though sometimes overlapping, styles or registers of musical performance. The first of these – the 'sincere' – is the one that most closely resembles the traditional approach to the film musical, where transparency and emotional communication are fore-grounded and heterosexual happy-ever-afters are the ultimate goal. Here, they are combined with the extra-textual familiarity of songs and stars, and in fact focus primarily on arguably the two biggest stars in *Mamma Mia!*'s firmament – Meryl Streep and Pierce Brosnan, in their roles as Donna and Sam.

Aside from two short moments of transition in and out of the narrative that bookend the film (both extracts from 'I Believe in Angels', sung by Sophie), all the numbers that are performed primarily with a sense of gravitas, realism or transparency focus on the love story between Donna and Sam. Numbers such as 'Knowing Me, Knowing You', 'Chiquitita', 'Slipping Through My Fingers', and 'When All is Said and Done', are all intended primarily to establish the emotional landscape of their relationship, whether by preparing it by allow-ing us a glimpse behind Donna's breezy exterior to the hurt and indecision that lies beneath, or through fleshing out Sam's somewhat one-dimensional character once his continuing feelings for Donna become clear. The moment where Donna and Sam's status as *Mamma Mia!*'s primary couple is cemented is their joint rendition of 'SOS'. Complete with single-sex chorus support for each of them and carefully balanced shots throughout, 'SOS' conforms with Rick Altman's notion of the duet as high point of the musical's 'dual-focus' narrative.[13]

As befits the idea that we are finally allowed sight of more than the surface level of Sam, this number marks the first extended singing in the film by Pierce Brosnan and is a good example of both the potential pleasures and perils of star audibility. Reviewers were generally less kind in their comments about Brosnan's singing than that of his co-stars, and whilst he often sounds vocally tense in many of his numbers, he is also perhaps the star playing furthest away from type here – James Bond and the musical comedy are not natural neigh-bours. Streep, in contrast, appears much more comfortable as a singer, and

– although firmly identified as a Serious Dramatic Actress with the Oscars to prove it – has had classical voice training and sang in several pre-*Mamma Mia!* screen roles.[14] Whilst Streep's apparent ease is able to soften some of the edges of Brosnan's often uncomfortable performance, it is perhaps the genre conventions of the musical itself that do most to provide a safety net here: we know how Donna and Sam's romance will turn out, which perhaps creates more space for co-existing hints of both pain and pleasure at their musical portrayal by Streep and Brosnan.

Streep's competence and comfortableness as Donna is a key facet of *Mamma Mia!*'s appeal. In a way that brings to mind Peter Kemp's discussion of Julie Andrews's highly personal but yet balanced singing voice, Donna, whilst audibly 'Streep' (allowing that frisson of recognition and its potentially distancing pleasures), does not overwhelm her material with 'egocentric appropriation [or] idiosyncratic embellishments'.[15] Instead, she delivers her well-known songs very cleanly, with relatively subtle vocal shading and styling used to personalise them and convey emotion. Even when Donna is allowed her most diva-ish of moments, bitterly singing 'The Winner Takes it All' to Sam towards the end of the film, Streep's rendition remains within the boundaries of what we might expect from a musical theatre performance. She saves her belting for moments of particular piquancy, resists any temptation to over-decorate, and instead allows the song itself space to communicate. Here, of course, is another layer of ABBA-related extra-textual meaning, with the strong perceived connections between the lyrics of 'The Winner Takes it All' and Agnetha Fältskog and Björn Ulvaeus's divorce, and similarities between the cliffside setting of Donna's performance and several sections of ABBA's music video for the track (which focuses primarily on Fältskog singing alone and isolated, including multiple shots of her walking by the coast). As with Fältskog, Streep personalises the song without interfering with the universality of its message – a balance between the private and the public that parallels the new and known aspects of pre-existing music in this kind of cinematic context. The success of Streep's portrayal of Donna is shown not only in the positive reviews received but in her subsequent casting as The Witch in *Into The Woods* (Rob Marshall, 2014) (which also features Christine Baranski), and perhaps especially her appearance in the title role of *Florence Foster Jenkins* (Stephen Frears, 2016) – Streep has established her singing credentials to the point that she can now be safely cast as a notoriously poor would-be opera singer.

Knowing Me, Knowing You: Camp, Comedy and Recasting the Familiar

Relatively conventional, if glamorously A-list, numbers like 'SOS' and 'The Winner Takes it All' demonstrate the extent to which *Mamma Mia!*'s feminist revisioning is built on a traditional base, highlighting performance as communication and resolution in a central love story. However, what sets the film – and often the jukebox musical – apart is the way that this initial layer of conventional romance and emotional transparency facilitates other scenes that knowingly embrace the musical's potential for camp, kitsch and deliberate rule-breaking. Peter Bradshaw's scathing review of *Mamma Mia!* describes a one-dimensional, high-energy but naive approach to the film's greatest hits soundtrack – a cast with 'no sense of perspective on the music'. But this ignores several shifts in emotional and physical register within the film that signal much more playful and often satirical approaches to ABBA's music, as well as the film's genre conventions and glitzy approach more broadly.[16]

Outside the romantic aspects of the central Donna/Sam storyline (and supporting Sophie/Sky pairing), *Mamma Mia!* is full of moments that poke fun at extra-textual associations and conventions. Sam, Harry and Bill's first appearance satirises not just the montage-sequence-as-introduction convention, but also the interchangeability of their three characters for much of the film, showing each of them setting off for the island in snappy shots that highlight their conventional good looks and sense of purposeful progress and virility. A thumping instrumental version of 'Gimme, Gimme, Gimme (A Man After Midnight)' accompanies this parody of screen masculinity. This wry approach to *Mamma Mia!*'s men continues for much of the film – Firth introduces his character as 'Bright. Harry Bright', whilst standing next to 007 actor Brosnan, and the muscled male chorus of 'Lay All Your Love on Me' cavort around the docks in a way that recalls the beefcake Olympians-in-training of Jane Russell's 'Ain't There Anyone Here For Love' in *Gentlemen Prefer Blondes* (Howard Hawks, 1953). Like its partner number, the large-scale female chorus 'Dancing Queen', 'Lay All Your Love on Me' focuses on ideas of gender-specific community and appeal – but whilst the all-shapes-and-sizes, dress-as-you-are female cast of 'Dancing Queen' celebrate their solidarity with an accessible but coordinated dance routine on the dock, the men's routine is positioned as intentionally 'sexy' after a seductive opening by Sky and Sophie, but one that falls short given the clownish effect of the flippers the chorus are wearing.

This gender-specificity of much of *Mamma Mia!*'s humour is an essential part of its positioning as a female-friendly text. Whilst Donna, Tanya and Rosie all feature heavily in many 'second register' numbers with their campy nods to comedy and satire, they do so most commonly in ways that place them in control, that make a feature of female community or solidarity, or that highlight the subjectivity of female leads in particularly striking ways, often drawing on aspects of gender-bending or role reversal.[17] Examples include the exaggerated point-of-view camerawork and 1970s-themed flashbacks of Donna's recognition of her former lovers in 'Knowing Me, Knowing You',

Tanya's playful taunting of a young male admirer in 'Does Your Mother Know', Rosie's relentless pursuit of Bill during 'Take a Chance on Me', and the early verses of 'Dancing Queen', which feature Rosie impersonating Elvis, and a dragged-up Tanya complete with tampon cigar.

This arch reimagining of the subjective significance of ABBA's songs – whilst leaving their sonic qualities largely intact – is first showcased in 'Money, Money, Money', a performance that establishes the run-down nature of Donna's business, her devotion to work not pleasure, and (in Tanya and Rosie's eyes) her related need for romance. This number makes a particular feature of outward-facing references that exploit the tension between the story-world of the film and the audience's (and the diegetic cast's) experience outside it. The song itself is somewhat of an outlier within ABBA's catalogue, drawing heavily on problematic Jewish cultural and musical stereotypes to communicate a desire for wealth in a way that treads an uneasy line between novelty and parody; a dual register of seriousness and silliness that also characterises much of *Mamma Mia!*. Donna switches in and out of sung delivery with asides about the ramshackle nature of the furniture, breaking the smooth transition to song at the number's opening; lyrics are over-literally choreographed with demands for payment by her chorus of employees; and Donna's delivery of the final line emphasises that it is a *man's* world as she straps on her tool belt and 'Aphrodite's fountain' cracks open in the courtyard beneath her feet. These 'real-world' moments ease us in and out of a fantasy midsection of the number that again takes the lyrics literally, with Donna imagining herself in 'Las Vegas or Monaco [to] win a fortune in a game' – a dream sequence complete with windswept hair, split-screen montage, pert sailor-dressed chorus routines and an epic long shot of Donna at the prow of a pleasure cruiser, with an enormous train billowing out behind her. This shot draws to mind similar ones in *Titanic* (James Cameron, 1997) and *The Adventures of Priscilla, Queen of the Desert* (Stephan Elliott, 1994) (Figure 7.1) – reference points that manage to nod towards both the silliness of over-serious love stories (*Titanic*'s on-boat pose with Rose and Jack has been much parodied) and their kitsch celebration in *Priscilla*'s embrace of diva culture (here, a lamé-clad Felicia lip-synchs to *La Traviata*).[18] This number – especially its central fantasy section – is high camp and meant to be taken as such. Cleverly, it not only evokes camp culture's celebration of the diva to portray Donna/Streep as a survivor, but also uses its over-literal interpretation of ABBA's lyrics and aspects of 'real-world' action to create the narrative space for her ultimate rescue at the hands of the 'rich man' whose world it is. It employs the conventions of musical performance as a storytelling vehicle, but also delights in their knowing over-exaggeration.

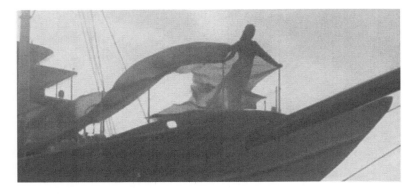

Figure 7.1 *Mamma Mia!*'s staging of 'Money, Money, Money' recalls *Titanic* and *The Adventures of Priscilla, Queen of the Desert*.

THANK YOU FOR THE MUSIC: THE JUKEBOX MUSICAL AS CELEBRATION

Closely related to these wryly camped-up numbers are those of *Mamma Mia!*'s third and final register of performance: the unashamedly celebratory, where little attempt is made to conform to the usual trappings of the musical genre and song and dance is enjoyed in stylised, artificial ways that bring to mind the 'musical moments' of non-musical films. This might seem like an odd distinction to invoke within the genre boundaries of the musical itself, but the particularly reflexive nature of the jukebox format brings a different feel to the performance-within-the-film trope that distinguishes it from the backstage or show musical. These numbers become less about the narrative of the film than about celebrating the act of performance through the very recognisability or ubiquity of the song itself – a position that narrows the distance between cast, character and audience via the potential implication that these performances exist for and by all three of them at once.

These 'musical moments' are signalled and managed in careful ways. Some of the largest chorus numbers in the film (for example, 'Gimme, Gimme, Gimme' and 'Voulez Vous', staged as part of the pre-wedding parties) are so chopped up by quick cutting and heavily stylised camerawork that any sense of 'realness' or community performance is challenged by an aesthetic much closer to that of the music video. The opening of 'Our Last Summer' uses the discovery of Harry's old guitar to motivate a nostalgic, self-accompanied rendition of a love song previously dedicated to Donna to present-day Sophie,[19] and the fully-fledged number 'Super Trooper' is inserted as a one-night-only hen party performance by Donna, Tanya and Rosie, appearing in their old guise of Donna and the Dynamos.

This sequence combines the sense of female solidarity and empowerment that is common to many of *Mamma Mia!*'s numbers with the performance-as-transformative trope of the musical, and a knowing awareness of how this particular idea has been taken up outside the confines of that genre – a key point of reference here is *Muriel's Wedding* (P. J. Hogan, 1994), where Muriel and Rhonda share a similarly positioned and life-affirming moment in a lip-synched rendition of 'Waterloo'.[20] Donna and the Dynamos dramatise several of *Mamma Mia!*'s key issues: in a film obsessed with 'finding yourself', nostalgia and the passing of time they literally embody their youthful past on the island, dressing and singing as their younger selves, and they also bring to life the musical tension between play-acting and realism that characterises the film's soundtrack. This is not quite the karaoke sequence or drag-style lip-synching of many musical moments, but it occupies a liminal and significant place between this and the more conventional performances of the backstage musical. We can hear Donna, Tanya and Rosie singing (and thereby Streep, Baranski and Walters), and care is taken to ensure that their individually recognisable voices are more audible as they are in shot, but of course they are singing ABBA's well-known material, in semi-disguise in 1970s costume, and as appearing as a resurrection of their youthful covers band, rather than their actual, older, individual selves. 'Super Trooper' is more than an enjoyable set-piece: it not only encapsulates the tension between past and present, recycled and original that runs through *Mamma Mia!*, but also the film's playful attitude towards these tensions.

This celebratory attitude is reinforced at *Mamma Mia!*'s climax, which, in a move that fully acknowledges that the primary appeal of the film is in its musical material rather than its plot, takes place after the final scenes of the riotous wedding breakfast and Sophie and Sky slipping away from the island at dawn. As the credits begin, so does the first of two extended performance sequences – 'Dancing Queen' performed by Donna and the Dynamos, and a full-cast rendition of 'Waterloo'. Both numbers take place on an open, 1970s-style dance floor against a black-cloth background, and everyone is in costume (Donna, the Dynamos, and other lead characters in glitzy 1970s disco outfits, and the supporting cast dressed as a literal Greek chorus complete with togas and lyres). Both of these performances are situated somewhere in-between the world of the film and the space occupied by its audience: as in 'Super Trooper', the gap between Donna, Tanya and Rosie and the stars who are playing them is dramatically narrowed, and the physical and musical setting of the number heightens this still further – the cast are visibly, campily lip-synching to a previous recording of themselves (rather than the original ABBA records), effectively dragging up as their own characters at the after-show party. There is no narrative motivation for these performances: they are purely celebratory, effectively a sing-along invitation to the audience and an encore that acknowledges the constructed nature of the plot-based performances that have preceded them. At the end of 'Dancing Queen', Donna steps forward and yells directly to camera – 'Do you want some more?' – a moment that of course primarily functions as Streep stepping forward to address the cinema audience, who can then be rewarded with the full ensemble performance of 'Waterloo'.

Mamma Mia! is a film that tries hard to have its cake and eat it – and arguably succeeds. In the tradition of the film musical it is genre fiction in the truest sense, repeating nostalgic patterns we find familiarly pleasurable, but with enough individuality (here partially provided by irony and knowing exaggeration) to keep it feeling fresh and perhaps 'guilt-free'. The film simultaneously reinforces and destabilises the conventions on which it is built and marketed, drawing on the intertextual connections and reference points of its cast, soundtrack and the musical genre itself. It delights in seeming to subvert these connections, especially in relation to issues of gender and age; in part to deal with some of the problematic politics of ABBA's musical material, but also to make a concerted appeal to a broad demographic – especially women, who have long been perceived as a key audience for the film musical. This is a tricky balancing act, but one that allows the film to exploit the nostalgia of the familiar whilst also poking fun at it – a wry, and often camp, way of presenting what is essentially yet one more iteration of the musical's heterosexual happy endings as something that feels more edgy, modern and that can pass, at least, as a feel-good 'feminist' film for the twenty-first century.

The conventional in the disguise of the edgy is not a new story in commercial filmmaking of course. But *Mamma Mia!*, and the jukebox show more widely, raises interesting questions about how the musical – a genre traditionally associated with the original, the virtuosic, the illusion of perfection, that extra level of suspended disbelief – manages to work its magic in a format where we are continually reminded of the unoriginality and commercial focus of the source material it is built around. The film's three 'registers' of performance – the sincere, the camp and the celebratory – are strategies that overlap and that are found elsewhere in musicals and in musical moment films. But the A-list jukebox musical's reliance on pre-existing texts and associations means that these registers take on a particular pertinence in both articulating and undermining ideas about stardom, the subjectivity of characters, cast, and audience, and notions of professionalism and quality. The audible imperfections and deliberate amateurishness of films like *Mamma Mia!*, *Moulin Rouge!*, and *Rock of Ages*, as well as other, more straightforward musical adaptations that cast big stars in unexpected roles (*Hairspray* [Adam Shankman, 2007] and *Chicago* [Rob Marshall, 2002], for example) may well create the potential for a more intense and personal experience of the utopian sensibilities and valorisation of community that are the hallmarks of the musical genre. A-list celebrities, ABBA's immensely successful hits, nostalgia, and exuberant performances are a heady combination, and one that has proved hugely successful with *Mamma Mia!*'s audiences: far from being parasitic or lazy, the jukebox musical offers us new ways to consume the pleasures of song, stars and spectacle. Feel that beat, watch that scene, dig the dancing queens.

NOTES

1. For example: Peter Bradshaw, '*Mamma Mia!*', *The Guardian*, 10 July 2008, available at <https://www.theguardian.comiculture/2008/jul/10/film.reviews> (last accessed 14 January 2017); Roger Ebert, '*Mamma Mia!*', available at <http://www.rogerebert.com/reviews/mamma-mia-2008> (last accessed 14 January 2017); Angie Errigo, '*Mamma Mia!* review', *Empire*, 3 July 2008, available at <http://www.empireonline.com/movies/mamma-mia/review/> (last accessed 14 January 2017); Melanie Reid, 'These dancing queens can be high art too', *The Times*, 14 July 2008, p. 22; A. O. Scott, 'Does your mother know you sing ABBA tunes?', *New York Times*, 18 July 2008, available at <http://www.nytimes.com/2008/07/18/movies/18mamm.html?_r=0> (last accessed 14 January 2017).
2. Pamela McClintock and Ed Meza, '"*Mamma Mia!*" still singing overseas', *Variety*, 12 September 2008, available at <http://variety.com/2008/film/features/

mamma-mia-still-singing-overseas-2-1117992112/>; 'Top films of all time at the UK box office', British Film Institute Research and Statistics, June 2015, available at <http://www.bfi.org.uk/sites/bfi.org.uk/files/downloads/bfi-top-films-of-all-time-june-2015.pdf> (last accessed 10 January 2017).

3. Kathy Hamilton and Beverly Wagner, 'An exploration of spectacular consumption at the movies: *Mamma Mia!*', *Journal of Customer Behaviour*, 2011, 10(4): 375–90.

4. Gordon Cox, '"*Mamma Mia!*" Closing: Broadway's female-driven blockbuster', *Variety,* 3 September 2015, available at <http://variety.com/2015/legit/news/mamma-mia-closing-broadway-musical-female-driven-blockbuster-1201585083/> (last accessed 10 January 2017).

5. Malcolm Womack discusses the repercussions of many of these changes on the film's construction of gender, noting how the film's emphasis on female friendships and the mother–daughter relationship works to recast ABBA's often problematic lyrics and interpersonal politics as a narrative of female independence and solidarity. Malcolm Womack, '"Thank you for the music": Catherine Johnson's feminist revoicings in *Mamma Mia!*', *Studies in Musical Theatre*, 2009, 3(2): 201–11.

6. For discussion of this album and its reception see Elisabeth Vincentelli, *ABBA Gold* (New York and London: Continuum, 2004).

7. Naomi Graber, 'Memories that remain: *Mamma Mia!* and the disruptive potential of nostalgia', *Studies in Musical Theatre*, 2015, 9(2): 187–98.

8. Significantly, though many of these leading cast members have appeared in screen or stage roles that have required them to sing, none of them are identified as musical actors, crossover stars or singers.

9. A useful overview of the key areas within scholarship on the film musical can be found in Steven Cohan, 'Introduction: musicals of the studio era', in Steven Cohan (ed.), *Hollywood Musicals: the Film Reader* (New York and London: Routledge, 2002), pp. 1–15.

10. Anahid Kassabian, *Hearing Film: Tracking Identifications in Contemporary Hollywood Film Music* (New York and London: Routledge, 2000), pp. 1–3. In common with most film musicals, *Mamma Mia!* also contains plenty of more conventional underscoring as well as musical numbers. Some of these cues are very short links, others are much more substantial instrumental versions of particular songs – but almost all of them contain recognisable thematic material drawn from ABBA tracks.

11. Michel Chion, *Audio-Vision: Sound on Screen*, trans. Claudia Gorbman (New York: Columbia University Press, 1994), p. 6. Similar ideas also apply to some dance forms as well – particularly tap, given its very audible nature – but this is less the case in *Mamma Mia!*'s deliberately low-key choreography, which certainly celebrates the physicality of movement, but not in ways that notably cross over into its soundtrack.

12. Jane Feuer, *The Hollywood Musical*, 2nd edn (Bloomington: Indiana University Press, 1993), p. 52; also Heather Laing, 'Emotion by numbers: music, song and the musical', in Bill Marshall and Robynn Stilwell (eds), *Musicals: Hollywood and Beyond* (Exeter: Intellect, 2000), pp. 5–13.

13. Rick Altman, *The American Film Musical* (Bloomington: Indiana University Press, 1987), pp. 16–27. In broader terms, *Mamma Mia!* both conforms and disturbs Altman's model. Whilst there are some deliberate gender symmetries across numbers such as 'Dancing Queen' (female large-scale chorus number) and 'Lay All Your Love on Me' (Sky's stag party equivalent), the film overall contains significantly more female-centred numbers.

14. Deborah Mellamphy, '"See that girl, watch that scene": notes on the star persona

and presence of Meryl Streep in *Mamma Mia!*', in Louise Fitzgerald and Melanie Williams (eds), *Mamma Mia! The Movie: Exploring a Cultural Phenomenon* (London and New York: I. B. Tauris, 2013), pp. 60–75.

15. Peter Kemp, 'How do you solve a "problem" like Maria von Poppins?', in Bill Marshall and Robynn Stilwell (eds), *Musicals: Hollywood and Beyond* (Exeter: Intellect, 2000), p. 60.

16. Peter Bradshaw, 'Mamma Mia! (review)', *The Guardian*, 10 July 2008, available at <https://www.theguardian.comiculture/2008/jul/10/film.reviews> (last accessed 14 January 2017).

17. See Womack, '"Thank You for the Music"'.

18. *Priscilla* is also a film that heavily features ABBA's music in ways that are often camp but highly effective. See Jonathan Rayner, 'Stardom, reception and the ABBA "musical"', in Ian Conrich and Estella Tincknell (eds), *Film's Musical Moments* (Edinburgh: Edinburgh University Press, 2006), pp. 99–111.

19. This rare moment of male musical agency in *Mamma Mia!* is an interesting one. Played partially for laughs by positioning Harry as the bumbling-Brit-abroad, but also containing the less comfortable spectacle of Sophie taking Donna's place in a love song performed by her possible father, the number initially relies on evoking the singer-songwriter archetype to present Harry's masculinity as alternative, non-threatening and desexualised. This moment (which predates the end of the film's brief reveal that Harry is gay) still revels in the perhaps unexpected pleasures of Firth-as-musician, but does not allow the celebration of this in the same way as with Streep, or even with Brosnan's more extended involvement in major numbers. After this opening section, 'Our Last Summer' quickly becomes a more conventional ensemble number for Bill, Harry, Sam and Sophie.

20. ABBA's music is also central to the construction of female subjectivity in *Muriel's Wedding*. See Catherine Haworth, 'Introduction: gender, sexuality and the soundtrack', *Music, Sound and the Moving Image*, 2012, 6(22): 113–35.

BIBLIOGRAPHY

Altman, Rick, *The American Film Musical* (Bloomington: Indiana University Press, 1987).

Chion, Michel, *Audio-Vision: Sound on Screen*, trans. Claudia Gorbman (New York: Columbia University Press, 1994).

Cohan, Steven, 'Introduction: musicals of the studio era', in Steven Cohan (ed.), *Hollywood Musicals: the Film Reader* (New York and London: Routledge, 2002), pp. 1–15.

Feuer, Jane, *The Hollywood Musical*, 2nd edn (Bloomington: Indiana University Press, 1993).

Graber, Naomi, 'Memories that remain: *Mamma Mia!* and the disruptive potential of nostalgia', *Studies in Musical Theatre*, 2015, 9(2): 187–98.

Hamilton, Kathy and Beverly Wagner, 'An exploration of spectacular consumption at the movies: *Mamma Mia!*', *Journal of Customer Behaviour*, 2011, 10(4): 375–90.

Haworth, Catherine, 'Introduction: gender, sexuality and the soundtrack', *Music, Sound and the Moving Image*, 2012, 6(2): 113–35.

Kassabian, Anahid, *Hearing Film: Tracking Identifications in Contemporary Hollywood Film Music* (New York and London: Routledge, 2000).

Kemp, Peter, 'How do you solve a "problem" like Maria von Poppins?', in Bill Marshall and Robynn Stilwell (eds), *Musicals: Hollywood and Beyond* (Exeter: Intellect, 2000), pp. 55–61.

Laing, Heather, 'Emotion by numbers: music, song and the musical', in Bill Marshall and Robynn Stilwell (eds), *Musicals: Hollywood and Beyond* (Exeter: Intellect, 2000), pp. 5–13.

Mellamphy, Deborah, '"See that girl, watch that scene": notes on the star persona and presence of Meryl Streep in *Mamma Mia!*', in Louise Fitzgerald and Melanie Williams (eds), *Mamma Mia! The Movie: Exploring a Cultural Phenomenon* (London and New York: I. B. Tauris, 2013), pp. 60–75.

Rayner, Jonathan, 'Stardom, reception and the ABBA "musical"', in Ian Conrich and Estella Tincknell (eds), *Film's Musical Moments* (Edinburgh: Edinburgh University Press, 2006), pp. 99–111.

Vincentelli, Elisabeth, *ABBA Gold* (New York and London: Continuum, 2004).

Womack, Malcolm, '"Thank you for the music": Catherine Johnson's feminist revoicings in *Mamma Mia!*', *Studies in Musical Theatre*, 2009, 3(2): 201–11.

8 BEYOND THE BARRICADE: ADAPTING *LES MISÉRABLES* FOR THE CINEMA

Ian Sapiro

Adaptations of Broadway shows were the mainstay of the film-musical genre at the height of its popularity in the 1950s and 1960s, with cinematic releases of Rodgers and Hammerstein's *Oklahoma!* (1955), *Carousel* (1956), *The King and I* (1956), *South Pacific* (1958) and *The Sound of Music* (1965), as well as other hits including *Guys and Dolls* (Joseph L. Mankiewicz, 1955), *Anything Goes* (Robert Lewis, 1956), *West Side Story* (Robert Wise, Jerome Robbins, 1961), *Gypsy* (Mervyn LeRoy, 1962) and *The Music Man* (Morton DaCosta, 1962). The popularity of the genre declined rapidly in the 1970s, but the release of Baz Luhrmann's *Moulin Rouge* in 2001 sparked something of a renaissance for the movie musical. However, there have been relatively few adaptations of stage musicals compared to made-for-screen offerings since the turn of the twenty-first century, and film adaptations of established shows no longer offer the sort of guarantee of success that they did fifty years ago.

Contemporary stage-to-screen adaptations have enjoyed mixed fortunes at the box office, with some, such as *Chicago* (Rob Marhsall, 2002), *Hairspray* (Adam Shankman, 2007) and, as Catherine Haworth discusses in her chapter in this volume, *Mamma Mia!* (Phyllida Lloyd, 2008), proving to be commercially successful. In these cases the films covered their production costs within a few weeks of opening in America and generated vast profits from screenings worldwide, but others have failed to match these returns despite being based on profitable and long-running Broadway properties.[1] *Rent* (Chris Columbus, 2005) opened in cinemas while the show was still running at the Nederlander Theatre, but fell short of recouping its $40 million budget – indeed, the release of the film coincided with a surge in ticket sales for the stage show, perhaps indicating that audiences opted instead to see the musical in the theatre.[2] *The Producers* (Susan Stroman, 2005) and *Rock of Ages* (Adam Shankman, 2012), the latter of which is considered elsewhere in this volume by K. J. Donnelly, fared similarly despite strong Broadway runs that were ongoing at the time the movies were released, demonstrating that translating Broadway longevity into Hollywood profitability is not always a simple task. Even *The Phantom of the Opera* (Joel Shumacher, 2004), which by the time of its cinematic release had been running on Broadway for sixteen years, lost money in America, and although its worldwide takings ultimately resulted in it doubling its original production costs, this was a far-from-stellar return for a film adapted from a stage musical with such global popularity.

It is against this backdrop of mixed success that director Tom Hooper and producer Cameron Mackintosh undertook a cinematic adaptation of *Les Misérables* (2012). Like many of its forebears, the stage show was still enjoying significant popularity on Broadway when the film was released, and also in keeping with other early twenty-first century screen adaptations of stage musicals, it received mixed reviews from critics and the public. While Kenneth Turan's *LA Times* write-up praised Hooper for 'finding ways to magnify the musical's ability to create those waves of overwhelming feelings in an audience',[3] Todd McCarthy, writing in *The Hollywood Reporter*, instead viewed it as 'heavily, if soaringly, monotonous'.[4] Singing was a central focus for many reviews, particularly the casting of the show but also the process by which the songs were performed and recorded. Indeed, while *Les Misérables* was by no means the first film musical to feature sound recorded live on the set, this apparently novel approach to vocal performance was much publicised in the lead up to the film's release.[5] In *Les Misérables: From Stage to Screen*, Benedict Nightingale and Martyn Palmer quote Hooper, who suggests that he 'became intrigued with this idea that the key to doing it was to do it live. I find with musicals on film that sometimes you don't quite believe in the reality of what you are watching'.[6] He acknowledges that *Les Misérables* was not even the first contemporary film musical to feature sound recorded live on the set, but goes on to state that:

> What hadn't been attempted before is singing live to this extent. [. . .] The other innovation is we decided to sing it almost entirely to live piano; this means take-to-take the tempo changes with the actors and it gives the actor the freedom of being in the moment.[7]

Despite wide-ranging exposure of this approach in the press and on social media, the new musical and technological processes developed on *Les Misérables* and the influence of this stage-to-screen adaptation on the future of the genre have been relatively unexplored. The project's team of music editors faced the significant challenge of creating the soundtrack using the shot footage, and to do so they had to overcome a range of issues not usually encountered in the production of films including matters of musical and performative continuity such as phrasing, dynamics, intonation and diction. The decision to cast mainly Hollywood actors rather than Broadway performers resulted in variable vocal performances – to which many reviewers of the film drew attention – and also obliged the music team to operate outside their normal practices, discussed below, in order to fully realise the sound world of the film.[8] In order to interrogate and evaluate the music-production processes that underpinned the filmic adaptation, and the resulting impact on mainstream practice, this chapter is informed by interviews I have carried out with some of the personnel who experienced and contributed to different parts of the process of creating the musical soundtrack for *Les Misérables*.[9] It also draws on a two-part feature in *Sound on Sound* in which supervising music editor Gerard McCann, production sound mixer Simon Hayes and some of their colleagues recounted much of their experience on the project, the only published source other than this chapter that addresses the adaptation from a musical or technical perspective.[10] Together, these resources allow consideration of the extent to which *Les Misérables* can be seen as a model for creating a contemporary screen adaptation of a stage musical, which, in turn, enables reflection on the further development of the genre post-*Les Misérables*.

The Music Team

The music team for *Les Misérables* was extensive, and an abridged version of the music credit list is shown in Table 8.1. Those interviewed for this chapter occupied a range of roles in the creation of the score: pianist, musical director, sound editor and music editor/programmer.

Jennifer Whyte was the principal 'live pianist' for the shooting of the film, and although she shared accompaniment responsibilities with Roger Davison, it was Whyte who played for the vast majority of the shooting. She describes the musical director of *Les Misérables*, Stephen Brooker, as 'Cameron [Mackintosh]'s right-hand man'. He is a vastly experienced theatre musical director, has conducted *Les Misérables* in numerous different countries, and was taught the score by the show's composer, Claude-Michel Schönberg. Neil Stemp was originally brought onto the project short term as a programmer, but stayed on as part of the music-editing team, and the final interviewee, John Warhurst, holds the credit of co-supervising sound editor for *Les Misérables*, which is both a completely accurate and entirely misleading job title. Warhurst explained this situation in his interview:

Table 8.1 *Summary of the extensive music team for* Les Misérables, *showing the range of roles held in addition to the number of professionals engaged on the project. Interviewees are indicated in* **bold.**

Role	People
Crowd Chorus Preparation	Michael England
Engineers	Chris Barrett, Fiona Cruickshank, Olga FitzRoy, Toby Hulbert, Sam Okell, Paul Pritchard, Simon Rhodes, Joe Rubel
Film Orchestrations	Anne Dudley, Stephen Metcalfe
Music Editing (and Programming)	James Bellamy, Christoph Bauschinger, David William Hearn, Robert Houston, Rael Jones, Gerard McCann, Matt Robertson, **Neil Stemp**, with Nick Hill
Music Mixer/Recordist	Jonathan Allen
Music Producer	Anne Dudley
Musical Director	**Stephen Brooker**
Musical Supervisor	Becky Bentham, with Catherine Greives
Musicians (including band for 'Master of the House')	Mark Berrow, Daniel Bhattacharya, Dave Daniels, Dave Hartley, Skaila Kanga, Ollie Lewis, Marcus Tilt, Jake Walker, Bruce White
On-set Pianists	Roger Davison, **Jennifer Whyte**
Supervising Sound Editors	Lee Walpole, **John Warhurst**
Vocal Coaching	Claire Underwood, Joan Lader, Linda Kerns, Liz Caplan, Mary Hammond, Mary Meyland, Roberta Duchak

I initially started as a music editor on the film and was taking care of all the vocals. Then we did some additional crowd recordings to enhance scenes like the riot in Paris, where the crowd has been added to make it really feel like a moment, and I took care of the crowd recording and all that side of it as well. When it got to the end of the process Tom [Hooper] said 'the vocals, the crowds and the music are probably most of the entirety of this soundtrack so I would like you to have the credit of supervising sound editor. It seems to be more appropriate for you in this film.'

Vocal Recording

Prior to *Les Misérables*, the established industry process for a film musical's sung numbers was to record the accompaniment first, have the vocalists record their parts while listening to this instrumental backing track, and then for the cast to lip-synch to the complete playback while shooting the film. As a result, a lot of musical work was normally undertaken in pre-production, before any footage was shot, and the music team therefore had a high level of creative authority over the resulting soundtrack. Recording the singing live on set for *Les Misérables* instead handed significant musical control to the cast, but before the filmmakers could proceed with their plan to effectively reverse the normal recording process, they had to ascertain whether the approach worked practically. McCann reports that 'we did some test shoots to be able to demonstrate the whole process from A to Z', Brooker recalling that the ABC Café scene was mocked up and used to assess the feasibility of the planned musical strategy.[11] The performers sang live on the set, and following shooting McCann notes that they 'tempo-mapped the vocals out and added a small 15-piece orchestra'.[12] Brooker feels that to some extent this experiment also tested his capability to lead an orchestra in the accompaniment of pre-recorded vocals, given that he was relatively inexperienced as a film-music conductor; fortunately for everyone concerned, all tests were passed.

Having established that the film could be made using the desired approach, the company embarked on a two-month rehearsal period starting in February 2012 that McCann suggests was 'very important because the entire cast came together as a musical theatre ensemble, and built up a sense of camaraderie that you normally don't get in a feature film where the actors get called in just for their own scenes'.[13] However, while the cast may indeed have utilised this period before shooting started to get to know each other better, the musical value of these rehearsals is questionable. Brooker reports that although time was set aside for rehearsing, these sessions tended to consist of 'people sitting around on the floor in a huge sound stage with a couple of tables and a coffee machine and a piano twenty-five feet away', and that in fact there were no vocal rehearsals ahead of shooting. Whyte recalls similarly that she 'sat in the corner of a room with Helena Bonham Carter and Sacha Baron Cohen and didn't play a note – I was there on hand but wasn't actually used'. Musical rehearsals instead took place on the set alongside the development of the visual component of the film, as the cast cultivated their vocal performances alongside their characters, settling into both over the course of several takes of a scene and, at times, many hours on set. This approach clearly fits with Hooper's ideal stated above of 'giving the actor the freedom of being in the moment', but as Whyte observes, 'it's a very expensive way to rehearse'.

Brooker suggests that if he undertook a similar project he would make full use of the rehearsal time to ensure that the music 'is so ingrained within a wonderful film actor to the best of his or her ability', making it easier to alter musical aspects of their performance such as phrasing, tempo and emotional nuance during shooting. Notwithstanding this, he notes that 'every single one of the leading actors arrived knowing every single thing', and Whyte suggests that rehearsals on the day of a shoot were very intensive:

> On the day of a specific shoot for 'Bring Him Home' or 'Empty Chairs at Empty Tables' or any of the big musical numbers, there would be quite a

significant amount of rehearsal. The room basically had Hugh [Jackman] or Eddie [Redmayne] or Sam Barks or whoever, plus me, plus all the people who were in charge – Tom Hooper, Brooker, Claude-Michel Schönberg, Cameron – all rehearsing to work out how we were going to do the song, and then that rehearsal would be transferred onto the set in order to work out how it was going to look physically before the filming started.

Once they were on the set, the principal cast determined the ultimate performance of a number, with the musical director effectively 'a security blanket for music' (Brooker). He was present only to offer guidance or clarification on an aspect of the music as needed, and to prevent significant musical problems from arising that would either adversely affect the overall musicality of the show (such as a number being at entirely the wrong tempo), or that might lead to issues later in the process. The cast wore small earpieces through which they could hear the offstage piano, and had to cope with the added anxiety of apparently singing *a cappella*, since no-one else on set could hear the accompaniment. The setup also placed significant pressure on the pianist since 'if you play a wrong note and there's even a flicker on their face it would register on the camera' (Whyte), potentially rendering a take unusable. The pianist could hear sound from the set through headphones – each principal actor wore two lavalier (lapel) radio microphones, and a boom microphone was also used where it could be kept out of shot – and a bank of monitors was set up in front of the piano on which they could see the multiple feeds of footage as it was being shot. Thus, although there was no line of direct communication from the set, the pianist could both see and hear the performers, and since much of the film was shot in close-up, Whyte acknowledges that she often had a better view of the singers' faces than she would have had in a theatrical production.

Several scenes required large numbers of people, but in contrast to the principal cast these film extras often had little to no idea of the music when they arrived for a shoot. In one such number, 'At the End of the Day', a significant proportion of the extras did not know what or when to sing, and Brooker recalls 'basically running up and down with a megaphone singing at them, and that was the rehearsal'. The large chorus numbers also posed a technical problem, since it was not possible to run '500 earpieces and lapel microphones, [and] we could [only] accommodate maybe 80 or 90 earpieces'.[14] McCann explains that the available earpieces were given to chorus members identified as strong singers, enabling them to lead the company, and additional boom microphones were used to capture the ensemble. However, Brooker notes that while the chorus singing was recorded, it was not necessarily all used in the final cut of the film. By contrast, Warhurst recorded additional crowd sound for the riot scene, which was dubbed onto the film after shooting 'to make it really feel like a moment', and states in *Sound on Sound* that 'a lot of the chorus material, like in "Master Of The House" and some other big chorus sections, was sweetened with overdubs to give extra width and size'.[15] These observations raise interesting and, in some respects, quite contentious points considering the 'live singing' concept employed in the film. Clearly in some of the larger scenes some of the recorded sound might not have been used – either for musical or other reasons – so although the sound heard in the film was indeed recorded live, it is not necessarily *all* of the sound that was recorded live. Conversely, when the live sound was not deemed sufficient to adequately represent the scenario depicted on the screen, sound recorded in a different place at a different time was added to enhance the film. Both of these strategies for working with chorus or crowd sound seem directly contradictory to the intentions of the director and producers to use the sound recorded live on set to make the experience more 'real' and 'believable' (to use Hooper's words) for those watching, and they demonstrate some of the challenges of the chosen musical approach.

The cast, and the principals in particular, were able to interpret the music freely, and this led to aspects of the music such as tempo, dynamics and even phrasing sometimes changing from take to take. This necessitated the music-editing team being involved and, for some personnel, on set throughout production, which is unusual. Normally when film music is recorded it is done to a click track, meaning that when the various takes are cued up together in Pro Tools to be edited into a master track the wave forms all align. In general, the vocal parts for *Les Misérables* were recorded without any sort of tempo guide, meaning that when Warhurst – who was the lead music/sound editor working with the picture editors during shooting – cued up the various takes of a scene in Pro Tools, there were often significant differences between the waveforms, making direct alignment impossible. He suggests that while he was able to navigate the various takes through recognising the shapes of the waveforms as representing the different lines and words of a song, the variability between takes caused problems during the editing of the film.

> When editors and directors choose takes they're looking at picture, lighting, facial expressions, and all these things, and they're not so concerned about the music slowing down because they just want it to look like that and then look like that. You sometimes have to tell them that musically it sounds like two takes stuck together, which isn't really a surprise because that's what it is! So from a technical point of view, when it came to putting it together we had all these complications arising from these takes not all sitting together. (Warhurst)

Critically, the audio and video were never dissociated from each other, so whenever the picture editor or director selected a particular take they were obliged to have both the picture and the sound since otherwise, as Warhurst points out, 'there was no point in making a live-sung musical'. In most cases suitable compromises were reached, with consecutive takes, especially towards the end of a shoot, often being very similar and allowing the team options in the construction of a sequence. Warhurst and his team also used Pro Tools's capabilities to stretch and shrink the audio as needed to smooth transitions between takes where there would otherwise have been noticeable changes, but had to do so in a way that did not compromise the vocal sound or the synchronisation. Importantly, and perhaps rather helpfully for the music editors, the filmmakers were not looking for singing of the highest quality as you might get if you saw *Les Misérables* on Broadway or in London because, as Brooker explains:

> we weren't doing a film of the show, we didn't want that; we wanted a film of the *book* with that score, so there was a conscious decision to buy into the rawness of it all and arguably the lesser musicality of some of it. They [the film-makers] were keen that it should suit the setting and capture the right emotion, with the rawness of some renditions actually a desirable characteristic.

The literary sources for musicals are sometimes used to expand parts of a story, but normal practice is that the theatrical works usually remain the primary materials on which film-musical adaptations are based.[16] As Brooker explained, a different approach was adopted for *Les Misérables*, with the show serving only to supply the film with a musical score. The characterisation and narrative were taken directly from the original story, Victor Hugo's novel, indicating the filmmakers' desire to create something distinct from the stage show. However, such specific intention was undermined significantly by the way the film was marketed, with the official trailer proclaiming the film to be 'based on the original stage musical Boublil and Schönberg's *Les Misérables*', and the official international trailer stating similarly that the source is 'Boublil and Schönberg's worldwide musical phenomenon'.[17] Victor Hugo is not mentioned at all. Paradoxically then, while the use of live singing was intended to emphasise the rawness of the characters in the novel and create something different to the theatrical work, owing to the way the film was promoted it instead served to link the movie more closely to the musical, blurring rather than defining the boundary between screen and stage.

POST-RECORDING THE ORCHESTRA

Although there was a corresponding piano accompaniment for each take of every cue – the offstage piano that the cast could hear in their earpiece while singing – there were two reasons why these could not be used to support the orchestral recording. Firstly, since the final edit usually comprised several takes cut together, the piano tracks would have had to be cut together similarly, and even then any Pro Tools manipulation applied to the vocal lines would also have to be applied to the piano music. Furthermore, since there was no direct line of sight between the pianist and singers, the piano was, unsurprisingly, usually not quite together with the vocalist, limiting its value as a guide for the orchestra. Indeed, Simon Hayes notes that despite being fundamental to the process of recording the vocal music in the film, the recordings of the piano accompaniments were thrown away once shooting was complete.[18] Having dismissed the possibility of using the piano tracks, once a complete song was edited, the music editors gathered as much synchronisation data as possible from the cut to help with the orchestral recording. Neil Stemp was one of the team tasked with using the synchronisation data to generate tempo maps, some of which he says were 'by necessity quite wacky'. The maps were used to create click tracks, and the team also reverted to old technology, grease-pen streamers, to help Brooker keep the orchestra synchronised to the recorded vocals.[19] It must not be forgotten, however, that despite all of the changes to underlying practices in music and sound recording and production, *Les Misérables* was still subject to normal filmic editorial processes – even once scenes and songs had been edited and handed over to the music team, they were often revised and edited further. This created more work for Warhurst and his team and the music editors plotting the tempo maps, and Brooker observes that McCann had to effectively reinvent one of the music editor's principal responsibilities; rather than editing music to fit new cuts of the film, he was constantly massaging click tracks so that when the orchestra was recorded it would match up with the recut vocal performances.

Once a click track was created and Brooker had practised with it, he worked closely with the music editors to adapt the clicks to better suit his conducting style and work with his understanding of the score. In the principal numbers the small number of vocalists involved enabled each singer to perform with greater freedom knowing that they were less constrained by having to stay in time with others, although 'the rule was that whoever was on screen, everybody else's vocal had to fit with that', to minimise any asynchronicity of voice and mouth.[20] Brooker identifies that the shifting tempi in the click tracks made them quite difficult to work with, giving an example of a click pattern as 'click . . . click . . . click . . . click, click . click . . click . . 1 . . 2 . . bang'.[21] As this suggests, it was sometimes difficult to anticipate when an actor might sing their next note, especially with pickups,[22] since after the last click of a bar there was a silence until the next click and that beat might not have been the same length as those preceding it. In 'Bring Him Home', for example, which has a running quaver accompaniment of the sort that permeate the

Les Misérables score, the orchestra is often left holding a note or chord at the end of a line of song for a little longer than seems comfortable. Had Brooker spread out the subdivision of the final beat he might have been late in catching the vocal line, but by pushing through it the orchestral accompaniment is left 'hanging', breaking up the musical line a little. By contrast, there are places where Hugh Jackman's vocal entries are early and Brooker has to move the orchestra on quickly so as to complete the supporting phrase and not be left behind. There are also occasional phrases where the vocal line is closely supported in the orchestration, and synchronisation is also sometimes problematic in this regard. It is notable that the starts of phrases or even bars often begin quietly and increase in volume quite rapidly over the first few notes, perhaps to mask any slight discrepancies of timing between sung melody and orchestral accompaniment.

In some cases a decision was taken to work without a click in order that the orchestral music might have the same sense of freedom as the vocal material, notably during instrumental transitions between sung numbers. The end of Valjean's soliloquy into the 'At the End of the Day' sequence is one such place; with the click in place the orchestral flourishes and running semiquavers sounded mechanical and lacked fluidity, so Brooker conducted this in free time, drawing on his knowledge of the show to pace the music and fill the required time. The first part of this passage is successful, with the orchestral flourishes heightening Jackman's sustained A flat, the re-entry of the orchestra timing perfectly with the action of him throwing his parole papers off the clifftop, and the next section of the music starting exactly as the camera reaches the street for the introduction to 'At the End of the Day'. However, the musical material feels slower paced than the corresponding visual activity of horses galloping in this part of the sequence, and indeed Brooker has to push the orchestra quickly through the final few bars before the chorus vocal entry at the start of the song in order to align with the reintroduced click.

Exceptions to the Approach

The vocal parts for one number were actually recorded to click in order to avoid significant synchronisation issues between vocal parts. The Act 1 finale, 'One Day More', features solo lines for Valjean, Marius, Cosette, Eponine, Enjolras, Javert and the Thenadiers as well as the chorus, and takes place across several locations. Whereas on stage all of these characters and locations coexist within the proscenium arch and can be led by a single conductor, in the film the actors are, by necessity, shot in a range of places including a moving coach, outside Valjean's house, the ABC café and the military headquarters. Brooker explains that the original plan had been to allow each of the principals to record their own part in free time, as with the rest of the film, but once the number got going the team realised the song would lose all musical coherence with this approach.[23] McCann reports that they

> establish[ed] a guide tempo during rehearsal, and in this case Russell Crowe, who was in the first scene, and live pianist Roger Davison finessed that tempo on set. This gave Hugh (Jackman), who was in the next sequence, a range of matching tempi he could work within, and from there we built a template for the entire song, and recorded the piano backing for it. This completely pre-recorded piano track was then used as a playback for shooting all the other cross-cutting scenes in this song.[24]

The fine detail of McCann's recollection is a little surprising, given that Crowe's character, Javert, only enters the song after passages for several other principals, and even though the song was shot out of sequence his limited involvement means he is a peculiar choice for establishing the tempo map for the number. Notwithstanding this, Brooker confirms that ultimately a click track was utilised and all parts were sung to the click, which probably made this song the simplest for the editing team to work with and the orchestra to accompany closely, despite its high level of musical complexity relative to the rest of the score. Interestingly, the impact of the click is not particularly noticeable when watching the number in the film, especially since the Thenadiers are slightly behind the accompaniment in places, though there is some clear choreography in the sequence – such as the cleaning of the guns – that would probably not have been so well timed without a click.

Just as 'One Day More' is an exception to the general rule of free singing employed in *Les Misérables*, 'Look Down' breaks with the practice of recording the vocal parts live on the set. Owing to the sheer amount of water involved, the vocal parts for this song were pre-recorded, and Brooker was in a frame above the set wearing white sleeves, conducting to try and keep the cast in time with the playback. While the approach taken is entirely understandable it is unfortunate that this is the opening number of the film, because in some respects it does highlight Hooper's concerns about the believability of the singing in film musicals – the singers' voices do not match the immense physical strain the characters are under despite 'people singing while pulling ropes, for it to sound as authentic as possible', and the sound is perhaps also a little cleaner for being recorded in a studio.[25]

ORCHESTRATION

One final notable impact of post-recording the orchestra is that the shooting of the film influenced the way in which the score was orchestrated. Anne Dudley and Stephen Metcalfe worked largely from the original stage orchestrations to create new scoring for the film, all of which was mocked up by Rael Jones for use in previews and test screenings in another change to previous practice; since the accompaniment is normally the first element to be recorded there is no need for mock-ups at previews since the final musical soundtrack is already available. In some cases a song went through several orchestrations; Brooker recalls that there were three or four versions of the orchestration for 'I Dreamed a Dream' because 'the initial orchestration was too busy and it got in the way of Annie [Hathaway]; well, her eyes really. So hence we ended up with that single tone at the top of the texture without any introduction, without any movement.' While the time required to construct and reconstruct orchestrations for a musical, especially one as dense musically as *Les Misérables*, is quite significant, it afforded the filmmakers an unprecedented opportunity to customise the accompaniment to the specific character of the picture and subtly differentiate the film from the stage show. Just as the actors responded to the dramatic situations in which they found themselves when performing the songs, so too the orchestral accompaniment and underscoring has a direct correlation to the picture, as the example offered by Brooker, above, demonstrates.

A NEW PARADIGM

The two-part *Sound on Sound* feature concludes with the thoughts of McCann and Hayes on the impact of *Les Misérables* on the future of the film-musical genre:

> 'Given how well the movie has done at the box office, one can say that recording movie vocals live on set does work', says Gerard McCann. 'I imagine that it will be difficult for any director to do a musical after this and handcuff him- or herself to pre-recorded tracks.' Simon Hayes agrees: [. . .] 'Shorter musical numbers in dialogue movies may still be recorded using pre-record and miming, but [. . .] from here on, sung-through movies will have to be sung live from start to finish. I don't think there's any other choice.[26]

By reversing the normal order of recording the music for a film musical *Les Misérables* broke the mould, and as the views of McCann and Hayes indicate, it appears to have created a new paradigm for the production of this sort of picture. To date there have been five stage-to-screen adaptations released since *Les Misérables* – *Jersey Boys* (Clint Eastwood, 2014), *Annie* (Will Gluck, 2014), *Into the Woods* (Rob Marshall, 2014), *The Last Five Years* (Richard LaGravenese, 2015) and *London Road* (Rufus Norris, 2015) – with *Annie* the only one not to utilise any live on-set singing.[27] All of the singing in *London Road* was recorded live (Warhurst), and *Into the Woods* and *The Last Five*

Years both employed a combination of pre-recorded vocal performances and live singing depending on a song's context,[28] but in each case a pre-recorded instrumental accompaniment was used, meaning that none of these film musicals offered the degree of flexibility that was granted in *Les Misérables*. This may be a factor of budget – at $61 million *Les Misérables* cost comfortably more than these other productions – but it might also attest to the significant difficulty of post-recording the orchestra, particularly given that a film itself usually remains in a state of flux during post-production. *Jersey Boys* overcame these problems by taking advantage of the live band present in the story and capturing all of the music on the set, but paradoxically the presence of the instrumentalists may have restricted the singers' interpretative freedom.[29] Whereas in *Les Misérables* the main purpose of the piano accompaniment was to help the performers maintain pitch and a sense of tempo, and the piano was therefore not always strictly synchronised with the voice, the singers in *Jersey Boys* had to ensure that the live band could stay precisely in time with them because that accompaniment would be used in the final release.

There have been a number of live television performances of stage musicals in the years since *Les Misérables*, starting with NBC's *The Sound of Music Live!* (2013) and continuing with two further offerings from that network – *Peter Pan* (2014) and *The Wiz* (2015) – ITV's *The Sound of Music Live* (2015) and Fox's *Grease: Live* (2016). NBC announced their first project in June 2012,[30] several months after shooting had begun on *Les Misérables*, and the film's live-singing strategy had already been much publicised by this time. While the television productions are stage musicals performed on the small screen as opposed to film adaptations, it nonetheless seems likely that the approach taken in *Les Misérables* had some impact on the way in which these programmes were produced, and perhaps how they were ultimately received by audiences.[31] The next cinematic stage-to-screen adaptation may well be *Wicked*, which is currently slated for release in 2019 (discounting Disney's live-action *Beauty and the Beast*, which is more of a screen-to-screen adaptation). Though it is too soon to know for certain, such is the impact of *Les Misérables* on the way music is presented in the genre that it is now highly probable that live singing will play a significant role in the recording and production of the film's score. Whether it will also include the harder part of the process – post-recording the orchestra – may depend on budget, the expertise and experience of those involved, and the continued development of sound and music technologies, but in the world of the contemporary stage-to-screen musical there can no longer be any doubt that when you 'hear the people sing' they are probably doing it live.

NOTES

1. Information on film production budgets and box-office takings referred to in this chapter have been synthesised from data on the following websites: *Box Office Mojo* (http://www.boxofficemojo.com/), the *Internet Movie Database* (www.imdb.com), *The Numbers* (http://www.the-numbers.com/) and the British Film Institute website (http://www.bfi.org.uk/education-research/film-industry-statistics-research/weekend-box-office-figures) (all last accessed 24 June 2016).

2. 'Weekly box office for *Rent*', *Internet Broadway Database*, available at <https://www.ibdb.com/Grosses/ViewProduction/4791/3> (last accessed 24 June 2016).

3. Kenneth Turan, 'Review: Vive '*Les Misérables*' in all its over-the-top glory', *Los Angeles Times*, 24 December 2012, available at <http://articles.latimes.com/2012/dec/24/entertainment/la-et-mn-les-miserables-20121225> (last accessed 24 June 2016).

4. Todd McCarthy, '*Les Misérables*: film review', *Hollywood Reporter*, 6 December 2012, available at <http://www.hollywoodreporter.com/review/les-miserables-film-review-398662> (last accessed 24 June 2016).

5. In the early 1930s, recording the sound alongside the picture was the only way in which the two elements could be entirely synchronised, and it was therefore common practice in film musicals from the era. More recently, Peter Bogdanovich's *At Long Last Love* (1975) and Alan Parker's *The Commitments* (1991) featured live on-set singing, though in both cases the backing tracks were pre-recorded.

6. Tom Hooper in Benedict Nightingale and Martyn Palmer, *Les Misérables: From Stage to Screen* (London: Carlton Books, 2013), p. 82.

7. Ibid. p. 82.

8. David Edwards, writing in the *Daily Mirror*, observes that Russell Crowe's 'warbling sounds like a cat being mistreated' and Anthony Quinn's *Independent* review criticises the singing of both Crowe and Hugh Jackman as 'strangulated' and 'an unlovely sound that keeps going out of tune' respectively. Charles Isherwood's *New York Times* review is similarly critical, noting that 'when it comes to the lead male roles [. . .] I found myself often yearning for earplugs', with Crowe 'never making anything resembling an appealing sound' and Jackman having 'a thin, nasal and unpleasantly metallic sound that quickly grew grating'. See David Edwards, 'Glum's the word', *Daily Mirror*, 11 January 2013, Features, pp. 2–3; Anthony Quinn, 'Heaven knows I'm miserable now', *The Independent*, 11 January 2013, p. 42; Charles Isherwood, 'On screen *Les Miz* dreams its dream, now extra large', *New York Times*, 4 January 2013, Artsbeat, p. 1.

9. Unless otherwise stated, all quotations from these interviewees are taken from the interviews carried out with the author: Jennifer Whyte, 6 May 2016; Neil Stemp, 9 May 2016; John Warhurst, 16 May 2016; Stephen Brooker, 22 May 2016.

10. See Paul Tingen, 'The *Les Misérables* sound team: part 1', *Sound on Sound*, April 2013, available at <http://www.soundonsound.com/people/les-miserables-sound-team-part-1> (last accessed 25 June 2016); Paul Tingen, 'The *Les Misérables* sound team: part 2', *Sound on Sound*, May 2013, available at <http://www.soundonsound.com/people/les-miserables-sound-team-part-2> (last accessed 25 June 2016.).

11. McCann in Tingen, 'The *Les Misérables* sound team: part 1'.

12. Ibid.

13. Ibid.

14. Ibid.

15. Warhurst in Tingen, 'The *Les Misérables* sound team: part 2'.

16. For example, the 2003 film adaptation of *The Phantom of the Opera* includes a

sequence outlining the Phantom's back-story that is drawn from Gaston Leroux's novel and does not appear in the stage show, though the musical itself remains the principal basis for the film.

17. Both trailers can be viewed on *YouTube*, with the relevant information appearing at 0:26 and 2:29 respectively: 'Les Misérables (2012) Official Trailer [HD]', *YouTube*, published 30 May 2012, available at <https://www.youtube.com/watch?v=xk5UStefYmE> (last accessed 18 August 2016); 'Les Misérables (2012) – Official International Trailer [HD]', *YouTube*, published 9 November 2012, available at <https://www.youtube.com/watch?v=EkHHHUk8RCw> (last accessed 18 August, 2016).

18. Hayes in Tingen, 'The *Les Misérables* sound team: part 1'.

19. A streamer is a diagonal line drawn across a series of frames of film using a grease pen so that when the film runs through the projector it appears as a vertical line that moves across the picture. The conductor can use a streamer to ensure they hit a particular point in the music at the right time, as the streamer hits the side of the screen.

20. Warhurst in Tingen, 'The *Les Misérables* sound team: part 2'.

21. While this is difficult to annotate clearly, the amount and type of punctuation between clicks and counts in this example should be interpreted as a stable pace for four clicks followed abruptly by a much faster tempo (the comma) that slows over the next few clicks to a new steady tempo that is slightly quicker than the original speed.

22. A pickup, in this sense, is an anacrusis – notes (and words) that lead into a new bar of music – rather than a device such as those found on electric guitars, that converts string vibrations into electrical signals for amplification.

23. This is particularly the case because the recordings were not quantised, since doing so would have reduced or even nullified the effect of the live singing.

24. McCann in Tingen, 'The *Les Misérables* sound team: part 1'.

25. Warhurst in Tingen, 'The *Les Misérables* sound team: part 2'.

26. Hayes in Tingen, 'The *Les Misérables* sound team: part 1'.

27. Indeed, the audible auto-tune in *Annie* only reinforces the 'produced' rather than 'live' sound of the score. See Ian Sapiro, 'You will know that she is our Annie: comparing three adaptations of a Broadway classic', in Dominic McHugh (ed.), *The Oxford Handbook of Musical Theatre Adaptation* (Oxford University Press, forthcoming).

28. Cody Collier, '*Into the Woods* will mix live and pre-recorded singing', *Guardian Liberty Voice*, 24 November 2014, available at <http://guardianlv.com/2014/11/into-the-woods-will-mix-live-and-pre-recorded-singing/> (last accessed 29 June 2016); Ramin Setoodeh, 'Jeremy Jordan on *The Last Five Years*, a *Newsies* movie and the end of *Smash*', *Variety*, 13 February 2015, available at <http://variety.com/2015/film/news/jeremy-jordan-on-the-last-five-years-a-newsies-movie-and-the-end-of-smash-1201433771/> (last accessed 29 June 2016).

29. Carolyn Giarina, '*Jersey Boys*: why Clint Eastwood decided to record the singing live', *Hollywood Reporter*, 21 June 2014, available at <http://www.hollywoodreporter.com/behind-screen/jersey-boys-why-clint-eastwood-713637/> (last accessed 29 June, 2016).

30. BWW Newsdesk, 'NBC & Craig Zadan/Neil Meron to present live broadcast of THE SOUND OF MUSIC!', 30 June 2012, available at <http://www.broadwayworld.com/article/Breaking-News-NBC-Craig-ZadanNeil-Meron-to-Present-Live-Broadcast-of-THE-SOUND-OF-MUSIC-20120629#> (last accessed 29 June 2016).

31. ABC News ran a story on the day of NBC's broadcast of *The Sound of Music Live!*

revealing that the von Trapp family were displeased with the casting of Carrie Underwood as Maria. They quoted Myles von Trapp Derbyshire, who asserted that the family 'had the conversations of who could play this role better and it was Anne Hathaway [. . .] who just won an Oscar for a similar situation' in her role as Fantine in *Les Misérables*. The following day this story was carried by several publications including the *New York Daily News* and *Los Angeles Times*, as well as being shared widely on social media, though some Twitter users responded with the assertion that Hathaway would have been a worse choice. Both sides of the debate appeared to be informed by perceptions of Hathaway's performance singing (and acting) live in the *Les Misérables* film, despite the demands of that project being quite different to those for a performance in a live television musical. See Michael Rothman, 'Who the Von Trapps wish could replace Carrie Underwood in *The Sound of Music Live*', ABC News, 5 December 2013, available at <http://abcnews.go.com/blogs/entertainment/2013/12/who-the-von-trapps-wish-could-replace-carrie-underwood-in-the-sound-of-music-live/> (last accessed 17 August 2016). See also Patrick Kevin Day, 'Who did the real-life Von Trapps want for *Sound of Music*'s Maria?', *Los Angeles Times*, 6 December 2013, available at <http://www.latimes.com/entertainment/tv/showtracker/la-et-st-von-trapp-family-sound-of-music-carrie-underwood-20131206-story.html> (last accessed 17 August 2016); Margaret Eby, 'Carrie Underwood "couldn't be more proud" of *Sound of Music Live!* – but Anne Hathaway was Von Trapp family's first choice for role', *New York Daily News*, 6 December 2013, available at <http://www.nydailynews.com/entertainment/tv-movies/carrie-underwood-proud-sound-music-live-von-trapps-wanted-anne-hathaway-article-1.1540076> (last accessed 17 August 2016).

BIBLIOGRAPHY

Box Office Mojo, *Box Office Mojo*, <http://www.boxofficemojo.com/> (last accessed 24 June 2016).

British Film Institute, 'Weekend box office figures', *British Film Institute*, <http://www.bfi.org.uk/education-research/film-industry-statistics-research/weekend-box-office-figures> (last accessed 24 June 2016).

BWW Newsdesk, 'NBC & Craig Zadan/Neil Meron to present live broadcast of THE SOUND OF MUSIC!', 30 June 2012, <http://www.broadwayworld.com/article/Breaking-News-NBC-Craig-ZadanNeil-Meron-to-Present-Live-Broadcast-of-THE-SOUND-OF-MUSIC-20120629#> (last accessed 29 June 2016).

Collier, Cody, '*Into the Woods* will mix live and pre-recorded singing', *Guardian Liberty Voice*, 24 November 2014, <http://guardianlv.com/2014/11/into-the-woods-will-mix-live-and-pre-recorded-singing/> (last accessed 29 June 2016).

Day, Patrick Kevin, 'Who did the real-life Von Trapps want for *Sound of Music*'s Maria?', *Los Angeles Times*, 6 December 2013, <http://www.latimes.com/entertainment/tv/showtracker/la-et-st-von-trapp-family-sound-of-music-carrie-underwood-20131206-story.html> (accessed 17 August 2016).

Eby, Margaret, 'Carrie Underwood "couldn't be more proud" of *Sound of Music Live!* – but Anne Hathaway was Von Trapp family's first choice for role', *New York Daily News*, 6 December 2013, <http://www.nydailynews.com/entertainment/tv-movies/carrie-underwood-proud-sound-music-live-von-trapps-wanted-anne-hathaway-article-1.1540076> (last accessed 17 August 2016).

Edwards, David, 'Glum's the word', *Daily Mirror*, 11 January 2013, Features, pp. 2–3.

Giarina, Carolyn, '*Jersey Boys*: why Clint Eastwood decided to record the singing live', *Hollywood Reporter*, 21 June 2014, <http://www.hollywoodreporter.com/behind-screen/jersey-boys-why-clint-eastwood-713637/> (last accessed 29 June 2016).

Internet Movie Database, *Internet Movie Database*, <www.imdb.com> (last accessed 24 June 2016).

Isherwood, Charles, 'On screen *Les Miz* dreams its dream, now extra large', *New York Times*, 4 January 2013, Artsbeat, p. 1.

'*Les Misérables* (2012) Official Trailer [HD]', *YouTube*, published 30 May 2012, <https://www.youtube.com/watch?v=xk5UStefYmE> (last accessed 18 August 2016).

'*Les Misérables* (2012) – Official International Trailer [HD]', *YouTube*, published 9 November 2012, <https://www.youtube.com/watch?v=EkHHHUk8RCw> (last accessed 18 August 2016).

McCarthy, Todd, '*Les Misérables*: film review', *Hollywood Reporter*, 6 December 2012, <http://www.hollywoodreporter.com/review/les-miserables-film-review-398662> (last accessed 24 June 2016).

Nightingale, Benedict and Martyn Palmer, *Les Misérables: From Stage to Screen* (London: Carlton Books, 2013).

Quinn, Anthony, 'Heaven knows I'm miserable now', *The Independent*, 11 January 2013, p. 42.

Rothman, Michael, 'Who the Von Trapps wish could replace Carrie Underwood in *The Sound of Music Live*', *ABC News*, 5 December 2013, <http://abcnews.go.com/blogs/entertainment/2013/12/who-the-von-trapps-wish-could-replace-carrie-underwood-in-the-sound-of-music-live/> (last accessed 17 August 2016).

Sapiro, Ian, 'You will know that she is our Annie: comparing three adaptations of a Broadway classic', in Dominic McHugh (ed.), *The Oxford Handbook of Musical Theatre Adaptation* (New York: Oxford University Press, forthcoming).

Setoodeh, Ramin, 'Jeremy Jordan on *The Last Five Years*, a *Newsies* movie and the end of *Smash*', *Variety*, 13 February 2015, <http://variety.com/2015/film/news/jeremy-jordan-on-the-last-five-years-a-newsies-movie-and-the-end-of-smash-1201433771/> (last accessed 29 June 2016).

The Numbers, <http://www.the-numbers.com/> (last accessed 24 June 2016).

Tingen, Paul, 'The *Les Misérables* sound team: part 1', *Sound on Sound*, April 2013, <http://www.soundonsound.com/people/les-miserables-sound-team-part-1> (last accessed 25 June 2016).

Tingen, Paul, 'The *Les Misérables* sound team: part 2', *Sound on Sound*, May 2013, <http://www.soundonsound.com/people/les-miserables-sound-team-part-2> (last accessed 25 June 2016).

Turan, Kenneth, 'Review: *Les Misérables* in all its over-the-top glory', *Los Angeles Times*, 24 December 2012, <http://articles.latimes.com/2012/dec/24/entertainment/la-et-mn-les-miserables-20121225> (last accessed 24 June 2016).

'Weekly box office for *Rent*', *Internet Broadway Database*, <https://www.ibdb.com/Grosses/ViewProduction/4791/3> (accessed 24 June 2016).

PART THREE

MUSICALS BY ANOTHER NAME

9 O BROTHER, WHERE ART THOU?: THE COEN BROTHERS AND THE MUSICAL GENRE CONTAMINATION

Stefano Baschiera

There is little doubt that music plays a crucial role in the Coen Brothers' oeuvre, both when considering the 'scored' original music built around the characters, and also when we think of the recurring diegetic performances of onscreen musicians. Their films are characterised by soundtracks that strongly intertwine with the narrative, to the extent that specific songs are already present at the screenplay stage.[1] The songs often create an ironic commentary to the scenes – as so called 'music-puns' – and strongly contribute to the feeling of temporal and spatial displacement, as well as the overall intertextual mash-up typical of the brothers' postmodern style.

Since their debut film *Blood Simple* (1984), the Coen Brothers have developed a recurring collaboration with score composer Carter Burwell and more occasionally, albeit very significantly, a professional relationship with musician and soundtrack producer T-Bone Burnett, which began with *The Big Lebowski* (1998), the first film to rely on pre-existing music.[2] As such, the use of popular music in the Coens' films remains one of their distinctive stylistic traits, mirroring the complexity of their work and attracting critical recognition, in particular assigning an authorship role to Burwell, and interdisciplinary scholarly attention. Among others, Jeff Smith rightly claims that, 'although popular music certainly contributes to the winking, ironic tone of the Coen brothers' films, it also serves very conventional storytelling functions by reinforcing particular settings, underlining character trait, and establishing mood and tone for specific scenes'.[3]

These storytelling functions of the music tracks are the focus of this chapter, in particular how they play alongside the other principal narrative frame characteristic of the Coens' cinema: that of film genre. In order to explore these elements, I propose to ideally organise their films according to the use of music, dividing their works into three overleaping categories: 'scored', 'sound-driven' and 'tracked'.[4] After considering the role that film genres play in their cinema, this chapter eventually investigates their engagement with the classical musical film genre.

The first category consists of the 'scored films', where a traditional music score follows the narrative development. These films rely on the collaboration with Burwell as composer of music themes, which are matched to the different characters and stress some of their background and recurring features. In fact, as noted by Randall Barnes, the aural aspect of the film is often present at the early stage of the writing, making sound an important component in the storytelling, as is evident in films such as *Raising Arizona* (1987), *Miller's Crossing* (1990) and *Fargo* (1996).[5]

The second category can be defined as 'sound films', where the music score works around subtraction and silence, leaving more room for noises and natural sounds. In these films Burwell works closely with the sound designer Skip Lievsay in order to create a soundtrack aurally less dependent on music. *Barton Fink* (1992)[6] and, even more, *No Country for Old Men* (2008) are the seminal examples for this category because of the very sparse use of Burwell's score and the reliance on other sound sources.[7]

Finally, the last category I would boldly put forward could be named the 'tracked-films'. It features films that strongly rely on a collection of pre-existing songs. *The Big Lebowski, O Brother, Where Art Thou?* (2000), *The Ladykillers* (2004) and *Inside Llewyn Davis* (2013) ideally belong to this category thanks to the soundtracks assembled by T-Bone Burnet, occasionally alongside Burwell's original score. Not only in these films do the chosen songs contextualise the story and dictate the pace of the editing – the title sequence of *The Big Lebowski*, built around Bob Dylan's 'The Man in Me', represents a seminal example – but they also closely contribute to the narrative. This happens in two different ways, either through an ironic commentary to the scene or because of the diegetic representation of the performance.[8]

The Coens consistently play with the source of the music, shifting back and forth from diegetic to extradiegetic, thereby often misleading the audience. As previously mentioned, on some occasions the categories overlap, creating interesting music textures. For example, one could consider a film such as *Inside Llewyn Davis* as an overlap between the categories of 'sound films' and 'tracked', with the diegetic folk songs as the only trace of music in a film otherwise surprisingly silent.

The types of songs selected for the soundtracks of the 'tracked' films are particularly noteworthy. From the use of folk music in *Raising Arizona*, specifically Pete Seeger's 'Goofin-off Suite', to the re-discovery of obscure tracks such as the version of 'Hotel California' by the Gipsy Kings in *The Big Lebowski* and 'Man of Constant Sorrow' in *O Brother, Where Art Thou?*, the Coens' soundtracks feature a relentless search for the less-known American music roots, including bluegrass and traditional folk, to the extent that Smith invites us to consider their work as that of music archivists.[9] Smith in fact argues that,

> on the one hand, the notion of the archivist serves to motivate the selection of unusual or unconventional material for the Coens' soundtracks [. . .]. On the other hand, by identifying Burnett's role in their productions as that of music archivist, the Coens reinforce their position outside of mainstream Hollywood. Like the archivist, the Coens' institutional niche is situated outside the nexus of commercial entertainment. Instead, the Coens align themselves with a culture in need of preservation, and thus embrace the values of marginalised folk cultures rather than corporatized mass culture.[10]

According to Smith, the selection of popular music in their films therefore offers a discourse of authenticity and historical continuity, highlighting how music in *O Brother, Where Art Thou?* and *The Ladykillers* contributes to the preservation and dissemination of vernacular music.[11] In *O Brother, Where Art Thou?* we witness the sudden popularisation of the ethnographic field recordings of Alan Lomax, present in the soundtrack, stressing the archaeological role of the film. What I find interesting is the question of 'authenticity' that seems to permeate the selection of music in the Coens' cinema within an oeuvre characterised by misleading signs and cultural references, lying characters and overall 'fakeness'.

From this perspective the use of music contributes to the creation of contradictions or ironic time/space coordinates, with music being the only authentic element in a clearly artificial narrative world. On occasions, diegetic music plays with misleading cultural references (*The Big Lebowski*) or engages with genre conventions and locations (*Raising Arizona, Intolerable Cruelty* [2003]).

Overall, the question of reality and authenticity does not usually feature in the thematic landscape of the Coens, despite the idealised indie mode of production characterised by an ironic detachment from Hollywood.[12] However, there is no doubt that among all the intertextual references typical of the Coens' filmmaking, in particular their references to literature and other films, it is in the selection of music, which they operate as a process of rediscovery and exhibition of forgotten tracks, that they create a comparable contemporary landscape akin to the work of Quentin Tarantino.[13]

Another level in which the music works is in the Coens' fascination for classical Hollywood manifested in their 'generic manipulation' of the syntax and syntagma of films noirs, westerns, gangsters and (slapstick) comedies, with elements of performative musicals briefly appearing in films such as *The Big Lebowski, O Brother, Where Art Thou?* and of course *Hail, Caesar!* (2016).[14]

COEN AND GENRE CINEMA: THE MUSICAL

Critics and scholars have not failed to notice the endless play of the Coen Brothers with genre and its intertextual connotations. From their debut *Blood Simple*, generic contamination has been at the centre of the brothers' idea of cinema and postmodern irony.[15] However, there is more than this. The Coen Brothers shoot films belonging to a specific genre in order to reflect on the genre itself. It is an imaginary structure that has been revealed to show the founding elements of the fictional world. The 'genre as contract' with the audience is signed and then betrayed and overcome, playing with the generic set of expectations, as happens with the 'this is a true story' incipit in *Fargo*.[16]

Moreover, the series of homages to the work of Raymond Chandler, James M. Cain and Dashiell Hammett, as well as the collection of cinematic references from classical Hollywood, contribute to underline the presence of an enunciator and remind that what the audience is watching is in effect a narrative artefact. The use of voice-over in several of their films, the onscreen narrators, and the stylistic excesses in the *mise en scène* contribute further to the reinforcement of the feeling of playful artificiality in the stories told.

The generic conventions play a crucial role in this regard, offering the Coens an opportunity to disassemble their syntactic and semantic elements, play with the narrative construction, and 'mix-up' the series of events that we come to expect for the development of a given genre, stylistic features and, especially, in its characters and tropes. Femme fatales, cowboys, crooks, millionaires, out-of-town dreamers, etc. characterise the Coens' filmography, often displaced in situations, places, and generic structures and conventions where they do not belong. *The Big Lebowski* can be seen as the clearest example of this genre contamination with its mix of witty humour, quirky characters, references to a past counterculture, and a noir novel structure; its soundtrack is central for determining the functions of the characters and important for the feeling of displacement of the generic syntax.[17]

The Coens' protagonists end up in situations that they do not belong to, they lie and they make stupid decisions; this recurrent feature can be found in the entirety of their filmography and it is constantly stressed by the score and music choices. The genre works as a first framing of the stories told, considered here as a set of instructions for the narrative development and conventions that are then mixed with that of another genre (from film noir and screwball comedy to melodrama) and reframed once again with a diegetic or extradiegetic enunciator, stressing the fictional storytelling aspect of their films.

Furthermore, there are several figures of reception inscribed in the Coens' work that put emphasis on the narrative frame. In fact, in *The Hudsucker Proxy* (1994) and *The Big Lebowski* the narrator addresses directly the extradiegetic presence of an audience. In the latter film, for instance, the cowboy narrator directly addresses the audience, talking into the camera and warning The Dude about his improper language.

Looking at the adoption of musical genre tropes in the Coens' filmography, we can see how its features appear throughout their work, mainly in three interconnected elements: artificiality, diegetic performances and homage. The first level of interplay between the Coens' films and the musical genre is the element of artificiality. As Barry Langford maintains,

> unlike the Western or the gangster film, the musical seems unencumbered by any ongoing commitments to social realism, historical authenticity or for that matter of any suggestion of performative naturalism (though the genre may embrace any or all of these at different times). The musical creates a hermetically enclosed generic world whose conventions and verisimilitudes are purely and peculiarly its own, and whose function is to enable and situate the musical performances that define the form.[18]

This is arguably what happens across the Coen Brothers' cinema, characterised by worlds where features of verisimilitude are constantly put into jeopardy. It is sufficient to think of the cartoonesque style and development of *Raising Arizona* to have an idea of it. If we consider the film musical as the genre with less ambition of 'realistic' likelihood, since the generic, thematic and stylistic elements dictate at least an acknowledgement of the artifice of the performance, we can see how the same attitude permeates several Coens' films. Indeed, considering that the film musical 'has always foregrounded its nature as generic construct and thus demanded the greatest suspension of disbelief by its audience', the Coens' films tend to work like a musical even when they are mainly based on other genres.[19] Here I am thinking of the different occurrences of when the narration stops and something else happens only for the visual pleasure (or amusement) of the audience. It may be a dream sequence (*Miller's Crossing*, *The Hudsucker Proxy*, *The Man Who Wasn't There* [2001]), a digression in the story (*Fargo*, *A Serious Man* [2009]) or a dream-like sequence or frame (*Barton Fink*); they stop the narrative and showcase the *mise en scène*, highlighting the stylistic qualities of the shooting. This is the case, for instance, in the recurring chasing of the hat in *Miller's Crossing* and the camera's subjective dive into the sink in *Barton Fink*.

The second level is that of the diegetic performances. The cinema of the

Coens features on several occasions protagonists who are professional enter-
tainers; playing an instrument, acting, singing or dancing, doing what in film
musical terms can be defined as 'performance mode'.[20] From *The Man Who
Wasn't There* to *Inside Llewyn Davis* and *Barton Fink*, these films show a
certain degree of *mise en abyme* of the cinematic apparatus through the presence of performers and audiences. In order to understand the use of performance in these films it can be helpful to look at the difference between the
notion of the integrated musical, in which the musical numbers are 'woven
into the narrative structure, motivated by character psychology and/or plot
development and expressive of the emotions, opinions or state of mind of the
singer(s)', and non-integrated, which are a collection of musical numbers as
'stand-alone spectacles connected only loosely'.[21]

Despite this division lacking clarity, it may be helpful when considering the
musical references in the Coens' films. For instance, the oneiric sequences in
The Big Lebowski and the performances in *O Brother, Where Art Thou?* and
The Ladykillers are undoubtedly integrated: linked to the narrative and the
plot development. Overall, the Coens' films show a peculiar fascination for the
moment of the performance. It is sufficient to think of how in *Inside Llewyn
Davis* Oscar Isaac not only plays the role of the protagonist but also performs
the rearrangements of folk songs, and in *Hail, Caesar!* Channing Tatum had to
learn how to tap dance, to understand how the camera 'capturing' the actors'
numbers has something in common with the more traditional musicals.

Finally, and strongly connected to the previous level, the third level is the
one of the 'musical homage'. This is case when the Coens' films are very
explicit in adopting stylistic and narrative features belonging to film musicals.
In a way not dissimilar to what they have done with film noir, gangster films
and Westerns, the playful reappropriation of the genre emerges on several
occasions, including dancing sequences, high angle shots and mass choreographies reminiscent of Busby Berkeley's films.

The musical performance, in the most classical manifestation with singing
and dancing, appears in a dream sequence of *The Big Lebowski*, with perfect
dream-ballets similar to the musical *Oklahoma* (Fred Zinnemann, 1955), and
in the backstage musical of *Hail, Caesar!*. The first features clear references to
Berkeley's choreographies, in particular *42nd Street* (Lloyd Bacon, 1933) with
the shot through the legs of the dancers and *Gold Diggers* (Busby Berkeley,
Mervyn LeRoy 1933) with the big dancing shadow of The Dude cast on a wall.
This is also the first time that the Coens employ musical-like costumes, inspired
on this occasion by the events of the film, summarised in the dream sequence.
Hail, Caesar! continues in this direction in its homage of the musical, featuring
a backstage musical typical of many classical integrated films. While the tap
dance over the song 'No Dames', with characters dressed like sailors, refers
to *Anchors Aweigh* (George Sidney, 1945), the aquatic scene with Scarlett

Johansson is a reprise of *Million Dollar Mermaid* (Mervyn LeRoy, 1952) and the synchronised swimming of the 'aquamusicals' starring Esther Williams.

Interestingly, in both cases of actual musical performance in the films, the narrative is suspended, the songs do not contribute or offer new information nor do they reveal sides of the characters. They are moment of 'pure' entertainment, revealing at the same time the artificiality of it.

Although an analysis of Burwell's score for *Hail, Caesar!* may undoubtedly be fruitful, I would like instead to focus on the specific film where the musical tropes, albeit not as clearly present as in the last two examples, are more intertwined with the narrative and which, as such, embodies the essence of the Coens' relationship with the soundtrack: *O Brother, Where Art Thou?*.

HOMER, OZ AND AMERICANA

Set in 1937 Mississippi, *O Brother, Where Art Thou?* tells the story of Ulysses Everett McGill (George Clooney), Pete Hogwallop (John Turturro) and Delmar O'Donnell (Tim Blake Nelson), three prisoners who escape from a chain gang in order to find a hidden treasure. After picking up Tommy Johnson (Chris Thomas King), a hitchhiker who sold his soul to the devil to play guitar, the trio perform at a radio station under the name the 'Soggy Bottom Boys' to make some cash. The popularity of the recorded song 'Man of Constant Sorrow' will become pivotal in the development of the story and the gaining of a pardon by the governor.

The film is loosely inspired by *The Odyssey* and once again features cinematic references that span from *The Wizard of Oz* (Victor Fleming, 1939) to Preston Sturges' film *Sullivan's Travels* (1941), in which one of the characters plans but never manages to shoot a Great Depression film with the title the Coen's work borrows.[22] Burnett's soundtrack lists a series of folk songs, gospel, bluegrass, dirges and traditional chants, which add historical connotation and, more importantly, are key to the narrative. Indeed, the diegetic performances dictate the rhythm of the film, with songs working to punctuate each stage of the story and the different encounters made by the three protagonists. It is significant in this regard that the soundtrack was recorded before the shooting of the film and in fact the involvement of Burnett, who worked on *The Big Lebowski* two years before, began at the final stage of screenwriting.

The Appalachian mountain folk song 'Man of Constant Sorrow', first recorded in 1922, was one of the archival discoveries of Burnett and contributed to the critical acclaim of the soundtrack due to it being exemplar of the 'authenticity' of folk music the film brought to global prominence.[23] For a detailed analysis of the songs and the ways they work within the film, I refer to the already mentioned work by Smith, which has a particular stress on a comparative analysis with the soundtrack of *Raising Arizona*.

Instead, what I would like to discuss here is how we can consider the film as a musical, in particular exploring the question of its performance mode not being limited to the music but also to other elements such as the choreography, the representation of audience, and the features that stress the creation of a fictional world. In fact, the digitally corrected colour by the cinematographer Richard Jenkins, in order to make the film look like an old postcard, the title card in the opening credit to remind the viewer of the *Odyssey* as a literary source for the film and, finally, the first encounter with a blind clairvoyant narrator, are all cues of the artificiality of the enunciation and the power of the storytelling. Several scholars have already pointed out the similarities between this film and the classical musical. Arthur Knight, for instance, claims that

> it is also a musical of a kind that even formalist genre critics would recognise. Since *O Brother* carefully, if fancifully, motivates all its performances and uses 'folk' music [. . .] it might even be seen as a formally integrated musical.[24]

From this perspective music starts right away from the opening titles, with a field recording by music archivists Alan Lomax and Shirley Collins of 'Po' Lazarus' performed by James Carter and the Prisoners. The song is presented diegetically in the film with the post-synch singing of prisoners in a chain-gang breaking stones. The rhythm of the breaking noise is the base of the song and the diegetic source of sound is made evident after a series of establishing shots of the Mississippi's countryside characterised by maize fields.

From the opening scene of the film the music is set as a crucial aspect of this fictional world and if we look at the very detailed categorisation of film musicals provided by John Muller and based on the different level of contributions of the music numbers to the plot, we can grasp how the opening song is a number which contributes 'to the spirit or theme'.[25] During the film there are several moments such as this, when the 'root music' is present to stress the importance of it in that time and place and the key characterisation in politics and everyday life. The diegetic musical support to the imprisonment of Baby Face Nelson and the performances during political rallies are further examples of this aspect. Establishing from the opening scene that music is an important part of this narrative world creates an expectation for the performance, which is one of the generic conditions of the musical.

Looking at the analyses proposed by Rick Altman, we can see instead how this film can be defined as a 'Folk Musical' considering how it 'projects the audience into a mythicised version of the cultural past'.[26] Memory, in fact, plays a central role and shows the tendency to glorify the past that 'takes place within that intermediary space we designate by such terms as tradition, folklore and Americana'.[27]

If the first purpose of music in *O Brother, Where Art Thou?* is to contribute to the spirit of an idealised time and space, later in the film there is a series of performances that are inextricable from the development of the plot. To categorise them based on Muller's categories would be complicated due to their overlapping nature. The scenes where the entirety of a song is performed are crucial for the advancing of the story: they cannot be erased without creating serious holes in the narration.

However, it is notable that the content of the lyrics does not necessarily add new information apart from re-establishing the condition of the world narrated. In fact, the song lyrics reaffirm the characters (such as 'Man of Constant Sorrow', 'Hard Time Killing Floor Blues' and 'Down by the River to Pray'). Interestingly, not all the new encounters of the three fugitives are framed with a song, but the musical performances play a key role every time a *group* of characters is introduced.

From the members of the Ku Klux Klan to the congregation going to the river for a baptism, singing 'Down by the River To Pray', the introduction of a group is the opportunity to have a choreographed performance that, despite not erupting into a dance sequence, shares features of the film musical. These numbers clearly advance the plot: the baptism dictates a change in the characters, the meeting with the sirens – attracted by the song 'Didn't Leave Nobody but the Baby' – sets in motion the disappearance of Turturro's character and the KKK scene leads to one of the main confrontations with the antagonists.

Such use of choreography is another 'music pun' as it is associated with a KKK rally to lynch Tommy Johnson. This is a further intertextual play, which refers to *Blazing Saddles* (Mel Brooks, 1974), another film that mixes genres with a high degree of film musical influence, and *The Wizard of Oz*. However, it also carefully places diegetic spectators (the three fugitives) in the performance space, offering a point of view from above of the choreography reminiscent of Busby Berkeley. Alongside the performance element, the question of the audience appears on several occasions during the film: in a cinema theatre, at the radio, in a live music hall, in a political rally. The ideas of stage and spectacle are central in the plot development and in the resolution of the film. This is true to the extent that it is the improvised performance of the trio in front of an audience that leads to the bigger plot point of the story. It is in fact the enthusiastic reaction of the spectators to the Soggy Bottom Boys that marks the defeat of the KKK leader and the triumph of the trio with a state pardon by the governor.

The active diegetic presence of the audience not only represents the enunciation frame of the film and suggests a reaction to the performance for the film audience, playing once again with genre expectations. It also links with the backstage musical (or show musicals for Altman), where the success of the characters' performance is central for the story. I am thinking of musicals such as *42nd Street* set during the Great Depression and where the chance of success for its protagonists, *in primis* the newcomer dancer Peggy Sawyer (Ruby Keeler), is linked to the reception of their show.

While the references to the *Wizard of Oz* are again mainly focused on the creation of a fictional world, in this case to be dominated by mass media, the musical structure follows closely the making of the performances. This is very distant from a 'lip-synch' musical mode where images show only some of the music production, usually singing or dancing.[28] Therefore, it is interesting to summarise which aspects of the musical genre appear in *O Brother, Where Art Thou?*, keeping in mind of course that there are no direct citations as in *Hail, Caesar!* and *The Big Lebowski.*

First of all, the semantic elements of the musical are present in the key role played by the recurring singing and playing in the world depicted by the film. This works both to create a temporal contextualisation and to rediscover what the Coens define as roots music: the backbone of American culture. Secondly, the genre contributes to the setting of the film in an extradiegetic way, with the association between the Great Depression and the Classical Musical.[29] Thirdly, we need to consider the different degrees of 'integration' in the narrative of the songs performed diegetically, in terms of lyrics and characterisation of the protagonists. Finally, we have the issue of performance that is a *mise en abyme* of the cinematic apparatus and reminds us once again of the fictionality of the world depicted and the inclusion of the audience.

From this perspective, *O Brother, Where Art Thou?* remains a unique experiment in the Coens' filmography. The next strongly diegetically 'tracked' films, *The Ladykillers* and *Inside Llewyn Davis*, did not consistently match the same level of narrative dependency on the performances of a musical narrative structure punctuated by songs and choreographic elements. Surely, performance is key for both the framing of the Greenwich folk scene and to grasp the relationship between characters in *Inside Llewyn Davis* and, more importantly, the role played by the representation of audiences in that film, being a single individual or a crowd, is not dissimilar to *O Brother, Where Art Thou?*. However, the content of the performance is more detached from the narrative, making it closer to films centred on music stars rather than film musicals.[30]

To conclude, we need to return to the latest work by the Coens, *Hail, Caesar!* as, I would argue, it is the moment where all the playing around with generic conventions becomes even more intertwined with their artificiality and the framing of the narrative. In several interviews Burwell confirms the challenge of writing scores for the different classical 'films in the film'.[31] Indeed, film's illustration of the work of a classic Hollywood studio – already briefly depicted in *Barton Fink*, albeit with a focus on the screenwriter's role – here privileges the genre-factory production: from the historical blockbuster to the Western. Two of the films shot 'diegetically' in the studio of *Hail, Caesar!*

are indeed musicals, paying homage to two different aspects of the genre, but both centred around the dancing and singing performance and highly choreographed scenes. The level of integration of these performances is, however, very loose. If they were removed the plot would not be affected by their absence.[32] They introduce new characters, but overall these scenes belong to the category of 'numbers which are completely irrelevant to the plot'.[33]

Interestingly, under this category Mueller lists

> numbers in which the major characters in the plot watch the performance along with the audience, but do not participate in it. The characters, for example, may go to a night club and let the plot pause as they are entertained, but otherwise unaffected, by performers who appear, do their routine, and then vanish.[34]

Despite the fact that the performers introduced do not vanish form the narrative of *Hail, Caesar!*, we can see how the plot stops to allow the character of Eddie Mannix (Josh Brolin) to watch the musical performance alongside us, the spectators.

While these integrated numbers overlap with the category 'contribute to the spirit or theme', it is paradoxically and semantically less relevant to the narrative than the use of musical performances in *O Brother, Where Art Thou?*, thus making it a mainly stylistic work for the Coens in a way not dissimilar to *The Big Lebowski*. Nonetheless, what is interesting is that the musical theme is constantly recurring in the Coens' oeuvre, waiting to become the main generic element of a future film.

NOTES

1. As Carter Burwell points out, 'In Joel and Ethan's films that feature of lot of songs, they are usually referenced in the script'; quoted in Daniel Dylan Wray, 'Carter Burwell on writing the soundtrack to the Coen Brothers' career', *Little White Lies*, 23 February 2016, available at <http://lwlies.com/articles/carter-burwell-coen-brothers-soundtracks/> (last accessed 5 September 2016).
2. See Tom Zlabinger, 'Listening deeply to Lebowski: one fan attempt to draw a musical map surrounding the Dude', in Zachary Ingle (ed.), *Fan Phenomena: The Big Lebowski* (Chicago: Intellect Press, 2014), p. 97.
3. Jeff Smith, 'O Brother, Where Chart Thou? Pop music and the Coen Brothers', in Ashby Arved (ed.), *Popular Music and the New Auteur: Visionary Filmmakers after MTV* (Oxford: Oxford University Press, 2013), p. 131.
4. On the differences between scored and tracked films, see K. J. Donnelly, *Magical Musical Tour: Rock and Pop in Film Soundtracks* (New York: Bloomsbury Academic, 2015), p. 8.
5. Randall Barnes, 'The sound of Coen comedy: music, dialogue and sound effects in *Raising Arizona*', *The Soundtrack*, 7 November 2008, 1(1): 15–28.
6. For an analysis of sound in *Barton Fink* able to reveal the collaboration between Burwell and Lievsay as well as the role played by the aural dimension in the Coens'

cinema, see Randall Barnes, 'Barton Fink: atmospheric sounds of the creative mind sound practices of the Coen Brothers', Off Screen, September 2007, 11(8–9), available at <http://offscreen.com/view/barnes_bartonfink> (last accessed 12 February 2016).

7. Dennis Lim, 'Exploiting sound, exploring silence', New York Times, 6 January 2008, available at <http://www.nytimes.com/2008/01/06/movies/awardsseason/06lim.html?_r=1> (last accessed 31 August 2016).

8. Of course, as already mentioned, these categories may overlap. I am thinking for instance of A Serious Man (2009), where the score of Burwell is on crucial occasions interrupted by significant silences, noises from unseen sources and extradiegetic songs. The latter is the case in the 'Goy's teeth' scene where the off-screen narration of the rabbi has 'Machine Gun' by Jimmy Hendrix playing in the background.

9. Smith, 'O Brother, Where Chart Thou?'.

10. Ibid. p. 149.

11. Ibid. p. 151.

12. Ibid. p. 150.

13. It is also important to point out the commercial and critical success of the soundtracks of the 'tracked?' films: O Brother, Where Art Thou? eventually ended up winning Grammy awards and selling almost 8 million copies.

14. See Rick Altman, 'A semantic/syntactic approach to film genre', Cinema Journal, Spring 1984, 23(3): 6–18.

15. Among others see Joseph Natoli, Postmodern Journeys: Film and Culture, 1996–1998 (Albany, NY: State University of New York Press, 2000), pp. 247–51.

16. Rick Altman, Film/Genre (London: British Film Institute, 1999).

17. See Tom Zlabinger, 'Listening deeply to Lebowski'.

18. Barry Langford, Film Genre: Hollywood and Beyond (Edinburgh: Edinburgh University Press, 2005), p. 83.

19. Barry Keith Grant, The Hollywood Film Musical (Malden, MA: Wiley-Blackwell, 2012), p. 3.

20. See Donnelly, Magical Musical Tour, p. 10.

21. Barry Langford, Film Genre, p. 85.

22. On the relationship between the film and The Odyssey see Margaret Toscano, 'Homer meets the Coen Brothers: memory as artistic pastiche in O Brother, Where Art Thou?', Film & History: An Interdisciplinary Journal of Film and Television Studies, 2009, 39(2): 49–62; doi:10.1353/flm.0.0125.

23. Among others, Ryan P. Doom argues that 'in many respects, the soundtrack from O Brother, Where Art Thou? overshadowed the movie as it went eight times platinum and ignited a blue grass revival. Produced by T-Bone Burnett, the sound created a rare non-musical musical'; Ryan P. Doom, The Brothers Coen: Unique Characters of Violence (Santa Barbara, CA: Greenwood Press, 2009), p. 109.

24. Arthur Knight, Disintegrating the Musical: Black Performance and American Musical Film (Durham, NC: Duke University Press, 2002), p. 235.

25. John Mueller, 'Fred Astaire and the integrated musical', Cinema Journal, 1984, 24(1): 28.

26. Rick Altman, The American Film Musical (Bloomington: Indiana University Press, 1988), p. 272.

27. Ibid. p. 271.

28. See Donnelly Magical Musical Tour, p. 10.

29. See Altman, The American Film Musical; Jane Feuer, The Hollywood Musical (BFI Cinema), 2nd edn (Basingstoke: Palgrave Macmillan, 1992); and Raymond Knapp, The American Musical and the Formation of National Identity, 2nd edn (Princeton, NJ: Princeton University Press, 2006).

30. See Donnelly, *Magical Musical Tour*.
31. For instance in Daniel Dylan Wray, 'Carter Burwell on writing the soundtrack'.
32. Arguably, this happens for all the 'inserts' from the films diegetically shot in the studio in *Hail, Caesar!*.
33. Mueller, 'Fred Astaire and the integrated musical', p. 28.
34. Ibid. p. 29.

BIBLIOGRAPHY

Altman, Rick, 'A semantic/syntactic approach to film genre', *Cinema Journal*, Spring 1984, 23(3): 6–18.
Altman, Rick, *Film/Genre* (London: British Film Institute, 1999).
Altman, Rick, *The American Film Musical* (Bloomington: Indiana University Press, 1988).
Ashby, Arved (ed.), *Popular Music and the New Auteur: Visionary Filmmakers After MTV* (New York: Oxford University Press, 2013).
Barnes, Randall, '*Barton Fink*: atmospheric sounds of the creative mind sound practices of the Coen Brothers', *Off Screen*, September 2007, 11(8–9), <http://offscreen.com/view/barnes_bartonfink> (last accessed 12 February 2016).
Barnes, Randall, 'The sound of Coen comedy: music, dialogue and sound effects in *Raising Arizona*', *The Soundtrack*, 7 November 2008, 1(1): 15–28.
Brophy, Philip, 'Carter Burwell in conversation', in William G. Luhr (ed.), *The Coen Brothers' Fargo*, Cambridge University Press Film Handbooks, general ed. Andrew Horton (Cambridge: Cambridge University Press, 2014), pp. 128–36.
Donnelly, K. J., *Magical Musical Tour: Rock and Pop in Film Soundtracks* (New York: Bloomsbury Academic, 2015).
Doom, Ryan P., *The Brothers Coen: Unique Characters of Violence* (Santa Barbara, CA: Greenwood Press, 2009).
Feuer, Jane, *The Hollywood Musical (BFI Cinema)*, 2nd edn (Basingstoke: Palgrave Macmillan, 1992).
Grant, Barry Keith, *The Hollywood Film Musical* (Malden, MA: Wiley-Blackwell, 2012).
Knapp, Raymond, *The American Musical and the Formation of National Identity*, 2nd edn (Princeton, NJ: Princeton University Press, 2006).
Knight, Arthur, *Disintegrating the Musical: Black Performance and American Musical Film* (Durham, NC: Duke University Press, 2002).
Langford, Barry, *Film Genre: Hollywood and Beyond* (Edinburgh: Edinburgh University Press, 2005).
Lim, Dennis, 'Exploiting sound, exploring silence', *New York Times*, 6 January 2008, <http://www.nytimes.com/2008/01/06/movies/awardsseason/06lim.html?_r=1> (last accessed 31 August 2016).
Mitchell, L. C., 'Dismantling the Western: film noir's defiance of genre in *No Country for Old Men*', *Genre*, 1 September 2014, 47(3): 335–56; doi:10.1215/00166928-2797327.
Mueller, John, 'Fred Astaire and the integrated musical', *Cinema Journal*, 1984, 24(1): 28–40.
Natoli, Joseph, *Postmodern Journeys: Film and Culture, 1996–1998* (Albany, NY: State University of New York Press, 2000).
Smith, Jeff, 'O Brother, Where Chart Thou? Pop music and the Coen Brothers', in Ashby Arved (ed.), *Popular Music and the New Auteur: Visionary Filmmakers after MTV* (Oxford: Oxford University Press, 2013), pp. 129–56.
Toscano, Margaret M., 'Homer meets the Coen Brothers: memory as artistic pastiche in

O Brother, Where Art Thou?', *Film & History: An Interdisciplinary Journal of Film and Television Studies*, 2009, 39(2): 49–62; doi:10.1353/flm.0.0125.

Wray, Daniel Dylan, 'Carter Burwell on writing the soundtrack to the Coen Brothers' career', *Little White Lies*, 23 February 2016, <http://lwlies.com/articles/carter-burwell-coen-brothers-soundtracks/> (last accessed 5 September 2016).

Zlabinger, Tom, 'Listening deeply to Lebowski: one fan attempt to draw a musical map surrounding the Dude', in Zachary Ingle (ed.), *Fan Phenomena: The Big Lebowski*, (Chicago: Intellect Press, 2014), pp. 96–110.

10 RACING IN THE BEAT: MUSIC IN THE *FAST & FURIOUS* FRANCHISE

Todd Decker

The Fast and the Furious (2001, hereafter *FF1*) – first instalment in the *Fast & Furious* film franchise (hereafter *FF*) (Table 10.1) – opens with a public service announcement by a blonde young man, who says to the camera, 'Hi, I'm Paul Walker starring in *The Fast and the Furious*. All the racing stunts in our film are performed in a staged environment by professionals with years of training and experience. So, with that in mind: be smart, dive safe, and stay legal.' *Furious 7* (2015, hereafter *FF7*) – seventh of a planned ten *FF* films – closes with a music video-style tribute to Walker, who died in a car crash on 30 November 2013. Walker was in the passenger seat when driver Roger Rodas, driving in excess of 80 miles per hour, crashed his 2005 Porsche Carrera GT into a concrete light post in a suburb north of Los Angeles in an area frequented by street racers and drifting enthusiasts. Both men were killed.

Walker's death occurred while *FF7* was still shooting and the extent to which his part had been committed to film was kept secret. And so, the experience of watching *FF7* when it opened in April 2015 was shadowed for viewers by the mystery of when and how – or, it became apparent as the film unfolded, if – Walker's character Brian O'Conner, a central figure in the franchise, would die in the film. Indeed, Brian survives to the final scene of *FF7*, where he is seen playing on the beach with his wife, Mia (Jordana Brewster), and young son, Jack. Three principal characters comment on the sight. Roman (Tyrese Gibson) – introduced as Brian's childhood friend and Walker's sole co-star in *2 Fast 2 Furious* (2003, hereafter *FF2*) – looks upon the young family and says one word: 'Beautiful'. Letty (Michelle Rodriguez) – who dies and is buried in *Fast*

& *Furious* (2009, hereafter *FF4*), returns a victim of amnesia in *Fast & Furious* 6 (2013, hereafter *FF6*), and regains her memory in *FF7*, looks at Brian, Mia and Jack but speaks only of Brian: 'That's where he belongs.' Dominic, or Dom, Toretto (Vin Diesel) – leader of the franchise's shifting team of drivers and thieves – continues Letty's focus on Brian: 'Home. Where he's always belonged.' Roman adds, 'Things are gonna be different now.' As Dom rises to leave, a minor character, new to the franchise in *FF7*, asks him, 'You aren't going to say goodbye?' At this moment, the soft piano and strings scoring the three friends' spoken farewells to Brian – readable as words of grief on the loss of Walker – comes to a pause: the piano falls silent, suspending all sense of meter; a pedal in the strings creates a sense of expectation, haloing Dom's response.

But just before Dom says 'It's never goodbye', a new piano melody enters, a melody known to many in the film's audience as the introduction to 'See You Again', a pop-rap track by black rapper Wiz Khalifa – familiar to *FF* fans from 'We Own It', the opening titles music to *FF6* – and featuring the young white pop singer Charlie Puth, who had just recently emerged on the national music scene by way of self-made YouTube videos. 'See You Again' was a phenomenally successful recording. It sat atop *Billboard*'s US Hot 100 chart for twelve weeks (tying the record for a rap track), briefly held the record for most streams in a single day in the US on the streaming service Spotify, and, according to the global recording industry group IFPI, was the best-selling digital single worldwide in 2015 with 20.9 million units (combining single-track downloads and track-equivalent streams).[1] The song's official video – mostly Khalifa rapping and Puth singing next to street racing cars, intercut with select clips from multiple *FF* films – is currently the second-most viewed music video in YouTube history, exceeded only by Psy's 'Gangnam Style'.[2]

As Puth's vocal begins in the film, an indescribably sad shot of Letty looking toward Brian and family (and the camera) initiates the franchise's musical farewell to Walker. Dom, it turns out, has gone for a drive. 'See You Again' could, perhaps, be understood as the music in his car – except Dom never fiddles with the radio. On a picturesque road, he pauses at a stop sign in his grey car and sits, lost in thought. A white car pulls alongside. It is Brian, of course. He looks at Dom, his best friend and brother-in-law, and says, 'Hey, thought you could leave without saying goodbye?'. Brian is shot from behind on the line; we do not see his lips moving, it might not actually be his voice. The two exchange looks from their respective driver's seats, as they had so often in previous films, poised here again as if at the starting line for a race. In voiceover, Dom/Diesel says his goodbye to Brian/Walker in past tense – 'I used to say I lived my life a quarter-mile at a time. And I think that's why we were brothers. Because you did too.' – and the screen goes to black just as Puth launches into the wordless wail hook of 'See You Again', a repeated, descending vocal line that comes across as a pop explosion of grief and loss. Tears were not uncommon among opening weekend audiences at this point – at least in my row of a packed suburban St Louis cinema. As the song plays, clips of Brian from across the franchise with all the major characters, some with spoken dialogue, invite the viewer to relive the *FF* saga in seconds. To close the sequence, the film returns to Brian and Dom in their white and grey cars cruising easily down the road. One last glimpse of Brian in his car, smiling over at Dom, has a glowing quality that suggests CGI; the shot likely assembled posthumously from existing footage, a shimmering memorial to Walker, the actor's beatified final film appearance. Then, in a symbolic shot, peaceful and fluid like almost no previous moment in the franchise, the 'brothers' part company, as Brian's car follows a fork in the road to the left while Dom's continues on. The camera tilts to the sky and goes to white. *FF7* and 'See You Again' end with the words *For Paul* flashed on screen.

FF7's extended musical goodbye to Walker taps the profoundly musical nature of the entire franchise. Musical sequences drawing on, and at times drawn directly from, popular music mark every *FF* film thus far. This globally successful action franchise relies heavily on popular music, tapping into an expansive if defined set of beat-driven genres: hip hop and electronic dance music mostly, with Latin, Asian and metal touches as appropriate to story location and character identities. The *FF* films share a cultivated, audio-visual aesthetic centred on the pleasure of watching cars, at rest and in motion, to the sound of potent, rhythmic, often popular music. *FF7*'s 'See You Again' montage mines the franchise's deep connection to hip hop along an especially pop-oriented vein but expresses directly the franchise's persistent use of popular music to structure and support images of cars and their drivers. And while 'See You Again' stands out within the franchise for its moderate tempo,

Table 10.1 *Franchise information for* Fast & Furious *films.*

	Title	Release date	Director	Composer	Setting
FF1	*The Fast and the Furious*	2001	Rob Cohen	BT	Los Angeles
FF2	*2 Fast 2 Furious*	2003	John Singleton	David Arnold	Miami
FF3	*The Fast and the Furious: Tokyo Drift*	2006	Justin Lin	Brian Tyler	Tokyo
FF4	*Fast & Furious*	2009	Justin Lin	Brian Tyler	Dominican Republic, Los Angeles, Mexico
FF5	*Fast Five*	2011	Justin Lin	Brian Tyler	Rio de Janiero
FF6	*Fast & Furious 6*	2013	Justin Lin	Lucas Vidal	London, Spain
FF7	*Furious 7*	2015	James Wan	Brian Tyler	Los Angeles, Caucasus Mountains, Abu Dhabi

sustained nature, lyrical qualities and extra-textual purpose, the sequence's combination of musical and visual elements draws directly on defining aspects of the franchise's remarkably consistent cinematic world.

This chapter details and analyses how music and image are combined in the *FF* films, defining the several and overlapping ways the franchise's signature action sequences function as musical numbers by another name. While some of these ways are typical for twenty-first-century action films, and thus illuminate the action genre more generally, others are unique to the car-centred world of *FF*. The franchise's characteristic clustering of street racing culture, popular music and male sexual fantasies are also described below.

Three sorts of car-specific action fuel *FF* narratives: (1) high-speed chases, often involving hijackings; (2) formal and informal street races; and (3) a cluster of street racing practices, such as the customising (or modification) of racing cars in garages and the display of cars in semi-public outdoor settings, grouped together here under the term *street racing sociability*. In formal terms within *FF* narratives, chases, races and street racing sociability are presented in more or less discrete units of varied duration, marked by specific if hybridised beat-driven musical styles and shaped to a remarkable degree by musical textures and forms. These are, in essence, musical numbers where the bodies in motion are cars and their drivers. (Only the franchise's ubiquitous and anonymous 'hot girls' ever dance.) *FF*'s car chases – a common narrative device in action films since the 1970s – are, unsurprisingly, rather conventional in their use of music. The original scoring used in chases typifies twenty-first-century scoring trends. Races and street racing sociability define *FF*'s storyworld, an original-to-cinema realm, based on characters created for the first film by Gary Scott Thompson, which has found great success in an era dominated by adaptations of pre-existing properties such as comics and book series. Popular music, both compiled from existing sources and recorded or remixed especially for *FF*, does crucial work defining the franchise's utopian world. Races, the street festival atmosphere surrounding them, and the joyful labour of working on cars are brought together in a realm of pure pleasure marked and instantly evoked by musical means.

CHASES

Chases typically function as set-piece action sequences of great narrative consequence within each film's crime and/or law enforcement plot. Starting with the first moments of *FF1*, a trope is developed across most of the series: a single large vehicle is either hijacked or brought to a violent stop by three smaller, sometimes identical, vehicles driven by Dom and his team. The size of the larger vehicle escalates: a semi-truck or eighteen-wheeler (*FF1*), a 'landtrain' of four tanker trailers (*FF4*), a bus taking Dom to prison (*FF5*), a massive tank, followed by a military cargo jet (*FF6*). *FF5* reverses the equation: Dom, Brian and Mia steal three sports cars from a moving train. *FF7*, with the larger theme 'cars don't fly', ups the ante: Dom, Letty, Brian and Roman each eject in a car, out the back of a cargo plane, parachuting to earth and landing exactly as intended on a twisting mountain road, where the quartet hijacks then destroys a gun-laden, bus-like rolling fortress. (*FF2* and *FF3*, with their tangential connection to the Dom–Brian saga, do not include high-speed chases involving one large and three smaller vehicles but both do include high-stakes chases.) With the exception of *FF1*, the plot-driven chases are fully musicalised with beat-driven original scoring typical of twenty-first-century action movies. Composer Brian Tyler's cue 'Landtrain' for *FF4*'s opening sequence offers a typical chase scene score. Music plays a major role marking important points of action, dividing the sequence into coherent narrative chunks, and generating an ever-escalating sense of danger.

The scenario involves Dom and company in the Dominican Republic stealing tanker trailers of fuel from a moving 'landtrain' – one truck and driver towing four tanker trailers – on a mountain road. The hijack begins when Letty jumps from Dom's car onto the endmost trailer. The first of two trucks in Dom's team pulls up behind the landtrain, reverses direction at full speed, and drives in reverse to within feet of the back tanker trailer. A member of Dom's crew tosses a hitch linking the truck – still traveling in reverse – to the trailer. Letty, meanwhile, sprays the hitch two trailers ahead with powerful chemicals, then strikes the compromised metal with a hammer, causing the hitch to break. The linked truck speeds off in the opposite direction with two stolen tankers. Initially, the hijack goes according to plan. A single driving beat, running at 128 bpm (beats per minute) and mixed with noisy sound effects, undergirds the above described action. Here, the beat-driven score's steady rhythmic energy suggests utter physical competence and driving mastery on the part of Dom and his crew. Tyler avoids hitting precise moments of action in the music except for one: the moment when Letty breaks the hitch – the achievement of the robbery – is marked by a thinning of the texture. Beat-driven scores built, like most electronic musics, in layers often employ sudden textural changes to mark events without stopping the beat. The musical forces used in 'Landtrain', however, suggest a conventional Hollywood orchestra, albeit with audibly electronic touches and 'produced' or altered sounds.

The attempt to steal the next pair of tankers goes awry when the landtrain driver spots Letty in his side mirror just as the second truck in Dom's crew successfully hooks to the remaining two trailers. The beat abruptly increases to 155 bpm as the driver takes aggressive defensive action: swerving back and forth, he endangers the now connected truck and causes Letty to fall. She barely catches herself on the ladder to the top of the tanker, where she dangles precariously. This state of affairs is solved initially by having Dom reverse direction at full speed to break the hitch so the second truck can pull free. Letty, however, is left hanging on the remaining tanker. Suddenly, the beat stops, though synth strings continue and crescendo, on a cut to the landtrain driver, who looks down the mountain road and sees a sharp corner at the end of a long, straight descent. The pause in the beat works to re-calibrate the physics of the scenario: an end-point to this chase has been posited and only so much space and time remain. The change in the music, specifically the brief cessation of the beat, reinforces this point of formal articulation in the action. After the pause, Tyler drops the beat back in at an even faster 171 bpm as Dom rescues Letty – she leaps from the trailer to his car; her jump marked by another thinning of the texture – and the landtrain driver bails out. The conclusion of the sequence, with even louder sound effects from explosions and such, uses a fourth beat texture, faster yet and deeper in the mix, which stops when Dom escapes by driving under the last tanker as it bounces down the road towards his car.

Tyler's score for the landtrain sequence contains no distinctive melodic motifs or themes and is undistinguished in its rhythmic content: the music is 'generic' in the sense that it sounds entirely typical of twenty-first-century action movie music. The cue paces the entire sequence and responds selectively to points of action. The score musically mirrors the formal shape of the sequence. Tyler's cue, heard without the image track, can be summarised in musical terms as a four-part form, with the predominantly rhythmic content of each successive section faster and more urgent than the previous. The film in its entirety and the score taken by itself are both aesthetic wholes. This approach to action movie music uses original, beat-driven scoring to grant a customised shape and formal boundedness to action sequences that are understood to be the 'meat' of these films. These elaborate dances for men and machines do not *require* scoring – the two hijackings in *FF1* are unscored – but the addition of beat-heavy music cued to events as they unfold and calibrated to communicate the varying stakes for the characters adds tremendously to the vitality of the chase topic, reinforcing story cues and character points in a context where danger is great and dialogue is minimal. By analogy with the genre of the musical, most of these chases are tightly integrated musical numbers, where action set to music has significant plot consequences. However, as the 'Landtrain' number suggests, in some cases *FF*'s chases function as kinetic spectacles of bodies in motion to a driving beat, thrilling set pieces offered primarily for the sheer amazement of the audience. In both uses, music marks the aesthetic boundaries of the chase.

RACES

The only acknowledged source for *FF*'s cinematic version of street racing is Kenneth Li's short 1998 *Vibe* magazine article 'Racer X'. Li describes 'an urban polyglot of Puerto Rican, Dominican, Chinese, Filipino, Jamaican, Italian and other ethnicities' in upper Manhattan devoted to 'tricking out low-buck Japanese imports like Honda Civics and Acura Integras' with powerful engines and exhaust systems and supercharged with tanks of nitrous oxide (or 'nos'), 'tattooing [these cars] like skateboards' and creating 'jet-fueled go-carts'.[3] Li's article, dating some three years before *FF1*, suggests this 1990s world of street racing was already being shut down by the authorities on actual streets and commercialised by moving the cars and drivers onto race tracks. *FF1* and *FF7* evoke the latter trend with visits to so-called 'Race Wars'. In the films, street racing endures as a twenty-first-century global culture, based in Los Angeles (*FF1, FF4, FF7*) and flourishing in similar forms in Miami (*FF2*), Tokyo (*FF3*), Rio de Janeiro (*FF5*) and London (*FF6*). *FF1–3* are deeply embedded in the world of street racing. *FF4–7* visit street racing as part of more conventional action plots: taking down a drug kingpin (*FF4*), executing an elaborate heist (*FF5*), keeping a doomsday weapon from falling into the wrong hands (*FF6*) and exacting revenge (*FF7*).

FF's races are impromptu yet formal affairs, jousts between boastful knights with no king present and always waged on a bet, whether for money or 'pink slips'. Several races involve four cars and drivers, usually with an appreciative crowd (*FF1, FF2, FF4, FF5*). The head-to-head, two-man challenge also recurs (*FF1, FF2, FF3, FF5, FF6, FF7*) and rivalries between two drivers arise within four-car races. Races celebrate speed for its own sake and for the purposes of male (in a few cases, female) assertion and competition outside the confines of any specific plot: races do not 'go' anywhere except to the finish line. They are challenge dances that always end with a clear winner.

The franchise's first race – coming just twenty minutes into *FF1* – sets a pattern for the visual presentation of street racing: many short shots both of individual drivers in their cars and wider angles showing multiple cars moving down the race route. On the soundtrack, this first race uses only sound effects. (Later races use music, as described below.) Consistent point-of-audition sound – relative to the camera's position, even when it is not in a 'safe' place – results in constant and abrupt changes in the mix. Prominent sounds, heard in sharp contrasts on the cuts between shots, include the competing roars of four differently-played engines – each time a driver shifts to a new gear (a percussive act involving feet and hand) the pitch of their car's motor changes – and the whooshing sounds of cars passing by fixed points along, including in the middle of the race route. Punching the 'nos' button proves an important point of narrative articulation here and in most races, as drivers are limited to two such tank systems and must choose wisely when to use them or risk being left in the dust. The 'nos' whoosh is a sound special to the franchise. Much of the race is spent in individual drivers' cars, where their actions and reactions can be registered, often in extreme close-ups of their eyes. Visually and sonically, this first race is a disjointed affair of sharp cuts.

The four-car race that opens *FF2* initially continues the effects-only approach on the soundtrack. But this sequence – taking five full minutes of screen time – lasts more than twice as long as the race in *FF1*. About one minute into *FF2*'s race, a rock-style groove with heavy rimshots on beats 2 and 4, running at 142 bpm, enters low in the mix. This music, with its timbral evocation of a band and consistent tempo (until the very end, when the drivers face an unexpected obstacle), works differently from the beat-driven music used in chases, as described above. Chases are always about more than just driving and use music to mark out larger phases in the action. Races are made of many small choices and observations, with no larger action arc beyond getting to the finish line first.[4] Continuous beat-driven music in a race functions less as added dramatic content and more as a formal element, binding together the swiftly-cut montage and keeping alive a sense of thrill.

FF3, a crucial film for music in *FF*, marks the first use of compiled and newly composed or remixed popular music for races. The remaining four films follow *FF3*'s lead. The pop music styles drawn upon for races are overwhelmingly beat-driven, where the musical interest lies in rhythmic repetition, textural change, superimposed layers and timbre rather than melodic shape, harmonic progression or large-scale forms. Races scored with compiled tracks include:

- Sean's race against a privileged football player in the opening scene in *FF3* – the only race in the entire franchise between two white men – which uses a near complete playing of Kid Rock's 1998 hit 'Bawitdaba', a very rare full-on rock record in *FF*.
- The first drifting race in *FF3* – Sean against DK, aka the Drift King – scored with the obscure 1995 track 'Speed' by the German digital hardcore group Atari Teenage Riot. At 162 bpm, 'Speed' sets the fastest tempo for any music used to score driving.
- Letty and Dom run their race through the streets of London in *FF6* to another obscure, beat-driven electronica track, 'Here We Go', a 2012 collaboration between two Russian groups – the duo Hard Rock Sofa and the trio Swanky Tunes. The race is effectively punctuated by repeated spoken statements of the track title, which function not as lyrics but as analogues for the short sentences tossed off by drivers in many *FF* races. The accented English of the voice saying 'here we go' adds an exotically 'European' touch.
- Letty's winning run at 'Race Wars' in *FF7* uses 'Blast Off', a 2014 collaboration between DJs David Guetta and Kaz James that builds on material from Van Halen's 'Ain't Talkin' Bout Love'.

As these diverse selections suggest, the compiled tracks used for races are not necessarily contemporary with a given film's story.[5] Electronica and dance music are favoured genres, with the chosen tracks sharing a mechanical, industrial, edgy timbre. Notably absent are hip hop or Latin selections, which are reserved for scenes of street racing sociability (see next section).

Another strategy for scoring races with popular music involves having pop musicians create original cues for races – in effect taking part of the original score away from the credited composer, whose contribution is limited to the chases and other narrative scenes.[6] In *FF5*, Dom and company require four police cars to execute their plan to steal a Rio drug lord's money. Driving away from the police motor pool where they stole said cars, Dom, Brian, Han and Roman find themselves stopped at a red light as if at a starting line. They proceed to bet $1 million on a quarter-mile race down an empty Rio street. When the light goes green, the four take off to the sound of a cue titled 'Million Dollar Race', credited in the film's clearances to writers and performers Edu K and Hybrid. Edu K is Edouardo Dornelles, a Brazilian producer and former lead singer of the Brazilian rock band Defalla. The cue includes a prominent vocal element, sung in Portuguese by Edu K and drawn from Defalla's 2000 track 'Popozuda Rock n' Roll'. Hybrid is a British, three-person electronica music group known for remixes: they contribute another besides this one to *FF5*. The track, a series of eight-bar phrases unfolding at 149 bpm, fundamentally shapes the cut of the race. As in all the *FF* races, the viewer's perspective shifts rapidly between the various drivers' faces and shots that give a sense of who is winning at any given moment. Director Justin Lin tells the story of the million-dollar race in eight-bar segments matched to the music. Several times he cuts from an individual driver to an expansive shot of all four cars exactly on the start of a new phrase when Edu K and Hybrid burst forth at a new, louder dynamic level. The combination of a sung vocal, which explicitly identifies the cue as popular in origin (even though it was made for the film), and the editing of the sequence along regular eight-bar phrases, felt more subliminally by moviegoers (especially those with experience dancing to such music), lends this race a formal clarity and purity. We are, together with these four friends, enjoying the rush of street racing in an aesthetically thrilling, visually uniform – the cars look the same – utterly controlled yet delightfully spontaneous stretch of musically organised time. This race, like almost all of the races in *FF*, has the utopian energy and infectious joy of a classical Hollywood dance number, except, of course, the only bodies in motion are the cars, which function as expressive extensions of their male drivers' agency.

'Home Sweet Home'

Every *FF* film includes the cinematic representation of street racing culture, a quasi-underground, quasi-public, thoroughly multiracial sphere – diverse within the larger non-white category – composed of cool cars, 'hot women', tough guys and loud music. As noted above, *FF1–3* dwell in this world while *FF4–7* make short but important visits. The connection between street racing in *FF* and any actual street racing culture is difficult to ascertain. Surely only a small minority of the audience for these films has direct knowledge of this realm – if, indeed, it exists anywhere in anything like the form presented along consistent lines in *FF*. And so, *FF*'s representation of street racing culture is something like a zone of free play for the franchise's makers, a world – like the depiction of racing – developed over *FF1–3* and referenced in *FF4–7*. Street racing culture, the essential special place *FF* takes its audience, involves two sorts of car-centric sociability: making (or the modification of standard cars into street racers in the quasi-holy locale of the garage) and showing (or the outdoor display of cars for the gathered crowds before and after races). I consider showing first, then making. Popular music shapes the content and form of both.

Just ten minutes into *FF1*, the viewer is initiated into the street racing world of Los Angeles at a pre-race gathering in a grand if grungy urban context: a wide alley between two massive warehouses. The scene begins musically, with two erotic female moans heard just as Brian declares to his auto parts dealer his need for not one but two big canisters of nos: the equation between sex and speed is succinctly and sonically made. The moans, mixed alternately to screen right and left – as on a record – mark the start of 'Say Aah', a hip hop track (created for the film) which plays on over the visual transition to the race: a time lapse image of night falling and cars gathering, their engines roaring. Only seconds-long, 'Say Aah' touches efficiently on several hip hop modes, continuing with a male voice singing 'Tell me what's the secret I'm missin' and Ima come an get it', followed by a female rapper, heard more as background rhythm. 'Rollin' (Urban Assault Vehicle)', a remix by three black rappers and one black producer of the white rap rock/nu metal band Limp Bizkit's 'Rollin' (Air Raid Vehicle)', fades in on a transition finessed by the sound of engines being revved, the franchise's defining sound effect.[7] This deep cut from Limp Bizkit's recent number 1 album *Chocolate Starfish and the Hot Dog Flavored Water* (2000) can be heard to both herald *FF*'s claim to occupy a cultural zone of racial mixing by way of musical genre hybrids and welcome white male rock and metal fans, Hollywood's perennial target audience, who are represented, of course, by Walker's Brian. Brian pulls into the crowded scene and stands beside his car, surveying a crowd clearly divided among groups of African American, Latino and Asian racers and their women, described in the original script as 'LA's tribes'.[8] Brian stands out: a 'snowman', says a leader of the Latino group. 'Furious', by rapper Ja Rule featuring Vita, fades in next after more engine noises. This revised, non-explicit, radio-ready version of the track 'F*** You', from Ja Rule's 2000 album *Rule 3:36*, was made into a video promoting the track and *FF1*, analogous to 'See You Again'. The cutting heard in the film includes Ja Rule rapping the line 'Do it fast. Do it furious', an instance of product placement in reverse: a song remade to insert a film title, then re-inserted into the film, typifying the intimate connection between *FF* and the popular music marketplace. (Only *FF1* and *FF4* include music supervisor credits, an astonishing omission in an era when such industry professionals, who manage the placement of popular music in film, began to receive credit equal to that of composers.[9])

Pre-race sociability involves examining cars, both their elaborate exterior decoration and customised engines, and checking out the throngs of 'hot girls' dressed in skimpy, flashy clothes.[10] Various designations for the women in race culture appear across the franchise's scripts and cast lists: 'babe', 'hot GIRLS', and 'MINISKIRTS' (*FF1*), 'cowgirl', 'beautiful girl' and 'sexy model' (*FF3*), and 'hot girl' (*FF4*, *FF6*). The *FF5* script details how the male characters should model proper appreciation of the scene: 'As they cruise by, Dom and Brian admire a TUNER HOTTIE IN WITH A PERFECT BUBBLE ASS in short shorts leaning under the hood of her car tweaking the engine'.[11] During Ja Rule's 'Furious', for the first time, one of these women is seen to be dancing, responding to the music. Indeed, all three tracks in *FF1*'s initial presentation of the street racing scene are hearable as vaguely diegetic in this environment where there are as many car stereos as there are cars. One script notes, 'a dozen different BASSLINES thump'.[12] Music is in the street racing air but across the entire series no main character is ever seen pressing play, actively choosing to listen to particular music. The music that defines the racing scene flows as an effortless aesthetic choice made by an unseen, or if seen unknown, tastemaker – a few street scenes include shots of elaborate car stereos or a DJ mixing live.

FF1's representation of the street racing scene is subtle and nuanced compared to that of *FF2* and *FF3*. But both later films draw on the original's use of hip hop to define the scene as essentially musical and definitively non-white. *FF2*, directed by John Singleton, opens with the complex rhythmic groove of 'Like a Pimp', from rapper David Banner's 2003 album *Mississippi: The Album*, playing over the Universal Pictures logo, which is 'modified' via animation into chrome rims. Banner had recently signed to a subsidiary of Universal Records after 'Like a Pimp', a single from his first, independently released album, drew major label attention to the young rapper. With Universal's support, 'Like a Pimp' charted on both pop (white) and black charts: #48 (*Billboard* Hot 100), #15 (Hot R&B/Hip-Hop Songs), #10 (Hot Rap Tracks). As *FF2* opens, the track's multi-layered rhythmic groove plays over street racing folks closing roads for a race. We arrive shortly at the starting line, a street festival atmosphere of cars and women, familiar from *FF1* but brighter and more self-conscious this time. Three car-and-driver teams are introduced: a dark yellow car with an African American driver attended by his girlfriend, the pair dressed in matching stylised athletic wear; a pink car, driven by Suki, a long-haired woman of indeterminate ethnic background, with a girl-power team of assistants; and a red-orange car belonging to a macho Latino who enters fondling the rear ends of two women polishing the hood. Presiding over the race like a master of ceremonies is the rapper Ludacris, with a massive afro, in the role of the mechanic, garage owner and tech guy Tej Parker (reprised in *FF5*, *FF6*, and *FF7*).[13] Needing a fourth car and driver for the race, Tej calls Brian, a blond white man driving a customised white import with blue painted and lighting embellishments, completing the visually fantastic lineup for the opening race.

Images of Brian speeding to the race through the streets of Miami are intercut with shots back at the starting line. The camera wanders around the cars, checking out four powerful and visually impressive sound systems and a b-boy dancing, suggesting that street racing may be hip hop's missing fifth element beside the standard four (graffiti, rapping, DJing, and b-boying). This second phase is scored with Ludacris's single 'Act a Fool', made for the film and released with a music video featuring cars and drivers from this opening race tooling around Los Angeles, *FF*'s spiritual home. Like so much of the hip hop heard in *FF*, 'Act a Fool', while anchored in black music, delivered strong crossover appeal, reaching #32 (*Billboard* Hot 100), #20 (Hot R&B/Hip Hop) and #10 (Hot Rap). The lyrics to 'Act a Fool' are, at least in part, about cars and street racing culture and the track ends with repetition of the film's title – on the model of Ja Rule's 'Furious' but nowhere near as serious. 'Act a Fool' is fun, slightly goofy but hip and knowing, exactly the qualities Ludacris brings to the franchise as a character and actor with authentic hip hop credentials. The opening to *FF2* repeats all the street racing tropes posited in *FF1* in bolder colours, broader strokes and more audacious designs. Crucially, the musical element – popular hip hop tracks occupying a liminal sonic space, not explicitly listened to by any of the characters but implicitly part of their world – remains the same.

If *FF2* brightens and stylises the street racing scene first glimpsed in *FF1*, *FF3* goes a step further, aestheticising the visual and musical presentation of pre-race sociability, rendering the mix of cars, women and music into a sort of music video, where almost all diegetic sound falls away and music takes the sonic lead. This expressive move removes street racing sociability from normative narrative modes and creates a fundamentally musical short hand for racing culture that subsequent films can easily and efficiently evoke. *FF3*, the only *FF* film lacking Walker, presents street racing in Tokyo through the eyes of Sean Boswell (Lucas Black), a white American high school student with a thick Southern accent, who is abruptly transplanted to Japan to avoid going to jail. Having arrived in Tokyo, Sean is approached by another American, a hip black teenager named Twinkie, played by the rapper Bow Wow, who happens to have a Sparko steering wheel on his backpack. Not yet in Japan for twenty-four hours, Sean finds a link to the street racing culture of drifting.

Twinkie takes Sean into a parking garage and, as the bell-like beat to the film's title track begins, the viewer – together with Sean – is plunged into a deeply familiar scene: cool cars, attractive women and hip hop. The track is by the Japanese rap group Teriyaki Boyz, who had recently released their first album for Def Jam Records, with co-writer and producer Pharrell Williams, an African American musician whose career rides the line between rap, R&B and pop along a similar track to the *FF* franchise. The soundtrack mix as Sean moves through the scene is almost entirely music. We are, for all sonic purposes, inside Sean's mind: amazed, excited and, yes, aroused. The only dialogue during the sequence comes when Twinkie tosses Sean a box of Kleenex, saying 'for when you blow your wad, man'. Sean just smiles at a joke every teenage boy in the audience surely gets but might resist laughing at too loudly. Director Justin Lin mixes implied POV shots from Sean's perspective with a lyrical roving camera that rises and falls, lingering in equal measure over spoilers and girls, shifting fluidly and sensually between slow and faster-than-normal motion. Sean sees a young man slap his female companion on the posterior – enhanced by a slap on the effects track, the only such diegetic sound – and two women link arms around each other's waists while sauntering sexily off – a teenage variation on the early *FF* films' persistent fascination with two sexualised young women kissing. Sex and speed, yet again, go together. At film's end, after Brian has triumphed in a head-to-head race, the distinctive bell timbre and rhythm opening the Teriyaki Boyz' track pre-laps a return to the festival-like atmosphere of the garage, a zone that can be created in seconds by way of popular music alone.

Lin's musicalising of the sociability of showing cars served subsequent *FF* films well. (Lin also directed *FF4–6*, so re-use of audio-visual tropes introduced in *FF3* can be understood as a director working variations on and making reference to his own work.) In plots that only touch on street racing culture, short musical segments act as signature moments, marking *FF4–7*, whatever their plot trajectories, as part of the franchise's unique aesthetic world. And while visual tropes of cars and women remain the same, the beat-driven popular music heard in each film changes, acting conventionally to indicate exotic locations and thematically to apply a specifically musical rhythmic energy, providing moments to just groove to music in the course of each film. Given the minimal importance of large-scale form for beat-driven popular music, short fragments of a track prove sufficient to cast the required spell. The mostly Latino street racing denizens in the Dominican Republic and Los Angeles in *FF4* enjoy the music of Pitbull, the Miami musician who sings and raps in Spanish and English.[14] In Rio for *FF5*, Dom and Brian pull into the familiar mix of cars and girls to the sound of 'Follow Me Follow Me (Quem Que Caguetou?) (Fast 5 Hybrid Remix)'. The scene is described in the *FF5* script as 'The hottest cars this franchise has ever seen. The hottest girls, too'.[15] Dom and

Brian look at each other and smile; Brian says, 'home sweet home', a moment reprised in the montage for 'See You Again'. The original 'Follow Me', by the Brazilian hip hop duo Black Alien & Speed, was released in Brazil in 2001, went on to score a car commercial for Nissan, and was re-mixed by DJ Fatboy Slim – all before its insertion as a 'hybrid remix' in *FF5*. The complementary yet distinct notions of hybrid and remix alike describe the way visual and musical elements are brought together in all the street racing festival scenes in *FF*, music often fulfilling the task of inflecting the visually similar scenes with local color. The 'hot girls' at the London car scene in *FF6* groove and writhe – at times, of course, in slow motion – to 'Roll It Up', a 2001 track by the Crystal Method, an American electronica duo. The capacious category of electronic dance music (EDM) works to characterise London as hip, European and energetic, exotic in a different way from the Latin musical touches heard in the previous two *FF* films. It also links *FF6*'s *Mission: Impossible*-style plot to street racing culture, crucially by way of a short visit to a familiar, deeply musical place. Near the start of *FF7*, Dom and Letty visit 'Race Wars' – last seen in *FF1*; Dom says of the festival, 'we invented it' – where the music is also EDM. Dom and the still amnesia-afflicted Letty drive into the scene, much like Bow Wow and Sean in *FF3*, to the sound of a track by house DJ Steve Aoki. As noted above, Letty wins her race to the music of popstar DJ David Guetta. All these scenes draw on *FF3* – a film that, while tangential to the Dom–Brian saga, proves essential to the franchise's aesthetic.

The sociability of the garage is also musicalised initially in *FF3*, further suggesting the importance of Lin for the *FF* aesthetic. Late in the film, Sean, Bow Wow and their Japanese friends work together to mount a Nissan high-performance engine in the chassis of a Ford Mustang. The film's loving depiction of the time, effort and expertise it takes to craft this custom ride and tweak it to top performance are set to a cue titled 'Mustang Nismo' by composer Brian Tyler. Writing in a beat-driven popular music mode, Tyler combines a hard rock guitar riff, introduced with delicious teenage melodrama on the first image of the engine, with electronica beats and timbres in a hybrid musical expression of the combining of import and American muscle. The cue approaches the urgency of music for a race but the images are calm and studied: drivers and mechanics doing serious work. A very brief sequence in *FF1* anticipates the 'Mustang Nismo' musical number, with the camera passing lyrically over special order parts overnighted from Japan. Missing from this short transition is the work of the mechanic who is also a driver, the interaction of man and machine as a cinematic topic, a technological sociability that cuts to the heart of the masculinity *FF* constructs around the milieu of street racing. *FF4* manages to integrate musicalised car modification into both plot and character development within the Dom–Brian plot. A montage of both men preparing their rides is scored by and cut to a rock guitar-heavy original cue. In *FF7*, the trope returns, this time as three men (Brian, Dom and actor Jason Statham as the film's villain) prepare their guns and other weapons for the final confrontation. Dom initiates the sequence by uncovering his signature black Dodge, a moment Tyler scores with the same guitar riff heard in *FF3* when Sean discovered the Nissan Nismo engine.

Each subsequent entry in an action franchise like *FF* makes an implicit promise to the return viewer to 'see you again', to deliver a cinematic experience at once familiar and new. The Jason Bourne action franchise – five films appearing in 2002, 2004, 2007, 2012 and 2016 – has unfolded across almost the exact same years as *FF*. Every Bourne film – including the fourth (*The Bourne Legacy* [2012]) with a score by James Newton Howard – begins with the composer John Powell's mournful descending and sighing melodic figure heard in the dark over the opening titles, the forlorn timbre of the English horn instantly inserting the audience into the expressive world of this mostly beat-driven franchise. *FF* has no such similar unifying melodic theme. Instead, each *FF* film similarly employs beat-driven musics as constituent parts of the franchise's cinematic topics of chases, races and street racing sociability. The multivalent differences between original dramatic scoring shaped to amplify action sequences (chases) and borrowed or custom-made popular music cues used to carve out the special realm of street racing (races, showing, making) reveals how music operates in powerful ways within the franchise. And while the narrative-oriented scoring can be understood within larger trends in Hollywood action film scoring, the mood-oriented or atmospheric popular music cues do more specific work, making and showing *FF*'s cinematic version of street racing culture even as they lend their musical content and form to cars and drivers and the ubiquitous 'hot girls' hanging out nearby.

Paul Walker's death forced a significant narrative inflection point upon the larger saga of the *FF* films. And while the makers of *FF7* were able to finesse Walker's death within the plot and grant his character Brian a happy ending, they had to acknowledge within the film that Walker/Brian would not – indeed, could not – be seen again in the next instalment.[16] The form of the music video proved an organic way to bid farewell to Walker/Brian, its codes and stylisation squarely within the musical character of the franchise, uniting clips of chases, races and street racing life in a powerful montage. As to musical content, the happy coincidence of hip hop and pop finding an increasingly comfortable meeting place in twenty-first-century popular music facilitated Wiz Khalifa and Charlie Puth's collaboration on 'See You Again', which in characteristic hybrid fashion for the franchise combines the foundational sound of the former – reaching back to Ja Rule's track for *FF1* – with the elegiac sentimentality of the latter – a vocal lyricism not previously called upon in *FF* until the necessity of mourning a real death was forced upon the franchise.

NOTES

1. Tshepo Mokoena, 'Wiz Khalifa breaks record for most Spotify streams in 24 hours', *The Guardian*, 16 April 2015; Global Music Report: State of the Industry Overview 2016, IFPI.
2. Available at <https://en.wikipedia.org/wiki/List_of_most_viewed_YouTube_videos> (last accessed 13 August 2016).
3. Kenneth Li, 'Racer X', *Vibe*, May 1998.
4. Two exceptions. The four-car race in *FF4* is integrated into the film's plot, which centres on Brian and Dom infiltrating a Mexican drug lord's operations. The stakes for the race are high and several drivers crash and die, something that never happens in any other race in *FF*. Even though the race is a highly structured, at times mildly humorous affair – with a dispassionate GPS device speaking directions in Brian's car – the scoring is more like a chase than a race. The same generally applies to the final race in *FF3*, a duel descent between Sean and DK down a curving mountain road. With high stakes for the plot, the score is, again, more chase than race.
5. Any attempt to locate specific films along any real popular culture timeline is troubled by the chronology of the franchise, which goes *1, 2, 4, 5, 6, 3, 7*. *FF4–6* all occur before *FF3*, which depicts Japanese youth excitedly watching the climactic race on their flip phones, a technology that was rendered passé with the introduction of the iPhone in 2006 (the year *FF3* was released).
6. One exception: composer BT's cue 'Race Wars' for *FF1* anticipates the practice of using a popular, beat-driven musical style to score both races and street racing sociability without calling on popular music professionals.
7. Rappers DMX, Method Man and Redman and producer Swizz Beatz are credited on 'Rollin' (Urban Assault Vehicle)'.
8. *FF1* 'D.A. Blue Revised' typescript dated 5 May 2000, by Gary Scott Thompson with revisions by Erik Berquist, John Pogue and David Ayer, author's collection.
9. *FF1*: Gary Jones and Happy Walters; *FF4*: Kathy Nelson. Producer credits on the soundtrack CDs show a pattern, with each film's director working with franchise producer Neal H. Moritz (credited on all seven) and selecting others who vary from film to film.
10. *FF* presents this sort of 'cruising' as a stationary activity with cars parked in orderly rows, a choice that facilitates dialogue.
11. *FF5* 'WHITE SHOOTING DRAFT' typescript, dated 16 June 2010, by Chris Morgan, author's collection.
12. *FF1* script, author's collection.
13. Ludacris is the most prominent of several rappers cast in speaking roles in the franchise. Among other African American rappers, Bow Wow plays a major supporting role in *FF3* and Ja Rule is among the drivers in the first race in *FF1*. The Puerto Rican rapper Tego Calderón appears as a member of Dom's crew in *FF4* and *FF5*. Hong Kong American rapper MC Jin plays a mechanic in *FF2*. And in *FF7*, Australian rapper Iggy Azalea has a cameo at 'Race Wars', where she briefly greets Letty. Beyond hip hop, the Latin pop and Reggaeton singer Don Omar plays a recurring role in *FF4* and *FF5*.
14. The Pitbull tracks used are 'Blanco (The Strictly Spanish Mix)', featuring Pharrell Williams and recorded and released as a single for *FF4*, and 'Krazy', featuring Lil Jon, a track from the 2009 album *Pitbull Starring in Rebelution*.
15. *FF5* script, author's collection.
16. Walker's spot as the leading white man, filled by Lucas Black in *FF3*, has apparently been taken by Scott Eastwood in *The Fate of the Furious* (2017).

BIBLIOGRAPHY

International Federation of the Phonographic Industry, *International Global Music Report: State of the Industry Overview 2016*, <http://www.ifpi.org/downloads/GMR2016.pdf> (last accessed 26 August 2016).

Li, Kenneth, 'Racer X', *Vibe*, May 1998.

Mokoena, Tshepo, 'Wiz Khalifa breaks record for most Spotify streams in 24 hours', *The Guardian*, 16 April 2015, <https://www.theguardian.com/music/2015/apr/16/wiz-khalifa-see-you-again-breaks-record-most-spotify-streams> (last accessed 13 January 2017).

Morgan, Chris, 'Fast Five "WHITE SHOOTING DRAFT"', unpublished typescript, 16 June 2010.

Scott Thompson, Gary, with revisions by Erik Berquist, John Pogue and David Ayer, 'The Fast and the Furious "D.A. Blue Revised"', unpublished typescript, 5 May 2000.

11 *KILL BILL*: QUENTIN TARANTINO AS A MUSICAL FILMMAKER

Geena Brown

Ever since the release of *The Broadway Melody* (Harry Beaumont, 1929), Hollywood has been producing musical feature films that have accumulated a specific repertoire of elements. With time, this coded canon of elements has filtered into other popular genres of mainstream cinema and has strongly influenced a wide variety of contemporary filmmakers. Characteristics that are associated with the musical genre consist of simple narratives with audio-visually spectacular moments, excessive set pieces that help to drive the narrative, and the explorations of themes such as glamorisation of exotic cultures and experimentation with traditional gender performances. Powerful emotions such as love and hate function as catalysts during instants of passion and conflict, and extraordinary bodies assert authority over luxurious sets by inhabiting it in remarkable ways. Musicals are spectacles, designed to captivate the attention of the audience with remarkable costumes, memorable movements and aesthetically pleasing scenery. But musical cinema is no longer the only genre to encompass and exhibit these qualities. Many of these conventions can be observed in what one might consider to be a completely unrelated genre: the Eastern martial arts genre. In 2003, Quentin Tarantino released a film that would highlight the porosity of assumed boundaries. *Kill Bill: Volume 1* (Quentin Tarantino, 2003) would intersect Eastern with Western Culture, animation with live action footage, and masculine with feminine gender performance within its protagonist. But most importantly, it would bridge the gap between the musical and the martial arts genres.

We could consider *Kill Bill: Volume 1* as a musical by any other name.

dancing or even running up walls, visually conveying and personifying feelings with their bodies.

Richard Dyer describes song and dance numbers as moments of escapism from the character's problems.[3] The story becomes secondary in these moments, so that the spectator may thrive in these flashes of intensified emotion. That sensation is then expressed cathartically through song, a trope which originally goes back to classical opera in which action would stop before the music began. Similarly, Rick Altman suggests the idea that dance routines in the American musical are often products of either romance or conflict.[4] He deliberates the idea that these routines are the result of intense emotions like love, shared between either the leading male and female roles, or hate between the protagonist and their enemy.

Kill Bill: Volume 1 encompasses a very basic narrative structure for a film that boasts a running time of almost two hours, but a number of 'excessive' action sequences are incorporated which assure that the film is memorable. After belonging to a group of assassins named the 'Deadly Viper Assassination Squad', led by the eponymous 'Bill', the Bride (Uma Thurman) makes the decision to forgo this lifestyle and attempt to pursue the path of the idyllic American family. However, on the day of her wedding rehearsal, her former business partners attempt to kill the Bride along with the rest of her wedding party, but fail to successfully end her life. The protagonist awakens after a four year coma under the impression that she has lost her fiancé, her friends and her unborn child, and sets out to seek revenge. Although this plot seems simple, Tarantino builds complexity in the narrative by incorporating detailed back-stories and sophisticated martial arts infused action fight sequences. As previously discussed, just as in the musical, these fight sequences occur at cathartic moments in which conflict overwhelms the characters, but these are not simply fight scenes; these are carefully choreographed, aesthetically pleasing and exquisitely edited set pieces that are designed to be memorable long after the spectator has finished viewing the film. Some of these pieces can last up to 10 minutes in length, and incorporate various different styles.

But despite this lack of narrative complexity throughout the American musical genre and *Kill Bill: Volume 1*, both case studies incorporate scenes in which music functions as a narrative device. If we look at the song and dance set pieces of *Singin' in the Rain* (Gene Kelly and Stanley Donen, 1952), then we can observe that they possess the clear purpose of conveying key narrative events alongside the comic relief and light-hearted entertainment that they provide the spectator with. Whilst discussing the topic of dancing as a narrative device within musicals, Michael Dunne argues that

> In some musicals – *Shall We Dance* and *Dirty Dancing*, for example – the principal characters are dancers, so that dancing becomes an agent

of narrative simply as an extension of their characterizations. In other musicals – *Top Hat* and *The King and I*, for example – dancing together develops the action of the plot in terms of the principal characters' romantic involvement. In still other musicals – *Carefree* and *Oklahoma!*, for example – dancing reveals subconscious elements of a character's personality, what Aristotle calls that character's 'thought'.[5]

Therefore, the dance scenes in musicals and the fight sequences in *Kill Bill: Volume 1* are similar in the sense that as well as providing extraordinary memorable moments, they are tools used to convey pivotal points of the story, be they important events or overall tone. But likewise, Tarantino often uses non-diegetic music to create atmosphere and reference the narrative in other parts of the film also. He uses popular music to queue action and foreshadow events that are about to take place. Examples include when 'Crane' by the RZA increases in volume and tempo as the Crazy 88 surround the Bride, and suggests meaning by recycling sound from alternative sources, or when then film's opening credits appear to Nancy Sinatra's 'Bang Bang (My Baby Shot Me Down)', adding context to the scene and emphasising that Bill and the Bride had previously been lovers immediately after she informs the antagonist that her baby is also his baby. As a result of these stylistic choices regarding sound, the meaning of the film's visual aesthetics change in direct correlation to the style of music which plays throughout the scene. Essentially, by exploring sound in this way, Tarantino utilises music as a way of driving the audio-visual relationship, and this sound can even influence the outcome of the scene during the film's post-production. One of the most prominent examples of this being how the filmmaker edits his scenes to fit the tone of his chosen soundtrack. As is discussed by Ken Garner whilst deliberating Tarantino's work, 'the music's rhythmic and thematic structure is [. . .] foregrounded throughout by the visual editing'.[6] The different elements of music such as rhythm and tempo can inspire the way that images are sutured together to create effect. In the scene where O-Ren (Lucy Liu) and her entourage arrive at the House of Blue Leaves, sound is used to personify the antagonists. It conveys the characters as powerful by increasing in volume as they enter the set, and tight close-ups of each villain are juxtaposed to create the illusion of an indestructible force. The rapidity of their movements as they walk through the corridor is decreased to match the tempo of the music, representing this group as a collected and powerful presence.

Aside from editing and choreography, parallels can be drawn between Tarantino's work and the musical genre in the ways that their sets are constructed, and how the characters interact with them to the rhythm of the films' music. Traditionally, musicals often exhibit extensive, aesthetically pleasing and luxurious sets; described by Steven Cohan as 'Crayola-coloured sets', the scenery is often rich with colour, extravagant textiles and beautiful props.[7] Once again, an excellent example of this is the 'Good Morning' set piece from *Singin' in the Rain*. In this routine, characters use their bodies to explore the onscreen space, making use of every aspect of its scenery to execute different dance moves. By doing so, Don (Gene Kelly), Cosmo (Donald O'Connor) and Kathy (Debbie Reynolds) are able to make the images more charismatic by using the set in creative ways. Dance functions here as a way of experimenting with how to navigate the luxuriously textured backdrop. As most of the other musical numbers from *Singin' in the Rain*, this dance routine makes use of all possible levels when dancing around the house, making use of everything from tables, chairs and countertops to benches, stairs and bannisters as platforms to perform upon. This unconventional use of home furnishings as performance tools allows the characters to build atmosphere and convey narrative in a way that is both visual and theatrical. Similarly, Tarantino also intends for his characters to utilise the space in such a way whilst creating new ways for them to interact with props and scenery. However, in doing so, he introduces the concept of experimenting with character positioning as a form of visual representation of power levels. For example, during the Bride's fight with the Crazy 88 at the House of Blue Leaves, he places Thurman's character in such a way that she is always represented to be in a position of control. She is persistently situated above or in front of her attackers, including moments where they chase her to upper levels of the restaurant, or where she stands upon a bannister whilst fighting with swords. The House of Blue Leaves fight scene is the jewel of this film, as can be observed from the way that it is so carefully framed by the walls of the restaurant like a traditional theatrical proscenium arch.

Fundamentally, in both Hollywood musicals and *Kill Bill: Volume 1* multiple bodies function together to create one fantastical spectacle; several bodies can be observed working together to create mesmerising shapes and patterns. These bodies are driven by music, as although appearing to move freely around the sets, their actions are tightly choreographed and instructed by the tempo of the music. Both Tarantino's characters and the stars of *Singin' in the Rain* can be observed utilising props to create interesting shapes with their bodies. But where Don, Cosmo and Kathy extend their physical performances by employing items such as colourful raincoats and umbrellas, *Kill Bill: Volume 1* incorporates various weapons such as Katana blades and Meteor hammers, which need to be handled manually, forcing characters to functionalise their bodies. Yvonne Tasker suggests that access to weapons represents a form of empowerment.[8] The intentions of these scenes across both genres are to use the body as spectacle by creating shapes and images that are to be perceived as bold and impressive by the spectator. These genres showcase the human form in remarkable ways, be it running up walls during Donald O'Connor's 'Make 'Em Laugh' sketch or performing surreal stunts, these sequences exhibit routines that push the body to its physical limits, disguising themselves as effortless tasks.

Editing and choreography offer additional ways in which the musical genre and Tarantino's cinema utilise the actor's bodies as spectacle. The issue of character positioning and synchronisation returns us to how they are explored in parallel ways for the purpose of using bodies to create aesthetically pleasing patterns and routines for the visual pleasure of the spectator. When discussing the filming of the Busby Berkeley musicals, Vera Dika states:

> In these films, the camera moved with ease and freedom, giving the illusion of gliding over, under, and around the represented objects. The effect was additionally created by the elimination of conventional editing strategies in these sequences. Instead, the musical performances were allowed to transform across various spaces like the unfolding petals of a flower [. . .] This creation of expansive space in the production numbers in some of these early musicals was then subjected to techniques that alternately rendered the image a flat pictorial plane. Most famously in the Busby Berkeley films, overhead shots looked down on performers arranged in changing kaleidoscopic patterns to flatten the image.[9]

Although the camera may not move as freely in *Kill Bill: Volume 1*, there are prominent shots within the fight scene which takes place in the House of Blue Leaves where we can see clear similarities to Dika's observations of character positioning in the Busby Berkeley musicals. For example, there are instances in which the camera pans from a medium close-up of the Bride's face to a long-shot of her from above to reveal her predicament as she finds herself suddenly surrounded by the Crazy 88. During this fight scene we also witness overhead shots in which the actors are carefully organised into a circle around the protagonist (Figures 11.1 and 11.2). As the Human Beinz's 'Nobody But Me' fades in, the Bride drops to the floor and begins to rotate on her back around the space constructed in the inner circle (Figure 11.2), much like the violinist in Berkeley's 'Shadow Waltz', who leads the other musicians by spinning on her feet as she plays (Figure 11.1). The Bride acknowledges that she is able to use her agile, carefully choreographed movements to attack each of these individuals from inside her sudden entrapment. The Crazy 88 are carefully positioned around the Bride, only advancing towards her at their cue in the routine so that the rhythm of their interactions runs smoothly, like a precisely choreographed dance routine. Although Tarantino never chooses to linger on these shots for long, these snippets display clear similarities, and the construction of these images suggests that his artistic vision for this fight sequence was highly influenced by dance sequences from the classical Hollywood musical genre. Despite executing different styles of movement, this martial arts scene

Figure 11.1 A still from the 'Shadow Waltz' sequence in Busby Berkeley's *Gold Diggers of 1933* (Mervyn LeRoy, 1933).

Figure 11.2 Stills from the 'House of Blue Leaves' fight sequence in Quentin Tarantino's *Kill Bill: Volume 1*.

is as precisely choreographed as the circles of dancers who create these kaleidoscopic frames in Berkeley's cinema. Both scenes consist of large groups arranged in such a way that their bodies move together to create suspenseful and entertaining routines. Tarantino synchronises his actors, as Berkeley does so well within his musical sequences, so that their bodies move together to create captivating routines which are executed in time to the rhythm of the music.

Non-diegetic music still remains dominant over the behaviour of Tarantino's characters, even when they are completing mundane tasks such as navigating the onscreen space. Alongside fight scenes, which are choreographed to the pace of the popular music that they accompany, the film incorporates a series of moments in which the character's physical movements are influenced, or even triggered, by sound. The corporeal movements of the Bride, along with other characters, often fit the pace of the non-diegetic music. A good example of this being the fast tempo funky seventies 'Trucker Theme' that accompanies the Bride as she first leaves the hospital. Although she has lost the use of her legs at this point in the film, having found access to a wheelchair means that her movement through the scene is quick and agile as she rolls through the hospital carpark looking for the vehicle to match her newly acquired set of keys. Her actions become sharp and jagged to suit this upbeat style of music as she turns her head to investigate her new surroundings. However, once discovering that the aforementioned vehicle is a truck, the music comes to a sudden halt, suggesting that the protagonist has encountered a physical task which, after discovering that she has temporarily lost mobility in her lower limbs, she will be unable to manoeuvre as freely. But it is not only the Bride whose movements can be influenced by sound. At the House of Blue Leaves, Japanese alternative rock instrumental piece 'Battle without Honor or Humanity' enters and leaves with characters as O-Ren and her entourage enter the restaurant, and the speed of the shot is decreased to meet the tempo of the music. In this moment it is not only the movement of the actors that is led by the musical queues, but also the editing of images and shot types. Between 00:19 and 00:20 seconds into the song, we hear three distinctive trumpet notes (which have been heavily synthesised). On the first and third notes Tarantino cuts closer to the group with O-Ren as a central focus point. In doing so, he successfully creates the desired ambience by foreshadowing action and constructing a tone that these characters bring with them.

Much like the modern musical, *Kill Bill: Volume 1* recycles pop records from different sources and makes extensive use of non-diegetic sound to influence onscreen action. There are other formal and stylistic similarities between Tarantino's films and the musical, and one prominent example already highlighted is the way in which *Kill Bill: Volume 1* demonstrates his fascination with the East and wuxia filmmaking. Wuxia films are a genre of Eastern cinema that exhibit astonishing martial arts fight sequences. Nicolae Sfetcu describes the genre's characteristics as 'action scenes centred on swordplay [. . .], featuring sophisticated action choreography with plentiful wire-assisted acrobatics, trampolines and under-cranking'.[10] The wuxia genre relies heavily on actors who have a background in dance to complete difficult acrobatic stunts, and quite often comparisons are drawn to Eastern musical cinema by critics.[11] Gary Needham states that 'the action scenes in wuxia films with graceful choreography [. . .], are often described as balletic',[12] and Kin-Yan Szeto argues that wuxia film choreography is based 'simply on the spectacle of action'.[13] It is a well-established motif of the Eastern martial arts genre to convey carefully choreographed violence as spectacle. Violence functions in the same way as a musical number, and *Kill Bill: Volume 1* bridges this gap by showcasing spectacularly choreographed fight sequences to recycled pieces of popular music. Tarantino's martial arts routines are performances that exhibit all of the conventions that we associate with a song and dance number from a musical, such as the pause in narrative, the sudden emphasis on sound, the physical excess of the human body, and complex and beautifully executed choreography.

As well as bridging the gap between the Eastern martial arts and the Western musical genres, Tarantino frames East Asian culture in parallel ways to how the musical genre does. Typically, the Hollywood musical has traditionally romanticised the unknown as 'exotic', meaning that foreign cultures are represented in these films as transcendent and enchanting. Examples include *South Pacific* (Joshua Logan, 1958) and *Flower Drum Song* (Henry Koster, 1961). The fictional cinematic reimagining of cultures that are unfamiliar to the spectator must remain fantastical, yet identifiable. On the subject of American musicals, Julie A. Noonan states that

> The 'exotic' is seen in opposition to the normal or natural viewpoint of the author, or in this case the central characters. Exotic is often used similarly to Other although with a mystical inflection. It denotes 'culture' as opposed to the 'normal' view of the defining body. The exotic can be far away as the 'East' is often characterized, or merely different within the West [. . .] Exotic seems to evoke curiosity in the Other, but it also read as dangerous.[14]

The 'Other', being any element that is not directly recognisable to the audience, is a key concept in the Hollywood musical canon. These representations idealise and glamorise foreign spaces, peoples and cultures, as, for example, the way that *An American in Paris* (Vincente Minnelli, 1951) portrays France. If the Other is unknown, it encompasses the potential to be 'mystical', for the spectator is unable to confirm its conventions or its limits. Alongside musicals that are set in exotic locations, many take place in the familiar territory of North America but still heavily reference exotic cultures through aural and visual aesthetics. Again, the 'Good Morning' dance scene from *Singin' in the Rain* is a good example, as it incorporates props and images from all around the world into its scenery. This striking iconography has been accumulated from a vast variety of countries with distinct and naturally identifiable cultures, such as England, Egypt and Spain, but all has been hyperbolised to create a rich, fantastical backdrop, much like the way in which Tarantino situates *Kill Bill: Volume 1* across a pan-Asian backdrop to showcase the culture. In conjunction with the scenery, this set piece also explores different music styles both visually and aurally in comedic dramatisations of various iconic international dance styles such as that of the Hawaiian hula dance, movements associated with the Spanish matador, the French can-can dance, and the English ballroom dance. All of these genres of music and dance are combined within this one spectacle of a routine to create something unique, outlandish and glamorous.

Tarantino's desire to maintain Japanese authenticity is prominent from his choice of Japanese popular music as non-diegetic sound. His decision to edit the scene in which O-Ren and her entourage walk through the House of Blue Leaves to Tomoyasu Hotei's alternative rock track 'Battle Without Honor or Humanity' suggests three things, the first being that music serves as a narrative device within the film that drives plot and character movement just as is executed within the Hollywood musical. The second is that the music builds upon the narrative, implying thoughts and attitudes of the onscreen characters, and the third, that Tarantino is directly paying homage to another element of Japanese popular culture. Composed by Japanese rock musician Tomoyasu Hotei, this track was originally written for the Japanese film *New Battles without Honor and Humanity* (Junji Sakamoto, 2000), a remake of Kinji Fukasaku's *Battles Without Honor and Humanity* (Kinji Fukasaku, 1973). By infusing the film with references to Eastern popular culture, Tarantino creates a hybrid aesthetic that advocates both his Japanese martial arts influences of the Eastern action genre and his influences from the North American popular cinema. As previously stated, Tarantino intended for the film to be an exploration of the fusion of these two cultures, and aside from the more self-evident visual elements such as props and settings, the filmmaker also plays with this concept using style and characterisation. The film experiments with the fusion of Eastern and Western cultures by emphasising O-Ren's character as mixed-race. Her cultural identity is explained as having both Chinese and Japanese ancestry, whilst being raised in a North American military base. This information is conveyed through the use of an anime sequence, just under eight minutes in length, which has been injected into an otherwise live-action Hollywood film. This sequence was inspired by traditional Japanese animation, and constructed for the film by an authentic Japanese animation studio Production I. G, who were also responsible for the animation behind *Ghost in the Shell* (Mamoru Oshii, 1995).

Finally, it is important to consider how both Tarantino's *Kill Bill: Volume 1* and the musical genre explore the construction of their heroines in parallel ways, and how they both create space for strong female representations. Despite the musical genre commonly revolving around largely conservative themes such as white, heterosexual couplings, they are progressive in their conveying of strong female figures. Traditionally, musicals are largely male-centric in their narratives, and often focus on a male protagonist's pursuit of a woman, but the structures of these films provide female characters with equal space to dictate the soundtrack, providing female characters with a platform to construct and determine their own representation. In doing so, these heroines embrace traditionally masculine-coded characteristics including power and independence. Tarantino's female protagonists, although traditionally feminine in appearance, can be perceived to behave in a rather masculine manner with regards to costume and choreography. This links back to Tarantino's references to the Eastern martial arts genre, as *Kill Bill: Volume 1* was released right in the middle of a cycle of popular Asian action films which featured strong female protagonists such as *Crouching Tiger, Hidden Dragon* (Ang Lee, 2001) and *House of Flying Daggers* (Yimou Zhang, 2004).

The classical musical was a space for elevated female roles, 'feminised' men and non-normative sexuality. Musicals convey stories of assertive leading ladies who break gender stereotypes by asserting authority over the onscreen space and taking control of their narratives. Not only do their fictional characters exude qualities that we traditionally associate with masculine performance, but so do their stars. When discussing former stars of American musicals, Stacy Ellen Wolf argues that

> Many women stars [. . .] exhibited performative charisma and power, including [. . .] Mary Martin, Julie Andrews, and Barbra Streisand. Some women performers, like Katherine Hepburn and Marlene Dietrich, exemplified masculine habits. Their performances, however, could be understood within the construct of the tomboy (as was Martin's, for example) or were softened by glamour (As in the case of Hepburn, Dietrich, and Garbo, all lesbian icons).[15]

In other words, many musicals focus on strong women who are confident enough to challenge traditional gender expectations. These popular figures were perceived to be constructed in such a way both on and off stage. Tarantino is an expert at constructing such bold, independent female figures within his films, and several examples reside within *Kill Bill: Volume 1*, including Uma Thurman's revenge-driven representation of the protagonist; O-Ren, the world's leading female assassin; Vernita (Vivica Fox), a fiercely protective mother who remains adamant that her child remain safe, and Gogo (Chiaki Kuriyama), a feminine young woman who refuses to be perceived as weak. Regardless of where these women stand on the spectrum of protagonist, antagonist or antihero, the filmmaker has constructed each of them as resilient feminist figures. Although censoring the Bride's name may dehumanise her to a certain extent, Tarantino films Thurman's character in such a way that she is a constant authorial presence within the onscreen space, especially within its action sequences. According to Lisa Coulthard, Tarantino frames his female action heroines in a way which is traditionally associated with male protagonists of the genre. She argues that

Most of the fight scenes in the film are between women and are choreographed and filmed in a way that is stylistically similar to those of any masculine-centred martial arts film or Western. These are duels, battles between equals; women fighters are never inferior to men [. . .] throughout the film, the Bride (Uma Thurman) controls the action, including the physical action of violent spectacle.[16]

Therefore, just as the headstrong female stars of the Hollywood musical display influence over the narratives of their stories, the Bride physically asserts her authority over the space in *Kill Bill: Volume 1*, especially within its fight scenes at the House of Blue Leaves. Throughout the fight scene the character grounds her position at the centre of the frame. As the Crazy 88 advance and the action encloses around, gravitating towards the Bride as a central focal point, the camera follows her, resulting in the spectator's attention being held on this character in a space where it is established that action and violence is happening all around. This is emphasised by the long-shot at the end of the Leaves' fight sequence in which Tarantino cuts to a shot of bloody corpses draped across the floor of the entire restaurant. We are reminded by this shot of the vast amounts of blood that have been shed within this scene, but this is the first time that the camera has left the Bride for long enough that we might realise how many obstacles she has overcome. The frames were otherwise restricted, only exhibiting images of her encounters with no more than a dozen enemies at a time. The Bride's actions are dramatic; she moves quickly and uses her body to fill the space with complex martial arts routines that drive her to inhabit the space both vertically and horizontally. According to Coulthard,

Each fight places gender (that of the heroine and that of her opponent) at the forefront. Fights with single women, collective groups, or male adversaries make use of unique fighting styles and weapons (knives, swords, martial arts) and offer particular outcomes [. . .] It is also important to note that fights between women occupy more screen time and are more developed in terms of choreography and style. Moreover, these fight scenes all feature moments of female bonding (connections made over the shared feminine concerns of children, pregnancy, lovers, mentors, or business success) that are conjoined with graphically violent action.[17]

In a similar manner to these conventions in the musical, Tarantino's female figures are robust, self-reliant women. He constructs his female characters in such a way that explores their strength and independence without compromising the elements that convey their traditional femininity, as Julie Andrews' characters in *Mary Poppins* (Robert Stevenson, 1965) and *The Sound of*

Music (Robert Wise, 1965), who perform assertive and authoritative roles such as a firm nanny and a governess whilst still dressing in feminine-coded garments and conveying a maternal nature. These women are determined, self-sufficient and intelligent, yet at the same time, matriarchal and intuitive. Much like the leading ladies of America's musicals, who dress practically and embrace the prospect of adventure,[18] these women exude power; they drive motorcycles, wield swords, work their way to the top of underground crime rings and face the prospect of death without batting an eye. Tarantino never attempts to conceal their femininity, but at the same time, his use of *mise en scène* to enhance his female cast as traditionally feminine never overshadows their authorial roles. Dressed in figure hugging motorcycle leathers, school skirts and traditional, elegant Japanese kimonos, it is never intended for these women to appear physically masculine, but their actions, and even a select few moments which they share together during the film's fight sequences, do otherwise display tendencies associated with masculine gender performance. According to Sharon Smith, 'traditionally the entire world is male', but just as the leading ladies of the American musical combine qualities of both genders to construct a powerful presence, Tarantino combines traditionally male-coded characteristics with female instinct whilst repurposing the female form as practical rather than sexualised to create successful, non-binary heroines.[19] Yvonne Tasker's definition of a 'feisty heroine', who 'offers an articulation of gender and sexuality that foregrounds a combination of conventionally masculine and feminine elements' encapsulates his female figures.[20] Uma Thurman's confident stance determines the Bride as the dominant presence within the scene. Her weapon, a Japanese samurai sword, traditionally coded as a phallic male symbol, is precisely crafted to personify her character and represent the power of the female form with its smooth, slender frame and gentle curves, whilst simultaneously encompassing a hidden strength. Yet again the female figure is symbolised here as meticulous, precise and deadly, rather than vulnerable, seductive and erotic.

To conclude, many elements of Tarantino's creative process appear to have been influenced by the American musical genre when constructing features in the style of the contemporary action film. Not only does Tarantino offer us a unique exploration of his musical influences, but understanding these references can help us to better appreciate his work. Therefore, whilst *Kill Bill: Volume 1* can be interpreted in a number of ways, it is not incongruous to read it through the lens of a musical. *Kill Bill: Volume 1* is a film that bridges the gap between the musical and the martial arts genres, as well as the gap between Eastern and Western cultures via its representation of the robust female protagonist. Aside from similar themes which have been transported from both the musical and martial arts genres, the filmmaker has chosen to construct his characterisation similarly. His leading female figures share with the stars of the classical Hollywood genre a number of character traits that challenge traditional gender roles and performances. They are resilient beings who are dedicated to the assertion of their own authority, at times contrasting with the ways in which Tarantino has constructed the physical appearance of their costumes, hair and makeup. The actors' performances are carefully choreographed and controlled in both *Kill Bill: Volume 1* and the stars of Roger and Hammerstein's classical musical cinema so as to function in such a way that the body becomes spectacle. Although for different reasons, such as dance and violence, the human form is instructed to move in extraordinary ways for the visual pleasure and fascination of the spectator, and moments of cathartic release are exhibited through song and physical expression. The illusion is created that both sets of bodies from both genres of cinema excel in skills that put strain on the human frame, despite the fact that the stars of the American musical from the late 1920s onwards were professional performers with backgrounds in dance, and the actors of *Kill Bill: Volume 1* received support from careful editing and special effects to accomplish their martial arts sequences. Essentially, the body is spectacle. It is intended to mesmerise the spectator by moving in incredible ways within both styles of cinema. Although executed in subtly different ways, both genres intend to impress their audiences with sound, dramatic movements, and spectacular bodies. Perhaps we should question our own pre-established definitions of a musical film.

NOTES

1. Jane Feuer, *The Hollywood Musical* (Bloomington: Indiana University Press, 1993), p. 130.
2. Barry Langford, *Film Genre: Hollywood and Beyond* (Edinburgh, Edinburgh University Press, 2005), p. 87.
3. Richard Dyer, *Only Entertainment*, 2nd edn (New York: Routledge, 2002), p. 29.
4. Rick Altman, *The American Film Musical* (Indianapolis: Indiana University Press, 1987), pp. 163–4.
5. Michael Dunne, *American Film Musical Themes and Forms* (North Carolina: McFarland & Company, 2004), pp. 67–8.
6. Ken Garner, 'Would you like to hear some music? Music in-and-out-of-control in the films of Quentin Tarantino', in K. J. Donnelly (ed.), *Film Music: Critical Approaches* (New York: Continuum, 2001), p. 195.
7. Steven Cohan, *Hollywood Musicals: The Film Reader* (New York: Routledge, 2001), p. 91.
8. Yvonne Tasker, *Spectacular Bodies: Gender, Genre and the Action Cinema* (New York: Routledge, 1993), p. 139.
9. Vera Dika, *Recycled Culture in Contemporary Art and Film: The Uses of Nostalgia* (Cambridge: Cambridge University Press, 2003), p. 178.
10. Nicolae Sfetcu, *The Art of Movies* (North Carolina: Lulu Press Inc., 2011), available at <www.lulu.com/gb/en/shop/nicolae-sfetcu/the-art-of-movies/ebook/product-17571668.html> (last accessed 10 January 2017).
11. Gary Needham, 'Fashioning modernity: Hollywood and the Hong Kong musical

1957–64', in Leon Hunt and Leung Wing-Fai (eds), *East Asian Cinemas: Exploring Transnational Connections on Film* (London: I. B. Tauris, 2008), p. 50.
12. Ibid. p. 50.
13. Kin-Yan Szeto, *The Martial Arts Cinema of the Chinese Diaspora: Ang Lee, John Woo, and Jackie Chan in Hollywood* (Illinois: Southern Illinois University Press, 2011), p. 55.
14. Julie A. Noonan, *The Sound of Musicals' Women: Tessitura and the Construction of Gender in the American Musical* (Kansas: Proquest, 2006), p. 89.
15. Stacy Ellen Wolf, *A Problem like Maria: Gender and Sexuality in the American Musical* (Ann Arbor, MI: Michigan University Press, 2002), p. 97.
16. Lisa Coulthard, 'Killing Bill: rethinking feminism and film violence', in Yvonne Tasker and Diane Negra (eds), *Interrogating Postfeminism: Gender and the Politics of Popular Culture* (Durham, NC: Duke University Press, 2007), p. 159.
17. Ibid. 160.
18. Wolf, *A Problem like Maria*, p. 53.
19. Sharon Smith, 'The image of women in film: some suggestions for future research', in Sue Thornham (ed.), *Feminist Film Theory: A Reader* (New York: New York University Press, 1999), p. 17.
20. Yvonne Tasker, *Working Girls: Gender and Sexuality in Popular Cinema* (London: Routledge, 1998), p. 68.

BIBLIOGRAPHY

Altman, Rick, *The American Film Musical* (Indianapolis: Indiana University Press, 1987).
Cohan, Steven, *Hollywood Musicals: The Film Reader* (New York: Routledge, 2001).
Coulthard, Lisa, 'Killing Bill: rethinking feminism and film violence', in Yvonne Tasker and Diane Negra (eds), *Interrogating Postfeminism: Gender and the Politics of Popular Culture* (Durham, NC: Duke University Press, 2007).
Dika, Vera, *Recycled Culture in Contemporary Art and Film: The Uses of Nostalgia* (Cambridge: Cambridge University Press, 2003).
Dunne, Michael, *American Film Musical Themes and Forms* (Jefferson, NC: McFarland & Company, 2004).
Dyer, Richard, *Only Entertainment*, 2nd edn (New York: Routledge, 2002).
Feuer, Jane, *The Hollywood Musical* (Bloomington: Indiana University Press, 1993).
Langford, Barry, *Film Genre: Hollywood and Beyond* (Edinburgh: Edinburgh University Press, 2005).
Garner, Ken, 'Would you like to hear some music? Music in-and-out-of-control in the films of Quentin Tarantino', in K. J. Donnelly (ed.), *Film Music: Critical Approaches* (New York: Continuum, 2001).
Needham, Gary, 'Fashioning modernity: Hollywood and the Hong Kong musical 1957–64', in Leon Hunt and Leung Wing-Fai (eds), *East Asian Cinemas: Exploring Transnational Connections on Film* (London: I. B. Tauris, 2008).
Noonan, Julie A., *The Sound of Musicals' Women: Tessitura and the Construction of Gender in the American Musical* (Kansas: Proquest, 2006).
Sfetcu, Nicolae, *The Art of Movies* (Raleigh, NC: Lulu Press Inc., 2011), <www.lulu.com/gb/en/shop/nicolae-sfetcu/the-art-of-movies/ebook/product-17571668.html> (last accessed 10 January 2017).
Smith, Sharon, 'The image of women in film: some suggestions for future research', in Sue Thornham (ed.), *Feminist Film Theory: A Reader* (New York: New York University Press, 1999).
Szeto, Kin-Yan, *The Martial Arts Cinema of the Chinese Diaspora: Ang Lee, John*

Woo, and Jackie Chan in Hollywood (Carbondale, IL: Southern Illinois University Press, 2011).

Tasker, Yvonne, *Spectacular Bodies: Gender, Genre and the Action Cinema* (New York: Routledge, 1993).

Tasker, Yvonne, *Working Girls: Gender and Sexuality in Popular Cinema* (London: Routledge, 1998).

Wolf, Stacy Ellen, *A Problem Like Maria: Gender and Sexuality in the American Musical* (Ann Arbor, MI: University of Michigan Press, 2002).

INDEX

Although on first glance it may be easy to label this film as (Western) action cinema, it incorporates all of the traditional features that are explored by the musical genre, and are often implemented in martial arts films. These include strong emphasis on its soundtrack and the action that is synchronised to it, and movement (violence, in this case) as choreographed spectacle. These striking moments are prominent in that they demand a narrative pause; commanding the spectator to focus on the protagonists' bodies and the physical excess of their performance, whilst also creating a space for women to dictate control over the soundtrack. *Kill Bill: Volume 1* is, therefore, the focus of this chapter, particularly in terms of how the film bridges the gap between the musical and the Eastern martial arts genres by encompassing and intersecting conventions of both. By observing how Tarantino combines these elements to create a hybrid piece of cinema, I intend to assess the common features that these two genres share. I argue that our understanding of what constitutes a musical film might not be as straightforward as we had once presumed.

Kill Bill: Volume 1 can be interpreted as a musical, not just owing to its exceptional soundtrack, but because of its emphasis on music and the influence that it holds over its character's actions. Traditionally, the musical film diegetically incorporates popular music, but what establishes musical cinema, as opposed to cinema of other genres which merely incorporates popular music, is the way that onscreen characters interact with these songs to create audio-visual spectacle. Although in more contemporary musicals there has been a turn away from dance, unlike the Busby Berkeley and Gene Kelly musicals of classical Hollywood, the onscreen images and sound are still communicating clearly with one another in *Kill Bill: Volume 1*. The audio-visual relationship creates choreographed sequences in which the action is dictated by the accompanying music, just as with the fight sequences in martial arts cinema. The film's intensified sound becomes primary to the point that it causes pauses in narrative that provide platforms for moments of heightened emotions to be conveyed physically. In both the musical and martial arts genres, the body functions as a physical manifestation of sound and effort. As can be observed in *Kill Bill: Volume 1*, the character's physical forms serve as visual metaphors for the intersection of aural and visual elements.

It is important at this juncture to discuss the way that the American musical transformed in the 1980s so that non-diegetic music could function within the fictional film world. Although onscreen characters often no longer created the music themselves, they would still interact with the film's soundtrack as it would influence the energy and tempo of their movements. Whilst establishing the genre conventions of the classical Hollywood musical, Jane Feuer suggests that

> The teen musicals of the 1980s represent a 'reconstruction' in the sense that they are not parodic or deconstructive of the conventions of the

classic musical. Rather, they introduce new conventions – the main one being the use of 'non-diegetic' rock music over the images rather than the use of diegetic music that defined the older form of musical film.[1]

This implies that although classical Hollywood musicals had previously consisted of diegetic set pieces that were produced, often vocally, during the scene by the characters (the Gene Kelly musicals of the forties and fifties, for example), the genre adapted in the 1980s so that modern musicals could explore contemporary rock and pop music tracks from their decade without the necessity of the sound's source inhabiting the onscreen space. After this decade, the definition of the Hollywood musical altered slightly so as to also encompass non-diegetic pieces. Recycled pieces of popular music were used within these films to create atmosphere and drive the narrative, despite the fact that they were not created or influenced by the onscreen characters; but instead, these non-diegetic pieces were used to provoke actions and movements from them, one example of this being the watermelon scene from *Dirty Dancing* (Emile Ardolino, 1987). Tarantino channels this element of the modern musical not only by using non-diegetic music to represent what is happening in the narrative, but also by recycling music from other recognisable sources of popular culture to build new layers of meaning within a scene.

But more interestingly than the way that sound effects Tarantino's world-building, is the way in which it influences his character's actions. Arguably, *Kill Bill: Volume 1* fits the genre conventions of the traditional American musical with regards to narrative, editing and spectacle, with one of the more prominent links being the use of choreographed movement. Memorable action sequences express the characters' intense inner sensations and showcase the actor's bodies as extraordinary, much in the same way as the musical uses dance. Whilst exploring the concept of dance routines in musicals, Barry Langford argues that

> Some or all of the musical numbers in even the most integrated musicals are to some degree 'excessive' in relation to their basic narrative function – inevitably, one might say, given the genre's basic contract with its audience, which is not storytelling as such but delivering memorable songs and [. . .] dance performances.[2]

This suggests that fans both identify and associate musicals with their hyperbolised song and dance sequences more so than recognising them for their plots. They encompass very basic narratives so as not to overpower moments of emotional climax: instances in which a character has reached the peak of the emotion that they are feeling and have no choice but to express this physically by breaking into song and/or dance as if the song and dance routine is its own entity that possesses them. The characters express themselves by jumping,